THE GROCER'S BOY
RIDES AGAIN

ROBERT MURRAY

Other Books by
Robert Murray

The Grocer's Boy:
A Slice of His Life in 1950s Scotland

The Spirit of Robbie Burns

THE GROCER'S BOY RIDES AGAIN

Another Slice of His Life in 1960s Scotland and Beyond

Robert Murray

The Grocer's Boy Rides Again: Another Slice of His Life in 1960s Scotland and Beyond by Robert Murray.

First published in Great Britain in 2020 by Extremis Publishing Ltd.,
Suite 218, Castle House, 1 Baker Street, Stirling, FK8 1AL, United Kingdom.
www.extremispublishing.com

Extremis Publishing is a Private Limited Company registered in Scotland (SC509983) whose Registered Office is Suite 218, Castle House, 1 Baker Street, Stirling, FK8 1AL, United Kingdom.

A CIP catalogue record for this book is available from the British Library.

ISBN: 978-1-9996962-4-5

Typeset in Goudy Bookletter 1911, designed by The League of Moveable Type.

Printed and bound in Great Britain by IngramSpark, Chapter House, Pitfield, Kiln Farm, Milton Keynes, MK11 3LW, United Kingdom.

Cover illustration shows Dundee, the River Tay and the Tay Rail Bridge.
Cover artwork is Copyright © James McDowall at Shutterstock (wraparound cover image)/Africa Studio at Shutterstock (central front cover image).
Internal illustrative sketches are Copyright © James Murray, all rights reserved.
Cover design and book design is Copyright © Thomas A. Christie.
Chapter heading illustrations are Copyright © Becky Stares at Shutterstock.
Author images are Copyright © Eleanor Jewson.

Internal photographic illustrations and diagrams are Copyright © Robert Murray and are reproduced from the author's personal collection, unless otherwise indicated. While every reasonable effort has been made to contact copyright holders and secure permission for all images reproduced in this work, we offer apologies for any instances in which this was not possible and for any inadvertent omissions.

MAP OF THE
COUNTY OF ANGUS

ABERDEENSHIRE

KINCARDINESHIRE

GLEN ESK

TO ROYAL DEESIDE

TO ABERDEEN

EDZELL

River N. Esk

GLEN CLOVA

GLEN PROSEN

BRECHIN

GLEN ISLA

River Isla

Lintrathen

RIVER SOUTH ESK

MONTROSE

KIRRIEMUIR

FORFAR

FRIOCKHEIM

To BLAIRGOWRIE

To PERTH

GLAMIS

ARBROATH

PERTHSHIRE

DUNDEE

CARNOUSTIE

MONIFIETH

To PERTH

FIRTH OF TAY

NEWPORT

BROUGHTY FERRY

Bell Rock Lighthouse

N O R T H

S E A

FIFE

St ANDREWS

MAP OF THE UNITED KINGDOM

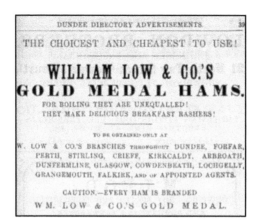

A vintage press advertisement for Wm Low & Co. Ltd.

Commercial College prospectus, circa the late 1960s,
showing the new campus on Constitution Road, Dundee

To my late parents,
daughters Carys and Wendy,
my grandchildren and my
late wife Gail.

THE GROCER'S BOY RIDES AGAIN

Another Slice of His Life in 1960s Scotland and Beyond

Robert Murray

PREFACE

I N my book *The Grocer's Boy: A Slice of His Life in 1950s Scotland* (published in 2018), I didn't set out to write a social history of the time. But somehow my story captured the emotions and imagination of readers of days gone by.

As I wrote about my boyhood days, I soon realised I was witnessing the ground-breaking changes going on in the retail grocery world. My early life straddled those life-changing moments which brought us the sophisticated grocery supermarkets of today. That book is about my early days in Carnoustie when – as an eleven year old – I delivered news-papers, then later pedalled around the streets of the town on my 'big basket' push-bike as a twelve year old message boy with the well-known Scottish multiple grocery company Wm Low & Co Ltd.

When I was fifteen, I became an apprentice with the firm, followed by my nervous start in 1960 as the company's youngest branch manager. Carnoustie, a small sandy-beach town on the east coast of Scotland – some twelve miles north of Dundee – had in the 1950s a population of around 5,000 and boasted a self-sufficient economy including a jute works, jam factory, foundry and cannery. In the summer months, the population more than trebled when holiday makers flocked in from the industrial Central Belt of Scotland. They were a welcome boost to the town's economy.

I was born in Barry, Angus: an inland village just two miles from the town. That earlier book tells the story of my very early life – walking through flooded roads to school, and my time at home with my mum and dad, brother Peem and sister Isobel. Despite our cramped living space, I had an idyllic young life playing safely in the yard and feeding the hens and rabbits we kept in our cottage garden. I can still smell the rabbit food – tea leaves mixed with oatmeal. It was such a distinct clean, warm and enticing smell that I used to nibble some of it on the way to the hutch... but I managed to resist tasting their dandelion diet when that was available!

On hearing the distant stirring sound of pipes and drums, mum used to take us to the side of Barry Road to watch soldiers marching towards Barry Buddon Army Camp. That, of course, was in the Second World War years, and nowadays I sometimes wonder if those men, on passing by, would have the sight of a mother and her children in their own thoughts as they went to war to save us all. Of course, we as children didn't realise that high emotion – despite (almost nightly, it seemed) listening to the long low drone of German aeroplanes high above us on their way home after bombing shipyards on the River Clyde near Glasgow.

Our small cottage, with its paraffin lamps and heaters, had a shared outside toilet with a 'sneck' which did not do a very good job of keeping the rickety door closed from the elements. The sound of mice (or rats?) scratching in the loft was an evening occurrence when the only other noise was the tick of our living room clock. These were some of my early memories.

In 1947 we moved to Westhaven, to a two-bedroomed upstairs flat with our own indoor private family toilet on the landing – what a luxury. This small fishing village on the east edge of the town proved to offer a new adventure wonderland for me and my friends Jim, Coffie, Ollie and brother Peem. For what seemed endless summer days we fished off the rocks, rowed fishing boats, played cricket and football, and lit our Guy Fawkes bonfire on a nearby grassy area we called 'the ballaster'. Westhaven was a carefree place in which to grow up, and my early experience as a newspaper boy and message laddie provided me with many lessons for life.

My first *Grocer's Boy* book recollects my delivery adventures along with my boyhood fun and rivalry with my message boy pals. The peace of those innocent young days, however, was shattered when – as a teenager – I gradually had to come to terms with the realisation that my mum was pregnant. My initial reaction at the age of thirteen was one of disbelief and embarrassment.

Of all the towns in the county of Angus in those days, Carnoustie was the only one not to provide a senior school, and the usual practice was for pupils to travel seven miles to attend Arbroath High School. Mum's nervous feeling was that she could not afford for all three of us to move on to complete our schooling at Arbroath, and so reluctantly I left the education system aged fifteen. My chosen area of work was to train as a radio and television engineer. But after six frustrating months, I – again, by luck – found myself commencing an apprenticeship within the grocery shop I had come to know so well. The many aspects of my training, and of the quirky "Go, go, greasy grocer, go" humour of my manager, is told in that first book, and I gradually advance to deputise for my boss.

3

After four years of work experience and evening class studies, I was offered – at the age of nineteen years and nine months – the job as manager of a branch in Dundee, and so my very nervous management days began. That nerve-wracking experience of first starting work as a manager in Brantwood Avenue, Dundee, is also contained in my earlier book.

Reactions to *The Grocer's Boy* have been warming, with many responses received at fairs, talks and interviews. Readers, many of whom didn't know either me or Carnoustie, connected with my story, and in many cases personal reconnections with people I knew in the past have materialised. By means of my book being sent on to family and friends in Commonwealth countries, I have been thrilled to have received favourable comments from all around the world. The experience has been truly amazing, and this 'follow-on' book has been prompted by those who enjoyed my nostalgic tales. I am most grateful to everyone who has taken the time to write to me with their thanks for bringing back their own long-lost memories.

Once my book was in print and readers approached me by various means to discuss the content, it became obvious to me that I had many more elements of my early life to relate. This story takes me from that first nervous management job, and then on to experience a bigger branch which at the time was experimentally described as 'self-selection'. At the time, I took it as a step into the unknown not only for myself, as I sensed my company's bold step into 'something different' in shopping habits and retailing methods. I can look back now and see it was the embryonic emergence of self-service stores, but no one could have foreseen the giant shops encompassing many departments which ultimately would denude high streets of shops offering butchery, fruit and vegetables, dry cleaners, tobacconists, to mention only a few – along with the disappearance of door-to-door bakery and milk vans. In my story, I give some experiences of the new problems which arose.

As I have said earlier, luck has been a constant factor in my life, and this book tells of the massive decision I had to make about whether to consider leaving behind my history of employment in the grocery industry and think about moving on to teach my trade within Further Education. Would I make the blunder of my life? Eventually, when my future seemed very dark, I – again, by luck – found an unbelievable opportunity which led me to new and exciting chapters in my life.

Following publication of *The Grocer's Boy*, I often found myself asked to give talks. As time passed, I realised that in addition to the nostalgia which my book generated, the theme which began to emerge was my luck. In this book, luck again seems to come to the surface. Just recently, however, I received as a gift the book *The Secret* by Rhonda Byrne, in which she relates very strongly the power of positive thinking. On reading it, I began to wonder if my many pieces of good fortune were luck after all – or was it really the power of my positive sub-conscious thinking that pulled me along? I was never aware of that, but *The Secret* has now made me think. "The doctrine of luck is the doctrine of the fatalist," I read somewhere recently, and so I now tend to believe my story is either one of faith or divine intervention. Whatever it is, or was, it has been my constant guide,

When in Dundee Central Libraries during one of my many book talks, I was astonished to be approached by a tall, friendly gentleman. He had heard about my book and revealed himself as John Allardice, an apprentice in a branch I managed in 1963 and who I had not seen for 56 years. After that surprise meeting he has re-introduced me to one of my former managers, John Thomson. Both are mentioned in this sequel. Another one of my many amazing pieces of good fortune which, along with others, are related in this book.

Like my first story, this does not set out to log social history – it merely gives one person's view of early life in the 1950s and 60s, and my adventures, scares, surprises – oh yes, and of course luck – which I experienced along the way.

By no means do I consider myself a 'writer', but wonderful life-changing moments in my past gave me some encouragement to write. When I was eleven years old, one of my classmates was seriously ill and everyone in my class was asked to write an appropriate well-wishing letter to Moira, who was a sickly girl. Of all the letters, mine was chosen, and my quiet nervousness to write was sparked into life. This was compounded when I jointly won the school's Robert Burns Prize (except fellow pupil Elizabeth's handwriting was judged to be better than mine, and she – to my everlasting dismay – picked up the trophy instead). In 1982 I had an article published in my local newspaper. I wrote about my feelings when I attended the funeral of a soldier, a local man who had been killed in the Falklands War. Those tiny but morale-boosting experiences gave me the modest notion that someday I should put 'pen to paper'.

These days I enjoy writing short stories within the Tay Writers group and, with their valuable help, I have embarked on this: my second *Grocer's Boy* book.

I trust you will enjoy it!

INTRODUCTION

Early Days

MUM and Dad had married in Montrose in 1939, and moved initially into rented rooms in nearby Monifieth to be near Dad's work on the main London/Aberdeen railway line. They then moved to the bungalow next door to the school in the small village of Barry, where I was born the following year. I don't recall anything much of those days, but many years later – to my mother's amazement – I described my crawl along a wooden-floor corridor with small carpets at the entrance to each room.

"Surely, you can't remember that!" she had exclaimed. "You were only two years old when we left that house."

Although I remember, for some unknown reason, that infant journey I must have made along the passageway, I didn't remember the arrival of my brother James ("Peem") in 1941. Strange, isn't it, how some less-important memories are retained while more significant ones are forgotten?

From the bungalow we moved to Annfield Cottage, another rented property, which was located at Barry Road, Carnoustie. Annfield was to be my home for nearly five years, during which time my sister Isobel was born when I was four years old. I walked to Barry school, about half a mile away, and have etched memories of Miss Bell – my teacher – and of sitting beside a gloriously warm fire with a metal guard around it. Apart from suffering school lunches and the lonely walks to and from school, I think I was a reasonably happy child and still recall the combined brisk smell of the fresh apple in my new leather school-bag containing my one infant-reading book.

A time arrived when the tiny dark cottage must have been insufficient, and the family moved to Westhaven – a small fishing village at the east end of Carnoustie, where we occupied an upstairs two-bedroom flat with our very own inside toilet. That move proved to be the most significant thing that ever happened to me in my childhood. Westhaven was a new world. My friends and I had joyous summers: we fished off rocks when the tide was out, looked after the clink-er-built fishing boats for the owners, and spent wonderful evenings playing rounders, cricket and football on a long grassy patch which we named 'the ballaster'. Winters saw us 'guising' at Hallowe'en, and buying an ever-increasing variety of fireworks with the proceeds. To this day I still remember the excitement of realising the state of the tide was right, and the subsequent buzz of activity to prepare hooks and lines followed by the dash to dig for lugworm bait as the tide re-ceded.

As I recall in my earlier book, the commencement of my delivery job was a landmark moment – my joy of complete freedom of fishing, boating and frolicking around our West-haven adventure playground came to a sudden end. It was during my early days at Westhaven when, at the age of nine, I found by accident – or luck – my first little job. Looking back, this piece of good fortune was to be the first of many which was to help steer me along my working life. The fortunate occurrence was when I was volunteered on Saturday evenings to fetch some DC Thomson-published *Sporting Post* evening newspapers and run with them to the railway station bookshop, for which I received my first pay of three pennies (1.25p in today's money). In time the lady who ran the book-stall also gave me a packet of Spangles – a famous brand of boiled sweeties, which were first introduced in 1950.

When I was about eleven years old, my brother and I started doing a morning paper round which required us to be up at 6.30am each day except Sundays. My weekly pay was four shillings (20p), which gave us a little pocket money and allowed us to pass some over to help mum's strained budget. Mum looked after us so well, for she would – on cold, wet and dark mornings – help us on our rounds. Bad weather and terrifying dogs were our only concerns.

It was while I lived at Westhaven that I, again by some large degree of luck, found a job as message boy for Wm Low & Co Ltd. My older pal Jim had very thoughtfully made it possible for me to get that job. The pay was thirteen shillings and sixpence (67.5p). For this, I had to work each day (except Tuesdays) from 4pm until 6pm and all day on Saturdays. I commenced in July 1953, the year of the Queen's coronation and the summer when Edmund Hillary conquered Mount Everest, thus securing his knighthood.

In addition to cycling around the town and countryside in all weathers, I was required to carry out basic tasks in the shop. In those days products other than canned goods were supplied 'loose'. Sugar arrived in 2 cwt sacks and had to be made into one pound or two pound bags, and I helped with filling. Likewise, I packed dried fruits and cereals into bags.

No fridge was fitted in the shop, and cooked meats, butters, lard and bacon were stored on marble slabs and covered overnight and at weekends by muslin cloth. Occasionally, I helped to cover up the products.

I had many experiences on my message bike with its bulky large basket fitted on the front. Facing winds was a severe test of stamina, but how I enjoyed being blown along on windy days – especially if I was wearing my bulky, bright yellow rain cape which (despite my mum's 'clear outs' after I left home) I still have to this day.

While the weather was a major element to contend with when out on my bike, there were other aspects of the job which required attention. These included learning the rudimentary jobs that needed done in the shop, including emptying mouse traps and disposing of waste paper. I learned to respect customers, and to follow instructions from the boss. Although I was unaware of it at the time, I was soaking up the whole business of diligence and honesty. I learned to balance priorities between the needs of the shop, the company, customers and myself.

There developed a friendly rivalry between myself and other message boys, and this strangely spun off into creating loyalty to my company. Another aspect of life as a message boy was that I began to feel the variations in seasonal business and the impact that this had on the stock we sold, the fluctuating deliveries and customer needs. In short, I was transported into a pulsating world which was dynamic and exciting.

When I had worries, I sat at my favourite secret place near the seashore to contemplate the changes and their impact. All that magic disappeared when I started my grocery delivery job.

The Message Boy Leaves School

The 1950s was a decade of major technical advancement – cars, television sets, washing machines and 45rpm records. It was a time when the 'old' continued to run alongside the 'new' – tram cars moved about Dundee city, and yet an increasing number of new cars were appearing on roads. Likewise, my mum was still using a scrubbing board and a mangle while very early twin-tub washing machines and spin dryers were introduced.

A major family event took place in 1955 – my parents were allocated, at long last, a council house at the west end of the town. The move to a three bedroom semi-detached villa-style property, complete with back and front doors and enhanced by a bathroom complete with bath, was for us like stepping on to a new planet. Hello "Planet Council House", farewell "Planet Cramped Cottage" and "Planet Flat".

In those days, pupils left school at the first recognised holiday immediately following a fifteenth birthday. For me, it was time to leave school in October 1955. My classmates had left in July at the commencement of summer holidays, but my departure date was October (the 'tattie holidays') before I could step out in to the world of work. Two others in my class were forced to wait until Christmas.

"I've found mine" said Peem, referring to the silver threepenny piece which he had found in his wedge of dumpling. On our birthdays Isobel, Peem and I always had a race to find one of the three silver coins wrapped in greaseproof paper. So now it was my fifteenth birthday, which fell during the holiday, and I had left school. It was not possible to continue my schooling – the time to go to senior school was when I was twelve, but in those days there was no way I could have rejoined my former classmates who had been attending Arbroath High School since I was twelve.

I had never thought of commencing work as an apprentice grocer, and with the major growth in television sets an engineering apprenticeship in radio and television seemed like a logical and up-to-date choice to make. Taking a moment, I went alone to the quiet place at the ballaster which I frequented when I wanted to think about problems or issues (like the time I was mortified by the realisation that my mum was to have a baby). I hadn't wanted to leave school, and yet there was no existing mechanism by which I could even try to ask the question. To this day I wonder what would have happened if I had gone to the headmaster and told him I wanted to catch up with my original group of classmates.

Arbroath then was a bustling and vibrant town with engineering works, a foundry and of course the harbour. As an apprentice engineer I found the change in pace, surroundings and colleagues all quite daunting. Expecting to get my hands inside a TV set, I found it frustrating to be assigned quite simple tasks such as sweeping the workshop floor (after all, I'd learned how to do that years before as a timid message laddie). Each evening I topped up acid batteries for customers who had sent them in for recharging, and quite regularly I had to unpack new TV sets and plug them in ready to be checked by a senior engineer.

Three senior engineers and third year apprentice Bob made up the staff complement, and though I enjoyed the banter and the comradeship a few negative elements began to appear. Being driven around Angus roads by apprentice Bob – a "mad" nineteen year-old driver – was one. Another, more seriously upsetting event was being told that I would never be allowed to work on fishing boats. The amazing background to that situation was that the fair-haired Vikings had left their 700 year-old mark on successive generations, and redheads like me were deemed to be bad luck. In effect, that meant my exciting prospect of working on boats would never materialise. A more fundamental problem existed. My late start in the college academic year meant I'd lost a year in starting my college engineering course. This was matched by an uninspiring weekly pay packet of only £1 and 10 shillings (£1.50). By the time my travel and lunch costs were counted, I was financially worse off than a message boy.

One evening in December, while waiting for my train home to Carnoustie, my father unexpectedly appeared on the station platform.

"What's wrong, dad? I thought this was your 'rest day'."

"I had to go to Montrose," he told me. 'Your aunty Mary has died."

I was astonished. "Gosh! How did that happen?"

"She died on the table?"

"What?"

"Yes, she had an operation on her appendix but died on the operating table".

It was the seemingly casual way dad told me that sticks with me to this day. Mary had never married, and I'd rarely met her when we visited her at granny's home in Montrose. When dad told me (my mum didn't yet know – there were no phones at home in those days), to my shame I look back and realise I didn't have the maturity to say the appropriate sympathetic comments to my father at the time. Only now do I realise that Mary may have had a boyfriend or fiancé during the WW2 years, and may have lost him in the war. Now there she was, dead at the age of 38, as a result of a simple operation that obviously went wrong. Can you imagine the questions arising with the health service today over such a tragic end? Poor Mary. Just sheer bad luck.

In the Spring of 1956, without any plan in mind, I – on impulse, on my way home – jumped off my bike and asked my previous boss in Willie Low's if I could start a grocery apprenticeship. After a slight scare that there may not be an opening, I was engaged as an apprentice. On reflection, I hadn't sat at the ballaster to agonise on the decision, which tells me I had a clear idea of what I wanted to do.

From Apprentice to Manager

It seems like yesterday when I reported for work on that very first day to start my work as an apprentice.

The familiar place I had not set foot in for just over six months was like going home or awakening after a bad dream. The smells of fruit and spices, cheese and fresh dairy produce felt comforting. Something inside told me I had made a big decision, and yet I wondered why I had ever left the grocery in the first place.

"Here, try this for size," said the boss, handing me a white grocer's coat. "It'll have to do you a week, so keep it clean."

He would not have known the sheer joy and pride I had while I put my arms through the stiffly starched sleeves. Then off he went, chanting "Go, go, greasy grocer, go" as he dashed off to prepare for the day's business. I was home.

It didn't take long for me to feel even more at home – I knew all the jobs to do. The buzz was there, and I was in tune with it. Along with my friendly rival Jock Brown and other pal Johnny Robb, I started the first year of night classes to study the Grocers' Institute syllabus. As time passed I learned every aspect of the business, and eventually was serving customers along with experienced staff. The boss showed me the more experienced technical jobs – everything from how to write price tickets and making window displays through to the book-keeping duties and ordering stock. Mr Munro, the area manager, was most supportive, and in due course I moved on to manage the shop when Mr Stewart the manager took a one-week holiday. Those teenage years provided a sound employment foundation for me, during which I graduated from my motorbike to a Wolseley 14 car and – along with my friends – enjoyed trips around the countryside and Saturday night dances.

Meanwhile, I had been studying my grocery trade subjects and, after three years, achieved membership of the Grocers' Institute. I had learned every aspect of the retail grocery trade, including the major trading periods such as Christmas and New Year trading when selling peaked. Looking back upon this time, shops were entirely counter service: we closed for one hour and fifteen minutes each lunch time, and had time off on only on one half-day and Sundays.

It was with great surprise when Mr Munro took me aside on one of his weekly visits to ask if I would like to manage a branch in Dundee. "It's a small branch called Brantwood Avenue," he told me, "but ideal for you to learn about management."

Another moment for me to sit at my favourite secret spot at Westhaven to ponder. Could I do this? *Should* I do this? My mother had a clever question for me: "Would you want to spend all your life working in the Carnoustie shop?"

The answer was obvious.

So the week prior to the Dundee holiday fortnight in 1960 I started my daily bus trips to Brantwood. After one week of working along with the existing manager, who was moving on, I was given the keys to the shop. Thankfully the two quiet weeks of the Dundee holiday period meant a trouble-free start to my management career.

A Young and Nervous Manager

At near nineteen years of age, I set out at the end of July to manage my first branch. It was a jolt to move from the known of Carnoustie to the completely unknown of Dundee – at least that part of Dundee, for I had occasionally visited the shopping area in the city. It was new and it was different, but I had no serious worries about the technicalities of running the branch. There were a few odd aspects. The shop sales area was probably less than a quarter of the square feet of the Carnoustie store's floor space, and the back shop was even smaller. The only store was a shed at the rear, which was just about adequate to hold the necessary stock.

I couldn't say I had any fears, but I certainly was ready to face the challenge and felt quietly confident and ambitious. The people in the area seemed friendly, although I have to admit I had to be on my guard. However, gradually I learned that there was a more relaxed and straightforward relationship between staff and customers. It was more down-to-earth than I had expected, with plenty of good humour. At the time I labelled it 'city' compared to 'small town'.

The shop was located on the lower slopes of the Law, Dundee's prominent big hill; a volcanic plug, I'd been told. With customers from three distinctly differing sections of the immediate area, I found it interesting. First, there was the nearest district comprising council house tenants. They had well-kept properties and tidy gardens, and the housewives were well-dressed and respectable customers. Across the main road – Strathmore Avenue – were privately-owned properties, and those customers were equally pleasant and obviously had greater spending power. The remaining third group lived in Beechwood council estate, which had a reputation for being tough. Beechwood tenants were a mixture of elderly people in economic hardship, and some workers. This last group mainly comprised of working wives who were employed in jute mills in the city. The practice for those hard-working people was to step off a bus, shop in my branch, and then walk home – half a mile away – with large bags of groceries. Sometimes they would ask me if my message boy would deliver. Those customers had an amazing, great sense of humour, and brightened up the shop with their down-to-earth chatter. It was a fascinating mix of clientele. I respected all of them. At that time I had no idea of so called 'socio-economic' groups – for me, they were all my customers wherever they lived and however they spoke.

One of the changes I had to deal with was the language – not that it was bad, I should say, but merely different. For example, I was struck dumb when a customer asked me for a "luppy o' tatties".

Winnie, my assistant at the store, came to the rescue.

"It's no a 'luppy'; it's a *lippe*. That's just the way it's pronounced – and it means seven pounds."

"Oh! Thanks, Winnie."

"Aye, and a half luppy is three and a half pounds."

I've never, so far, discovered the origin of the word 'lippe'. In addition to unique Dundonian terms were Scottish words and phrases used by the Beechwood customers. I found them warm and comforting, as my granny and grandad used similar terms. One customer – a Mrs Reilly, who worked in a jute mill – was brilliant at finding the right words for the occasion: "Eh'll need tae get awa hame early; my mithers no' weel. The doctor's been in tae see her, and she's up tae high doh." On another occasion, she teased the message laddie when he told her he'd a few early deliveries to make before getting to her place. "Yer a wee scunner, son! Nae tip for you the day!"

Sales improved, and I was determined to see my branch climb the sales increases chart. My sales level was the smallest in Mr Munro's area, but my increases on the previous year continued to develop and eventually I reached the top spot. In time I purchased a Ford Prefect car, which gave me immediate flexibility – now I could travel to and from the shop as and when it suited, without the discomfort of waiting for buses. In my enthusiasm, I realised that I could also use the car to drive into town and do the banking, and although there was a system for branches to obtain a delivery of supplementary orders I occasionally drove to the company's central warehouse and picked up stock directly. I worried about every penny; that is, sales coming in and expenses going out. By nature I was a worrier, probably a bit like my mum. An indication of my stress was that I found myself driving from home to the branch and somehow finding myself miles along my route without knowing how I got there. I have been told in later life that this kind of incident is caused by stress. I didn't feel stressed nor over-anxious at the time, but I was very conscientious.

At my first Christmas at Brantwood I developed the idea of producing a 'Christmas box', containing a collection of festive and normal products such as a box of chocolates, a Christmas pudding, a few crackers, cake, tea, sugar and so on. It wasn't meant to be a luxury box, but a practical gift. I used old tomato boxes and lined them with Christmas paper. Once I added up the total value of the contents, I added a margin of profit. The origin of my idea was that I had prepared one for each of my grandparents (without adding the extra profit, of course!). I drove to Montrose and Dunninald to deliver them. I don't think I was trying to show off, but I suppose I was trying to say "I'm a manager now, granny, and here's what I've cleverly done for you."

During my first winter at Brantwood, the higher altitude was obvious – the snow remained long after the icy streets in the city centre and Carnoustie had melted. During a dark winter night, thieves broke into my shed at the back of the shop. This was an entirely new experience for me, and I telephoned Mr Munro immediately. I was hugely impressed when two detectives came to investigate. The intended 'loot' – cases of Heinz soup and parcels of sugar – were left lying outdoors at the foot of the rear fence. The police told me the culprits must have been disturbed. Lucky for me the stock was intact, but I had to gauge if any other stock items had been stolen – which seemed unlikely. It was a strong reminder that I was in a city, unlike my sleepy wee capsule in Carnoustie.

In the February of 1961, my uncle Bill – the former Chief CID Inspector of Aberdeen – died, and I wanted to attend his funeral there. It was my first time off during my time at Brantwood, and I picked up my uncle Alan – Bill's brother – in Arbroath on the way to Aberdeen. Alan had at one time run a fruit and vegetable shop in Montrose High Street, and I found we chatted all the way there and back about shops and management. It was the first time I could honestly say I felt able to discuss retailing and my early experiences. I clearly recall driving past the road leading to his mother's (my granny's) home. I discovered I was able to speak on equal terms with my older uncle and, for a while, I reminisced about holidays Peem and I had enjoyed at granny's croft cottage.

CHAPTER 1

April 1962:
"I'm a Manager Now!", or
"How Did I Get Here?"

"**M**AKE sure she's out of gear and keep your thumb tucked in on the handle." My dad's firm advice rang in my ears. No ignition keys or fancy start buttons in those days. Holding my breath, I 'cranked' the engine with the starting handle.

Running late, I had dashed to my car and noticed a thin film of soft ice on the windscreen. Thank goodness the harsh wintry days of ice and snow were, hopefully, passed by now, but then one never knows when the demarcation line will fall between winter and spring in this part of the east coast of Scotland. It was a cold morning, but not one that was going to rip off my wiper blades – as had often happened when they were frozen to the windscreen and carelessly not switched off by me.

Running back and forth between the choke control on the dashboard and the starting handle at the nose of the car was a time-wasting and disagreeable task. The position of the choke had to be gauged – too much and the engine flooded, too little and my pride and joy would need more gentle words... but never a kick. My message bike in times gone by had never given so much trouble, and all this energy was a nuisance. But it was a routine part of my life now, and a different world from my wet and miserable days as a message boy.

Come on now, my perfect Prefect pal: third time lucky... please! I gently coached my 1954 Ford Prefect and, with a burst of high revs, she was suddenly alive. Throwing the handle on to the floor behind the driver's seat I at last clambered in and, swishing off the soft ice, I was – in my mind, at least – 'airborne' and ready to 'fly' to the shop I managed at Brantwood Avenue some twelve miles and forty minutes away in Dundee.

"Showers are forecast, Robert – better take your coat," mum had advised me as I prepared to leave the house. "James has gone away to work with waterproofs because he's working outside today."

"It's a shame. He's not very well, is he?"

"Not at all. I think he's a bit run down these days. I put a kaoline poultice on his sore throat last night, and he's suffering from chilblains on his toes and hacks on his hands too."

"I think he's feeling down about not getting word about a job," I suggested.

"We'll need to give as much help as possible," mum said as she nervously twisted her hands on her pinnie.

"Yes, mum. I'll be home about half-past one – it's half-day today! Poor Peem; it's a shame."

James, my younger brother – otherwise known as 'Peem' – worked outdoors and started at 7am. He routinely had to watch the weather.

It was a few minutes past 7.30a.m. on a Wednesday morning in April 1962, and I looked forward to my short working day as I drove up the 'raised-beach' hill in Carnoustie called West Path and headed for the main road which ran between Arbroath to the east and Dundee to the west.

You've wasted valuable minutes this morning, Robbie... *but not as bad as the times when you had the overcoat tangled under the bonnet.*

My mind recaptured those annoying delays – and it was a pleasant feeling not to have the troublesome old coat under the car bonnet, as was my practice in the hard frost and icy days of winter. I say troublesome because often, in my haste, I had a reckless habit of setting off with the unseen coat still in place only to find several hundred yards later my car shuddering to a halt with sleeves wound tightly around the fan belt. The coat had been dad's idea, and it had served me well, but there was no such need today. By far the most treacherous condition I had to take great care with was black ice, which was often prevalent in early spring mornings. Looking like rain on the road, it had claimed a share of road deaths for as long as I could recall. I'd been constantly warned about it by my dad, and had many narrow escapes on it while out on my message bike in years gone by.

Arriving at the T-junction with the main road (or 'toll road', as we occasionally referred to it), I turned left and settled in my seat for the journey to Dundee. As I drove to the city, often referred to as one with a history of 'jute, jam and journalism', my thoughts took me back to August 1960 when, at the age of 19 years, I had first been appointed manager of Wm Low's branch at Brantwood Avenue. According to my area manager I was the company's youngest manager. Quite a lot had happened since those first shaky days, and yet I was still nervous for I found that in the retail grocery trade one could never totally relax – there was always the chance of having to face the unexpected.

In my little world I had begun labelling the chapters in my life as being like 'planets'. My 'home' planets were Barry, Westhaven and now Carnoustie. In work terms, my first planet was 'Carnoustie' – a happy training base – followed by my adventurous 'space' journey to Planet Brantwood. In my imagination, I moved around planets in my space suit.

Wm Low & Co Ltd was a well-known and highly successful Dundee-based multiple retail grocery organisation which had traded since 1868. The Carnoustie branch – where I had served my apprenticeship – had operated since 1894, and by 1900 the company traded through a hundred branches across Scotland. In my boyhood days when I'd started work as a paper boy and grocery message laddie, I'd had some nervous moments. But now, whilst feeling the pride, I was in an anxious state.

It hasn't sunk in yet, Robbie, has it? You are one of a growing band of successful managers of a major Scottish company. So stop being so nervous. You wouldn't have had the promotion if you weren't seen to have the potential.

I reflected on my lucky start, at the age of twelve, as a message boy with the company. Jim, my pal, had miraculously arranged the job for me. In an attempt to get into the modern technical world I had, on leaving school at the age of fifteen, taken a job as a radio and TV apprentice engineer, but then I made my momentous decision to leave the TV traineeship and ask Ian Stewart – my Carnoustie branch manager – if I could start as an apprentice grocer. Years of day release and night classes had paid off, and here I was driving to my work as a manager in my own four-door pale green 'Fordie' – complete with a pair of flashing orange indicator 'ears' on the roof. Alex Reid, the garage owner in Carnoustie, had kept an eye open for a reliable second-hand car for me.

"I think I can get one of the latest designs for you, Robert; the shape with the mud guards built into the main body, a heater and only one previous owner." Alex had contacts and had nodded and smiled as he told me.

As I recollected that conversation, I was reminded to open the flap near my left knee and allow more warm air from the engine to invade my cold 'cockpit'. How did I manage this? What luck? I still couldn't believe it, for now I have exciting news again. My boss Mr Munro, the area manager, told me only last month that he wanted me to manage a bigger branch in Logie Street, Lochee – about one and a half miles from Brantwood. So, I would soon be wearing my space suit to whizz to 'Planet Logie'.

How big a planet will Logie Street be, and what will the atmosphere be like?

But this good news now presented me with a serious nagging doubt, for I had heard nothing more from Mr Munro. Had he changed his mind about me? Had some other manager been preferred? Had the customer who complained to head office about one of my assistants created a doubt in my boss's mind? Mr Munro had told me I wasn't at fault, but was that true – or had he merely been trying to make me feel better? Had a 'black mark' been created? Or perhaps he had noticed my shop blinds weren't up at nine o'clock one morning when I had been badly delayed by a road blockage, when a car and lorry had collided on the Arbroath main road?

Come on, Murray; there you go again. You must stop being so negative – none of those problems were caused by you.

* * *

As I fleetingly went through my early recollections and those distracting fears, my mind took me back to a more comfortable event which I will forever associate with my start as a message boy – a professional journey that would take me into the retail grocery world.

It was the July of 1953, I was twelve years old and The Open golf tournament was being played on the Championship course at Carnoustie. Mr Stewart, my manager, had given me time off to see the final moments. The first time The Open had been played at Carnoustie was in 1931, when Tommy Armour won, and later in 1937 when Henry Cotton secured the prized trophy. These early events had established Carnoustie as a real test on a 'links' course. Carnoustie hosted the famous event a further five times, the most recent being in 2018 when Italian Eduardo Molinari beat all his rivals.

"It's golf history, Mr Stewart."

"Alright, Robert. Don't forget; you'll need to do all your deliveries before you enjoy watching golf. Remember I'll still be here, so bring the bike to the back door when it's all over," he had told me. Picking up the feeling he wasn't interested in golf, I realised he had given me a unique chance to see the final stages of the tournament which had not been held in the town for sixteen years. He had added his peculiar "Go, go greasy grocer, go," chant at the end of his comment, so I could sense he was quite relaxed about it.

I couldn't help it – instantly, I recalled all the events of that dramatic day, which will forever be inextricably linked to my start as a message boy. It had been an unusually eventful summer. Princess Elizabeth was crowned Queen, and I witnessed her coronation on my friend's television set – one of only a few in the town, he had told me. Then Edmund Hillary and Sherpa Tensing ascended Mount Everest, creating a huge sense of achievement for the nation. Now, another exciting national event was taking place – but this one, "The Open", was right on 'my doorstep'. In those days the tournament ended on a Saturday, and now it was the last nail-biting day of play.

There had been much commotion in the town for the approach of this world-famous contest. Nearly two weeks earlier I had begun my job as a message boy, and earlier on this pulsating day I had rushed around town to make my deliveries as my boss had allowed me time to see the closing stage of this most prestigious golf event. The previous week I had been asked to make a special delivery of fresh fruit to the Bruce Hotel in the town where the most prominent man in golf, and tipped to be the winner, was temporarily resident – none other than the American Ben Hogan. What fired my imagination was that he had arrived early to practise on the course, and was reported to require special daily baths in the hotel to aid his damaged back caused by a car accident. I learned much later that the standard bath in the hotel was reportedly too small to allow him to fully stretch, and that he had to make trips to Dundee to find a suitable facility. I remember my school pal Alan Craigie telling me, with incredulity, that he had seen Mr Hogan practise by driving golf balls into the sea. "Gee, Robbie, he must be rich," Alan had told me. "I'm going to look for the balls when the tide goes out!" I imagined the American golfer may have consumed the apples and pears I had delivered, and I felt a naïve schoolboy rapport with the great man.

With a gallery of probably no more than two hundred people, there were no obvious security arrangements and not a TV camera in sight. Come to think of it, I didn't pay to watch – I had merely walked on to the course. Kneeling in the front row on the edge of the green – and I mean the exact edge, where the fine cut by the Shank's precision lawn mower had dictated the line – I settled down to witness history. Now, on a dull calm day, the scene was the 18th green of the famous course, and Ben Hogan was about to make a putt to win the Claret Jug trophy. I was all too aware of the tension.

A hush descended – a pregnant pause.

In those carefree days I played a lot of golf with my brother Peem on the smaller Burnside course and was accustomed to the fresh smell of newly cut grass, but as I knelt there in my short trousers that sense seemed more pronounced – yet dimmed somewhat by the offensive cigar smoke which hung lazily over the area. No one dare move or make a noise. I felt stinging on my legs, and looked down to see an army of red ants crawling over me – and, worse still, climbing their way up inside my pants. Frozen stiff with fear, I couldn't speak, gasp or cry out. For what seemed an age, my hero addressed his ball and seemed to take an eternity to mentally prepare for the shot of his life. To my massive comfort, his lengthy putt sent the ball into the hole, and an almighty cheer echoed around the green. I leapt to my feet and brushed off the offending insects with as much relief, I guess, that the winner had felt with that history-making last strike of his ball.

Mr Hogan was presented with the iconic trophy, and said how happy he was to receive it. Then, amongst other tributes, he said in his distinctive American accent: "I have found Carnoustie to be a wonderful place, and the people so helpful and friendly." At that moment I wanted to shout out "And I delivered your fruit!"

That was it; I had to dash back to the shop. I had my own world to address – in relative terms, as important to me as Mr Hogan's famous achievement had been in the world of golf.

* * *

The blast of a car's horn disturbed my reverie, and looking in my mirror I saw a large black Wolseley car with the driver's face staring out angrily. "How did I get here?" I gasped. Arriving at the 'circle' (as a roundabout is described in Dundee) at the east end of the city bypass, known as the Kingsway, I realised I must have missed a few opportunities to join the flow of traffic. This was not an unusual occurrence; somehow, quite amazingly, I found that I had driven on 'auto pilot' for several miles along that main road with its dips and bends. Usually I would be preoccupied by worries about business: had I bought enough vegetables to see me through till Saturday evening, or had I overestimated the baskets of tomatoes I had purchased? But today, I had allowed Ben Hogan and niggling worries about Mr Munro's delay in confirming my move to crowd in on me.

Robbie, someday you're going to come a cropper. Maybe even driving around the circle the wrong way! Just think of the chaos that would be caused if you were off work due to an accident.

Looking back at those dangerous moments, I realise that – although there were no radios, mobile phones or CD players in cars in those days – it allowed too much of the equally-dangerous practise of thinking... or perhaps I should say day- dreaming. Quite suddenly, it seemed, I was parking my car in a road space beside the shop. It was a couple of minutes after ten past eight. Good timing to start prepping things for the day, with blinds up at 8.30. After all, I antici-pated it was going to be the usual busy forenoon of a half day.

Looking to the west, I could see dark clouds forming. *Mum was right – she always was good at reading the weath-er.* Even as a message boy I had learned how much weather had an impact on business. Rain was on its way, but thankful-ly no staff or customers were waiting for me at the shop doorway – unlike the time when I appeared at 8.20am, only to find Mrs Cruickshanks who commented, "Whaur have you been son? Yer at the coo's tail the day! I ha'e tae hurry, I've an early bus to catch!"

This was the lady with a clever (and lucky) wee dog called 'Spot', who obviously enjoyed salmon and who – his owner claimed – could recognise cans of it going into her shopping bag. She would mouth the words "And a can o' salmon" and then say "Just haud yer wheesht and put the can in a paper bag, son, so he disnae see." This was always her request. For all I know Spot had probably long before worked out the body language and the verbal signals of her cautionary words, and so knew he was on to a 'winner'. But would you believe it? A dog called Spot that could read labels on cans of salmon! A well-named pet.

Mrs Cruikshanks, a regular customer, was a good enough reason not to be late. But the fact that Mr Munro, my boss, lived very close to the shop was an even more important motivation not to be seen arriving rather tight for time – or worse, late!

CHAPTER 2

April 1962:
"A Worrying Delay", or
"Half-Day Rest"

"A H'M in an awfy hurry, son. Can you open up? I just need a loaf and quarter o' boiled ham," a shrill voice said. I opened the door and looked out. It was Mrs Cox from Beechwood, frantically knocking on the shop window.

"Alright, Mrs Cox; come in. What's the problem?"

"Oh, my neighbour's lum went up this morning. The fire brigade had tae come and pit oot the fire. She's had nae breakfast. I telt her I'd get something quick for her breakfast." Another unusual, exciting start to a day. But it indicated how people helped each other out.

As expected, it was a busy Wednesday morning in the shop. Winnie and Isobel, my full-time assistants, were serving almost continuously at the counter, and I was preparing a space in the back shop for I was expecting – at any minute –

the weekly 'general order' which would arrive on the back of the Bedford flat-bed lorry from the company's Dundee warehouse in Bellfield Street. I remember thinking, because of the heavy showers, that Eddie the driver would have the tarpaulin draped over his load today. No net in those days!

My other thoughts were that my increase in sales had led the area manager, Mr Munro, to suggest meeting the additional cost for a part-time assistant, and I was hopeful the young lass I had interviewed could start within a week.

You didn't have to ask for another assistant, Robbie. The boss saw your increasing sales figures. You worried about the increase in costs of more staff, but Mr Munro could tell you needed help. Stop being so worried about everything.

Just as I saw the lorry with its precarious load chugging to a halt on the emphasised camber of the road, the black phone – sitting on its matching cradle with a circular dial device and located on a narrow ledge in the back shop – suddenly rang out. For some strange nervous reason, I had a habit of guessing if calls were likely to be good or bad news; on occasion a fruit and vegetable supplier would call for an order, or Head Office would ask for some information. But the timing of today's ring seemed to herald something not so good. My predictions were not always correct but, somehow, I persisted with my illogical nervous habit.

"Hello, Robert. How are things today?" It was Mr Munro.

"Fine thanks, Mr Munro," I replied.

"Robert, just a quick call to say that your move to Logie Street has to be delayed."

This statement magnified my growing fears.

Don't go and over-react now, Robbie. Just bide your time. You can't put your space suit on yet.

34

"Oh, that's a pity. Is there a problem, Mr Munro?"

"I'm trying to juggle people around, and I can't find your replacement. Your move could be a month away."

Eddie would be bringing stock in through the back door at any moment, and – clutching the phone with its persistently annoying twisted and frayed short cord – I put my head around the doorway to the front shop and noticed a queue of customers had formed and help was needed.

As so much was happening, I didn't have time to formulate any questions. I merely said, rather hastily, "Don't worry, Mr Munro. That'll be alright." I tried to give what I thought was a managerial response. My immediate concern was that my boss would think my reaction was one of seeming haste and disregard.

"Speak with you next week, Robert," was all that he said. Then I heard his phone go down.

* * *

"Lucky dip today, Mr Murray?"

Jings, Robbie. It's not been a lucky one so far, but you can't tell Eddie that!

"Will I have the winner this week?" I joked as I put my hand inside his mucky but nonetheless inviting lucky bag to pick a number.

Pushing his spectacles further up his nose, he replied, "Oh, go on. Ye'r a lang time deid!" – his usual response to my routine jocular remark.

To run his 'sweepie', as he called it, Eddie – while on his travels – collected two shillings from his 'clients' (managers and staff) who picked out a number from his well-worn and tatty cloth bag. The number was checked against the list of football matches listed in the *Sunday Post* every week, and the person with the highest number of goals scored in a match won the handsome kitty.

As I passed over my florin, I teased Eddie: "You know, I read in the *Courier* that a well-known Broughty Ferry minister has been sounding doom and gloom about our sick society throwing good money away on bingo."

Eddie had a ready reply. "Aye, but that's a posh part o' the world. They don't do 'sweepies' there." Turning, he added, "What about you this week Isobel?" The ever-hopeful driver looked expectant while Isobel came into the back shop to fill a bag of potatoes. "No way, Eddie. I've more chance o' winnin' £50 at the next Twist Marathon in the JM!"

I knew Isobel was a keen and fit dancer. She was referring to the recent energy sapping non-stop 'Twist' competitions held in the famous Dundee ballroom.

"And you, Winnie?" he asked as she washed her greasy hands.

"I'm saving my money for a ticket to a Joe Brown concert someday. I've got his latest, 'Picture of You' – it's great. Hope he comes to Dundee sometime soon."

Putting all thoughts of Mr Munro's call and Eddie's kitty to the back of my mind, I dashed to help at the counter before Winnie and Isobel increased their 'help us please' sighs.

* * *

It was noticeable that half-day mornings were particularly busy. It had been the same on Tuesdays when I was an apprentice in Carnoustie branch. Now, in Dundee, each Wednesday was my half-day and once part of the 'order' had been put on shelves or into store and I had 'cashed up', I headed home to Carnoustie.

All through my training days Mum had been a constant support to me. "Well how are things today?" she enquired as I entered the kitchen through the back door.

"All fine, mum – but I've just been told my move to Logie Street has had to be delayed." I don't know why I blurted that out so abruptly.

"Oh dear," she replied as she laid a soup bowl at my usual place on the kitchen table. From the window she had seen me arriving in the street, and would be ready in a few minutes to serve my soup.

"What's it today, mum?"

"It's your favourite: homemade Scotch broth. But I've put a 'wee ticky' more carrots in it this week. It's the last of dad's carrots from his sand-pit in the garden."

"Lovely." I liked mum's word 'ticky'. It was her own word, and it was homely.

"Dad's on late shift, but he had to set off early today. He had to take his bike on the train from Carnoustie to Arbroath, then cycle to Lunan Bay signal box. He was busy tidying his shed this morning."

"Will he have to bike home from Lunan when he finishes at 10 o'clock?

"Oh, yes. There'll be no train that stops at Lunan station after 6 o'clock, but he'll still have to be on duty to operate the signals for 'fasts'." (By 'fasts', she was referring to fast long-distance trains as opposed to slower local trains.)

"Hope it doesn't rain."

"I hope not too – he's got a sore throat, but he's resisting the kaoline."

I'd told mum and dad a few weeks earlier that I had been offered to manage a larger branch. The move had been planned, at that point, to take place in a week's time. This was of great encouragement to me. I had been aware that my sales were growing, and I had confidently come to expect that each week would beat the same week the previous year.

After my brief explanation to mum about the delay, she was relaxed. "Mr Munro will have a lot on his mind," she reasoned. Mum always had a canny way of making things seem simple and acceptable.

"I'm not worried, mum. It's just that I had hoped to make the move next week as planned, because my college exams will be next month. Now they'll clash when I take over my new branch."

Come on, Robbie. You're a big boy now.

* * *

Part of my half-day routine was to read out to mum pieces of news from the paper. Knowing she didn't stop doing things around the house all morning, I knew she welcomed my little skip through the pages. Dad, although free during the morning, had – by the look of the pristine newspaper – not yet read it, and I had a quick look at the unopened *Courier* (The *Dundee Courier & Advertiser*) and noticed something unusual. "You'll have to be careful when you visit Dundee now mum," I observed.

"Oh? Why's that, Robert?"

"Because there are going to be 'panda crossings'!"

"Is there a circus coming?" she asked.

"Nothing as exciting, mum. No, it's the name used for a safer crossing on busy roads in Dundee. It says here that zebra crossings are thought to be dangerous because people just thought they could walk on to the crossing and vehicles would automatically stop. Pandas will have a button to operate a green light, to indicate when it is safe to cross. There'll likely be a few pandas along Princes Street in Edinburgh too!" I mischievously added with a laugh.

"Don't remind me of that."

My tease was that on a family day out to Edinburgh at one point, we were all up on the battlements of the Castle when mum said, "Oh, look at that policeman on a horse directing the traffic away down there at a T-junction on Princes Street!"

We all kept looking around and asking, "Where, mum? Where?"

"Look! I can see him!" she insisted.

This went on for many minutes, and we nearly gave up when dad discovered that mum had seen a statue of a rider on horseback in Princes Street Gardens, in direct line with Princes Street. Later, when we walked along Princes Street, I noticed the statue which I think was the one mum had been referring to.

"Look at that, mum! It wasn't a policeman directing traffic at all. It's a statue in memory of the Officers and Men of the 'Royal Scots Greys', with a senior officer astride a horse. The inscription reads: "In Memory of those who gave their lives and commemorated their victories during The Boer War, 1899 to 1902." Mum had a great ability to laugh at her own little mistakes, and we kept that story going for years.

"Well, look out for pandas, mum!" I smiled as I turned over a page. It was always a joy to have some time with mum on my half-day, and dad too depending on the timing of his shifts. That's when I could help him in the garden. It was a time to catch up on family events, as well as read the news and listen to the popular songs of the time. I remember Danny Williams' 'Moon River' and Cliff Richard's 'The Young Ones' were favourites then. I had another look at the *Courier* and called out to mum, "I see there's been a bairn drowned in a burn near Montrose." As soon as I read out the story, I guessed mum's instant reaction.

"Well, you see? I was right to give you a spanking that day!"

Mum was referring to the time I had wandered nearly half a mile away from home with some other four year old boy along the banks of the Barry Burn, almost to the point where it flows under the railway line. I had simply disappeared and, when she caught up with me, she pulled down my pants and gave me a real sore spanking. I remember it vividly, because some Anderson Grice foundry workers were shouting and applauding from a high crane. Today I can only imagine the panic mum must have been in back then.

Changing the subject as quickly as possible, I moved on. "Looks like there will be a road bridge across the Tay after all. It says here the George Wimpy Company is to use a steamer and a land-sounding launch to do test borings along the line of forty piers for the planned road bridge."

"That'll be a huge help," mum said. "How easy it will be to get to Fife then."

"And listen to this! 'The new Overgate will offer the finest battery of food trading shops in Scotland. Housewives will be able to buy everything from walking distance'."

"Well that's good news, Robert," mum replied. "Do you think you could be managing a shop there someday?"

"I doubt it, mum. They will likely have bigger shops then. Remember, I'm managing a small branch."

"Maybe someday you will do that."

"But here's more news. Dundee seems to be on the 'up'. This article says that the goalposts at Riverside are to be removed to allow a Piper Apache aeroplane to land and provide a city-to-city link."

"Will that be a big aeroplane?" asked mum.

"No, it says here it will be a four-seater."

"That must be good for business." I was always impressed by mum's down to earth understanding of the world.

I recall in those days thinking that Dundee was making huge changes. Each time I read the newspaper, there were reports of big decisions being made: the Tay Road Bridge, air transport, city redevelopment and new Overgate plans, along with City Council efforts to bring in American investment. The early 1960s was a period of great change.

"Oh, mum, listen to this," I said, spotting something else. "Burton's the tailors have got a big advert in the paper today."

"What? More bargains?" she enquired.

"Yes, that's right. Made to measure suits, for as little as £11 and 10 shillings."

"But you had a new suit only two years ago!"

"They're offering so many extras nowadays. It says here: "Design your own outfit". You can choose your own colour and quality of material with extra pockets, special linings, waistcoat option, with or without turn-ups on the trousers and different styles of lapels."

"That sounds like the thing soldiers used to talk about. What was it called; something like 'the full Monty'? But do you really need one, Robert?" I should explain that 'The Full Monty' was a reference to the amount of money (twelve shillings and sixpence) soldiers received when they were demobbed after WW2. The highest amount paid out was based on the purchase of a complete three-piece suit from Montague Burton's – hence the term the 'Full Monty'.

"Not really, mum. But it's good value to keep in mind."

"If you have the money, why don't you get your next suit in a year or two from Mr Irvine in Station Road? He's got a good reputation."

"He's a one-man specialist tailor, mum. His prices will be too high for me. I don't see how he'll compete with the Burtons, Colliers and Hepworths of this world." Mum, I could tell, didn't think I needed a new suit, so I changed the subject. "Anything good on TV, mum?" I asked as I neatly folded the paper ready for dad's return.

"Don't know, but *The One O'Clock Gang Show* ended just before you got home. Oh, it was a really good laugh today. It's just a lot of silly nonsense. Larry Marshall was taking the mickey out of Charlie Sim and Dorothy Paul today. Remember how you always watched the show on Fridays when they dressed up as school bairns being cheeky to Jimmy Nairn, their teacher in the classroom?"

"Carefree days, mum."

She looked concerned. "Are you not enjoying your manager's job, then?"

"Oh yes, it's fine. There's never a dull minute, and my sales are good."

"Are you worried about the delay?"

I sighed. "It's just that it all seemed ready to happen, and suddenly it's been put back. I only know what Mr Munro tells me. Maybe there's something going on that I don't know about."

"Surely you would know."

"There's no one I can speak to. My old boss once told me that managers chat on the phone because they like to get a warning that Mr Munro's on his way to their branch. Do you remember when I was a message boy in Carnoustie, I had to rush back to tell the boss I had seen Mr Munro's car parked in Park Avenue? I could never understand why any manager needed such a warning."

"I'm sure there will a good reason for the delay," she suggested reassuringly.

"Maybe I should be chatting on the phone to other managers, to hear what's going on. But I don't really know them."

So, what was the news out there? I wondered... was there something I should know?

What are you worrying about now, Robbie? You've never had a problem with anything Mr Munro has said or promised in the past. You'll have to start believing in yourself.

Mr Munro had always been reliable and straight with me, so I put his call down to some genuine problems he must have encountered. My real disappointment was that two weeks previously I'd told my two Carnoustie pals, Jim and Alan, that I'd be moving on in one week. Jim was my boyhood hero. He had told me everything I needed to know about fishing and boats at Westhaven. He was nearly three years older than me, and we had shared a huge history of adventures growing up in our wonderful Westhaven world. He had served his time as a joiner/carpenter, been called up for National Service in the Scots Guards, and was now a policeman in Dundee. By chance, a few months previously, he had spotted me at the doorway of the Brantwood Avenue branch as he cycled along on his duties. Since then he had occasionally stopped off to chat. Alan, on the other hand, was my school classmate who inspired me to start work as a radio and TV mechanic. He was now working in Dundee and occasionally looked in to see me in the shop. It was always such a good feeling to keep in touch with my old Carnoustie friends. But now they would have to find out that my move wouldn't be happening as planned at all.

CHAPTER 3

April 1962:
"Peem Needs Help", or
"The Dog and Dish"

"I'M off for a run in the car, mum," I called out as I put on my raincoat.

"Before you go, can I ask you to have a word with James tonight?" mum asked me. "I'm concerned about him; he's very down just now."

"What's wrong?"

"He's worried about finding a job."

I knew my brother Peem had spent about four years at Duncan of Jordanstone Art College, Dundee, and since June last year had been doing casual work until he found a job in the art world.

"Alright, mum. I'll do that."

"Don't you go worrying about your own problems now, too," she said anxiously as she tidied the kitchen table.

Suddenly I realised mum was now worrying about both me *and* my brother.

"No, it's alright. I'm just going for a chat with my former colleagues at the shop."

* * *

After catching up with mum's news, I decided to drive along to my previous branch shop in the town where I had served my apprenticeship. A quick chat was always welcome with my former colleagues and Ian the manager, with whom I had recently developed some gentle sparring about our relative positions on Mr Munro's monthly sales percentage charts. It was rather a sad way to spend my half-day holiday.

One of the disadvantages of working in the retail grocery trade was that Sundays were the only days not worked. Saturdays, being so extremely busy, meant that it was a late finish with some exhaustion. Sunday was the only day for a long 'lie-in', and then it seemed it was time for mental preparations for the week ahead. Half-days had a similar restriction, in that little could be done in the few hours of an afternoon. This was especially true in winter. Looking back, I wonder why, in the summer months, I hadn't played golf on my half-days in Carnoustie. But I have come to realise that I actually spent my time doing night school homework. Now on Wednesdays I had no-one to play golf with, as Tuesday was the town's half-day and my former golfing classmate Jock Brown – also an apprentice grocer – had left Carnoustie and was now working with a food-canning company.

Come on now, Robbie. You must build up some confidence. Things are going well. There's nothing wrong keeping in touch with Carnoustie branch, but you should start to think about getting some golf on your half-day. Get out and get some fresh air.

What I really wanted was some quiet time to reflect on Mr Munro's phone call, but I had developed a pattern on occasions of popping in to see my old workmates. Looking back, I can only think that I had still an emotional tie with the Carnoustie branch – it was my grocery trade 'nursery', where I had been trained and advised for five years. Nobody stopped work to speak with me; that was the way it was. No time to stop and chat, and I too would not have wanted my staff to stop and chat in my own branch.

"Well, how's the Greasy Grocer the day?" said my old boss in his usual humorous way as he dashed past carrying a side of bacon.

"Fine," I replied. "Still plugging away." Which was my usual answer, without bragging about my increasing sales and my move up the league table of shops' sales increases. Unlike Brantwood, Carnoustie branch had steadily increased sales so that its percentage increases were difficult to achieve, whereas I had scope to improve from a low base and move up the boss's chart of successes. Although my friends were busy dashing about on duty, there was still time for some quick fire wise-cracking and gentle banter. My old boss's usual chant was still as quirky and humorous as before: "Still time to come back here and help us out! Go, go, greasy grocer, go!" he would say as he moved about the shop with his characteristic grin. I was always determined never to boast about my sales increases, but Ian enjoyed the banter and I relished the fun too.

"Have you heard, Robert? Big changes coming!"

"Oh really?" I said, sensing one of Ian's teases on the way.

"Yes, Carnoustie may be having a new extension and refurb – so you might be knocked off your perch in Mr Munro's league table!"

"But I may be running a supermarket someday," I replied with good humour. Of course, it was just bravado, but for effect I breathed on the nails of my folded right hand and rubbed them on my coat. This was just Ian's way of winding me up. It was actually a great compliment for me to even have that kind of exchange with a highly-respected manager. Ian had been a great help to me in my training days, and I respected him hugely. I never went into his back shop, as I regarded that as no longer my domain. I knew he didn't gossip with other managers; nevertheless, I made no comment about my delayed move to Logie Street. I had always taken the view that I wouldn't want Mr Munro to think I had "gossiped" about anything.

After what was merely a brief "hello and cheerio", I left my friends to get on with their work without interruption. My mind was set on parking at Westhaven, over-looking the sea. Since my earliest boyhood days, I had a favourite spot at which to sit and mull over any problems or issues. Today was no different, but instead of sitting in the long grass with birds singing and crickets chirping around me – as they had done years before – I was now comfortably cocooned within my Ford Prefect. My thoughts began to wander. I could see the rocks where, a few short years ago, I fished with my pals Coffie, Ollie, Jim and Peem. I recalled the incident where Ollie was nearly drowned, and remembered the days where we knew every step across every rock to get to our favourite rock, 'Dargie'.

The longer I recalled those fishing times and the deeper my recollections of those carefree days became, I thought of our giant playground which stretched from Buddon Point to the Bleachfield and all the risky and naughty things we did. We burned dead marram grass in springtime, causing the police to make a surprise visit (and leading us to scarper), guddled sticklebacks in Craigmill Burn at the Bleachfield, and fished for trout at the sluice further upstream at Craigmill Den. One of our more dangerous exploits was to attempt our own versions of army training on the nearby army assault course at Barry Buddon, possibly equalled by smoking Woodbine cigarettes under the upturned boats in winter. Five Woodbine ciggies came in paper packs of five for eight pence (approximately 3p), and we kept matches loose in our pockets so mum didn't hear them rattle in a box. Yet we survived those wonderfully risky, dangerous and happy days.

How had I, in that short time, become a manager? Yes, I had done all my night classes, but I never dreamt it would happen – nor had I pushed for it to happen. And only a few months ago, by yet another piece of luck in my life, Alex Reid the garage owner had mentioned to my dad that he had his eyes on a good second-hand car with low mileage for me. Now more news about something I didn't seek: a bigger branch. Why had this delay really happened?

You're beginning to sound like you don't enjoy this management world. What's wrong with you? Are you scared of a bigger branch?

Would it still take place? Had my boss decided against the move? Did he want me to experience a bigger branch as an assistant manager, perhaps? I had heard that sort of thing did happen. Years later, I learned that managers in the city regularly phoned each other with titbits of gossip or news, and certainly with a warning call that "Munro is on his way!" In all of my experience at Carnoustie branch, I had never been aware of Mr Stewart, my manager, making or receiving calls from other managers. I was a new face in Dundee and had no prior connection with Dundee managers, so I was not in the loop of personal calls. There seemed no need for me to warn other managers that "Munro was on his way", as I had nothing to fear. As far as I was concerned, he could turn up at any time. I could never understand why managers needed warnings.

Alan, my former school classmate, had now completed his apprenticeship as a radio and TV engineer. It was he who had the idea of training in the future technology of television. He had left school a few months before me, and was partly influential in my decision to follow his lead – only to find I soon missed the hustle and bustle of the grocery trade. While out and about in his company van, he had by chance noticed me while I happened to be at the door of the shop. Jim, my hero from my Westhavem fishing and boating boyhood days – and now a Dundee Bobby – also looked in from time to time. For me, there was some comfort in having two Carnoustie friends to chat with. Both would now look for me at the Logie Street store and be puzzled by my absence. No phones at home in those days, and the very idea of mobile phones would have seemed then like something out of a *Flash Gordon* movie.

By far my greatest concern was that the exams for the retail management course, which I had been asked to commence last September at Dundee College of Technology (known locally as 'The Teck', or 'Teckie'), would take place about the same time as Mr Munro wanted the move. The latter would have to take precedence. Only two other managers from Wm Low attended the course: Jim, manager of a large shop in Dundee – physically the biggest branch in the city – and Tom, manager of one of the busiest branches in Fife. I was very much aware of being one of the 'select three'. There were retail managers, owners and directors from other companies on the course, and – since it wasn't only orientated towards grocery – I was learning exactly what the course was offering: the Principles of Retail Management. It was a two-year course, and year one had commenced almost seven months earlier. The current subjects were Scots Law, Work Study, Merchandising and Economics. I'd had a jarring moment when the College Head of Department interviewed me and used the word 'paradoxically' during the discussion. I'd had no idea what the word meant. This had two effects on me: one, get home and look up the dictionary, and two, how am I going to get anywhere with this course when I don't even understand the words they use?

Come on now, Murray! You wanted to go to Arbroath High School, and now you're studying subjects you could barely spell when you were doing your grocery evening classes.

Our economics lecturer had recently mentioned that Professor C. Northcote Parkinson was to visit Dundee. The Professor's well-publicised two principles were given a good airing in the classroom. One was "Expenditure rises to meet income," and the other, "All work expands to find time available for its completion." We had some lively discussions, with good practical examples within the retail trade. The exchanges of ideas and experiences within the class were valuable, and I felt it was a definite level up from anything I had previously studied. My anxiety now was that I wanted to do well – especially with my two more experienced company colleagues being in the same class.

You must be seen to do well, especially as everything so far had gone smoothly since you took over the Brantwood branch. You've coped with a few adventures since those nervous early days. Come on now, Murray. You're worrying again. Everything has gone smoothly, and stocktakes have proved you have produced good profit performances. Do you realise how many times you speak to yourself?

The day-to-day routines had worked out well enough. The staff and suppliers had been co-operative, and the few new Dundee terms used by customers – although initially quite confusing – had now become second nature (lippes and loafs being my obvious early pitfalls). In thinking about my life so far, I concluded that by far one of the best developments for me had been getting my car. It had changed my working life. As my sales grew, I increasingly found that I ran out of stock – which was an encouraging problem to have – and the car became invaluable when, during those mid-day breaks, I collected 'supplementary orders' from the company warehouse in Bellfield Street. Jim Anderson, the warehouse manager, was always chirpy and cheery and gave me help to put the boxes in my car. Today it's inconceivable that a manager would drive his own car to pick up stock at a central warehouse. In hindsight, I didn't give a thought to my car insurance policy, but it didn't seem necessary in those days.

The acquisition of my car, registration CTS 540 (TS was one of the two initials used for vehicles registered then in Dundee city, the others being YJ), previously owned by DC Thomson, had been well-maintained and was hugely beneficial, as my flexibility was now improved greatly. At lunchtimes, when the shop closed, I was able to drive into the city centre and park immediately outside the Royal Bank of Scotland in Reform Street, pick up my bank bag (which I had carefully deposited in the night safe the previous evening) and obtain a supply of change for the till. This was the moment I could have a quick chat with my school classmate Bill McGregor, who worked there, but those meetings had come to an end when he finished his training and secured a banking job in India. Lunchtimes were a slight problem. I had tried on occasions to eat a sandwich in the back shop, but found it too monotonous and uninspiring. Eating lunch on the premises made it a long day. By a chance meeting, I started joining some Carnoustie acquaintances for a bite to eat at the Dundee Pasteurised Milk restaurant (the 'DPM' or, as Dundonians called it, 'the DP and M') in Reform Street, but one day I noticed a lady at the next table giving her dog a lick of food off her plate! Nicknaming the place "The Dog and Dish", I never returned and started to eat at Draffens' 'cottage' restaurant instead – which was a little more expensive for my liking, but was at least 'dog free'. All that had not been as horrific as at the café in West Port, Arbroath, during my radio and TV apprenticeship days where – one lunchtime – I found a piece of newspaper floating in my soup. That was bad enough, but the piece still visibly read "Death Notices" with the words "Suddenly at Dundee Royal Infirmary..." very obvious. It was not a comforting thing to read at the start of a meal.

As I sat there with the rain driving in from the sea, I tried to convince myself of one important fact: my attitude was to keep on top of everything around me, and I felt I was doing quite well until one day Mr Munro asked me, "How do you feel things are going here for you, Robert?"

"All fine," I replied.

"Just remember to assert yourself."

He didn't say why, and he didn't elaborate. Although I knew what the word 'assert' meant, I never asked him why he had said it. All that happened was that I became more conscious of my own behaviour. That was the only piece of advice I was ever given about managing, but the observant Mr Munro must have seen the need and I knew immediately I had to respond.

You see, Robbie? You must develop some strength. Mr Munro has seen the need. So, do it!

To balance my general good fortune, however, I had suffered a few incidents in winter. With icy roads being a problem, I found it difficult to get traction on my rear tyres. I partially solved this issue by filling up two large sacks with sand and leaving them all winter in my car boot. It became normal practice to pack them in the rear space at the end of autumn, when bad roads were expected. Dad had given me that idea, as well as his clever plan to put a coat over the engine.

Now, as I sat there in my car on a dismal wet half-day holiday, I recalled the day when, on my way to work I was caught in an early morning blizzard. Cars were slipping and slithering all over the roads. It was difficult to say the least. Some cars were abandoned but there was no way I could simply not turn up and open the shop as usual at 8.30 am. By taking obscure routes I managed to arrive at Brantwood exactly on time and luckily with no customers or staff shivering at the door. Looking back now, I can see I was in a similar situation as my father had been in. He had set off from Westhaven at 4.30am on a fifteen mile journey on his pushbike to 'man' the Longforgan railway signal box at 6am, and was caught in a blizzard. He kept going and managed to get there late, but still in time to operate the signals to allow the early morning Aberdeen/Glasgow passenger train to make its way. I still have the letter he received from the railway chief thanking him for his determination to keep the line open despite his ordeal.

I sat in the car and looked out to the rocks and the incoming tide, and momentarily thought how lucky I was to have my father's practical advice. It became rather cold as I stared through the rain streaks on the windscreen. It was time to return home.

Listen, Robbie. Whatever you do or think won't change what's in Mr Munro's mind. Just get on with things and start thinking on the bright side.

"I hope you've not been away worrying about the delay, Robert," Mum said as I shook the rain off my coat as I walked into the kitchen.

"No, no, mum – not at all. It's just good to catch up on the news along at the Carnoustie shop," I responded with some inaccuracy while trying to remove her fears.

"That's good," mum smiled. She then added, "It'll be James' 21st birthday this November. It's a long way away, so we must keep a date in mind for his party. I think he needs cheered up a lot."

"Yes, mum. I'll keep that in mind."

"And Isobel's 18th birthday will be on the 26th of July – we'll need to do something special."

Isobel, my oldest sister, was the keen dancer who had won prizes as a young girl with her 'Irish Washer Woman', 'Sailor's Hornpipe' and 'Highland Fling' performances. What a shame that, years previously, she could practise only when the McLagan's – who lived in the flat below us – were out. It was time to read through some notes for my exams which were few weeks away, so I disappeared to my room upstairs. Tea would be ready in about a couple of hours.

CHAPTER 4

April 1962:
"Sharing Our Worries", or
"Peem's Problems"

"TEA'S ready now! Come along; it's steak pie, and then rice pudding with raisins!" mum called from downstairs. We enjoyed the delicious steak pie, then mum cleared away the plates. That was our cue. "One, two, three..." we all chanted slowly in our ritualistic way as mum opened the oven door.

"Here it comes now!" Mum added in the spirit of the grand presentation, and we all gathered around the large duck-egg blue enamelled dish with the dark blue rim as it emerged from the oven to watch the skin of the rice pudding ripple with heat. Wednesday meals were so special, and that is something I also now realise – that mum too must have savoured those times when we were all there, and even more especially when dad was on early shift.

What a lucky laddie you are, Robbie Murray!

Earlier, mum had been nervously darting back and forth to the living room window and looking for Peem. This was nothing new: she always liked to know what was going on in the street. Peem had obviously come into view. "Here's James coming now. Oh dear, he's looking quite down." She turned to look at me. "Don't say anything to him yet. Wait till after tea," mum suggested as she nervously twisted a dish towel in her hands and dashed to the kitchen.

James, or Peem (a popular local nickname for a boy christened James in this part of the Scotland), was a year younger than me. As mentioned earlier, from 1957 until 1961 he had been attending Dundee's respected Duncan of Jordanstone School of Art and Architecture. Like me, he wasn't allowed to leave school until he was fifteen – except in his case, his birthday was in November and he was not permitted to leave until Christmas 1956, resulting in him not commencing Art College until the September of 1957. But for the last year, with no jobs in the offing, he had been doing manual work with a nearby potato merchant known locally as "Tattie Thomson". This made me realise that while I had been engrossed in my modest advancement over the last few years, I had not been so closely involved in following my brother's progress – especially about finding work.

Peem had been keen on drawing and sketching, and had taken an interest in dad's artistic works. I remembered when, in 1961, he revealed his complete course portfolio which he had prepared for his possible future employment interviews. I was staggered at the quality of what he had achieved. Drawings and sketches of human muscles – legs, arms and torsos, along with nudes and compositions of such a variety. And all perfect examples. "Peem, they're all so brilliant! You could frame all of them as classic drawings," I had enthused at the time. I could tell he was thrilled to show off his work, and it made me realise that while I had been so busy managing a grocery shop, Peem had been developing and was now exhibiting real artistic talent.

Isobel, my seventeen year old enthusiastic Highland dancing sister, now a legal secretary, had arrived home from work and 'Baby Jean' – now eight years of age – was playing on the living room floor with her scrapbook. Only dad, being on late shift, was absent. It was Wednesday, and we were all together. Those were chatty times, when we talked about music and TV. Looking back, I see how rare and special those periods were. When I think of it now, I realise how little quality time we all had at that age. When we were younger it was different; in good weather we went for Sunday walks around the town, and when wet or cold we played board games like Ludo, snakes and ladders, and draughts at every opportunity. Gradually we developed our own job and free-time interests. Isobel, I remember, couldn't stop talking about Cliff Richard's 'Please Don't Tease', while Baby Jean – in her own way – used to sing 'Please, No Teas'. I can also recall that Isabel was ecstatic when she listened to 'The Young Ones' – "That's about me!" wee Jean used to call out.

Jean was quite a little mimic in her own way, and we all had a laugh when she asked us to play 'My Old Man's a Dustman' by Donny Lonegan, as opposed to Lonny Donegan, which was her own contrived little joke about his name. We all wanted to hear our own favourites. Peem preferred Elvis Presley and Acker Bilk, but still strummed his guitar whenever he got the chance. He had come a long way from his first renderings of 'Hang Down Your Head, Tom Dooley'.

Looking back at those times, I realise I must have been more than a bit boring and far too serious about pop – although I did enjoy the slower numbers such as 'Moon River', which was popular then. My first impressions of new songs and the singing stars of the day were always slow to develop. It is only now, with hindsight, that I recognise the bright new talent which came on the scene in those early 1960s days.

After all those years I look back and value even more those rare moments together as a family, for sadly – all too soon – we each went our separate ways.

* * *

After our meal that evening, Peem and I went to our room and chatted. Surprisingly, he raised the subject of our futures by asking me about my progress.

"What are your job plans then, Robbie?" he asked me.

"Well, I suppose I'm going to get bigger branches to manage. But it's a tough job, and a lot of hard work looking after stock and watching out for theft and losses."

"Do you enjoy it, though?"

"Yes, I do," I replied. "I get a buzz out of making things happen and seeing results, and I enjoy meeting people."

"You must be earning good money. You've got yourself a car already."

Peem's comment seemed to indicate a comparison he had already drawn between us. I detected, not his jealousy, but rather some frustration.

"My car's a must, and I'll need it even more when I take over a bigger branch. But I've just been told today that the move will be delayed. That's a bit of a worry – I'm not sure why it's happened." This was my attempt to let him see that things didn't always go smoothly for myself either. "What are your work plans, Peem?" I prompted.

"Not sure. You know I left college last year, and I've been working with Tattie Thomson? It's good money, but it's boring and I'm not going anywhere. I'll soon be twenty-one, and I feel like I've done nothing. All I've done so far is work for him during my long summer holidays to pay my way through each year. All I ever got from Angus Education Department was a grant of £200 at the start of year one." His sense of dejection was obvious.

Peem's a perfectionist, Robbie. He needs help. Do whatever you can.

"Have you written to any prospective employers?" I enquired.

"I have, a few. But there's not a lot going on around here. Sometimes I don't even get a reply."

"I don't know anybody in the art world, but I'd think your best chance will be to keep sending off letters. Even if there's no job advertised, just write and enquire."

"I feel I've spent four years for nothing." My brother looked dejected.

"You mustn't give up, Peem," I insisted. "I'm not an artist, but I know your work is brilliant. It's only a matter of time. Depends what kind of work you want. Does it have to be commercial?"

"All I know is that the best chances for work seem to be with DC Thomson in Dundee, and it's very difficult to get a job there."

Thomson Press was – and still is – a prominent newspaper and comic publishing company long established in Dundee and London, publishing many titles such as *The Courier*, *The Sunday Post*, *The Beano* and *The Dandy* and a whole host of others.

"I think you're right. Just keep plugging away," I reassured him. "Something will turn up. Remember the last time we spoke about jobs? We were in my car on the way to uncle Will's funeral in Aberdeen."

"Yes, I remember. Uncle Alan, you and me. We had a good chat that day about only getting somewhere in the world with hard work." Peem was referring to the day in February the previous year when I drove him and mum's brother Alan to the funeral of their oldest brother Will. That conversation had been more significant than either of us had realised at the time.

CHAPTER 5

April 1962:
"Down Memory Lane and Advice from Uncle Alan", or
"Guided by Family Background"

A S happens at funerals you often learn more about the person when they've gone and it's too late to ask questions. I remembered keenly that conversation the three of us had had on the way to Aberdeen. Alan had told us of Will leaving school at age fourteen, and how he had worked in a farm bothy until he was nineteen when he joined the police service. Like his dad (my grandad), Will was a tall, strong man. He had progressed through the ranks doing his spell, amongst others, of point-duty at Union Street, Aberdeen, and eventually becoming a Detective Chief Inspector. Alan himself had been in the police force too, but an unfortunate car accident left him side-lined. He had subsequently owned and run a fruit and vegetable shop in Montrose, and he and I had some interesting chats about the retail trade. He was, I felt, an entrepreneur at heart who just missed his chances.

"Peem, the message that day from Alan was that uncle Will had – like you – worked hard on a farm before he progressed. But equally, Alan's own ambitions had been quashed only by bad luck. So, don't let things get you down too much. Things take time. Don't give up."

"The best thing I remember about that day," Peem observed with a grin, "was Alan's stories about Woodside."

Despite the generation gap, we had found our stories and observations of holidays and events at granny and grandad's Woodside Croft were little different from Alan's day. The croft, part of the Dunninald estate, was near Montrose. Grandad was grieve (a Scottish term for an 'overseer', farm bailiff or manager) on the farm at Boddin, and eventually served over forty years for Mr Robertson the farmer there. Amazingly, he also ran his own croft on which – by some Herculean effort – he managed to grow crops and potatoes. Peem and I holidayed there often, helping to gather potatoes, pick fruit and doing little jobs.

On an Open Day at Dunninald Castle in 2009, I took mum for a look around the castle and grounds. Mum, then aged ninety-five, was always keen to visit the place where she, as a young person, was a cook. We met Jonathan Stansfeld, then into his eighties.

"Hello, are you Mr Stansfeld?" ventured mum.

"I am indeed," said the tall, distinguished gentleman.

"Oh, you must be Jonathan, then?"

"Yes, that's correct," came the cultured reply.

"You must have been about five years old the last time I saw you!" mum said with conviction.

"Goodness me!" The startled landowner recoiled a little.

Mum went on to explain that she was Bella Taylor, the daughter of George Taylor who had farmed the croft for many years.

"Oh, yes: we refer to that as 'Taylor's Strip' now", Mr Stansfeld informed her.

At this, mum let out a joyful gasp.

"Yes, no doubt about it. Your father kept a tidy croft. My family were always most impressed."

Mum was quite emotional when she realised her family name was now part of the history of Dunninald Castle. She went on to recount to me how the Stansfeld family kept a tight watch over the estate. It was then I realised that when Peem and I were playing around the croft while on holiday, we were constantly reminded to behave ourselves.

"The 'Laird' will be 'oo't and aboot', so behave yourselves now!" was grandad's oft-repeated warning.

Looking back now, I realise that life on the croft was a time-warp. I imagine it could have been life on any Scottish farm over the past two or three hundred years. It was the croft and the simple but hard life granny and grandad had that help me so much to relate to the kind of world in which Robert Burns must have grown up. When studying Burns at school, I found a close affinity with everything he wrote. Although life in the countryside must have been harder in Burns' time, there was a sense that not much of the attitude and contentment had likely changed over the years. It was this close feel to nature I gained at granny's home which gave me the vivid touch of country life Scotland's National Bard painted in his poetry.

The highlight, for me, in this idyllic world was granny looking after Maisie, her one cow, which came to the gate of the field without fail at 4pm to be milked in the byre which formed an integral part of the croft cottage. We were told to be quiet during the milking, when Maisie would be chewing hay. While milking – which was not a quick affair – granny wore her special knitted woolly hat while she pressed her head against Maisie's side. A welcome task for Peem and me was to have a chance to make butter in granny's churn, which resembled a large sweetie jar with a whisk inside and a fitted handle on top. It was a long slow process, and it became increasingly harder to keep churning as the rice size globules of butter began to form.

"That's fine now, boys. You've done well. You can go out and play again," she would say. And off we would go, leaving Granny with the difficult bit.

Grandad's world centred on the other two fields which made up the croft's acreage, where he harvested potatoes and grain.

Alan was so enjoying the chat about the 'old days' during that trip to Aberdeen. He obviously had not had anyone in recent years to share his love of farming life with. He gave us tales about mechanised 'tattie' diggers, how the grieve of a farm had to measure the size of 'bits' which pickers had to work on, and how farm workers had to lift such heavy baskets of potatoes high to fill the carts.

"They must have been very strong workers," Peem commented.

"They certainly were. Although tractors replaced horses and the methods of digging had improved, the labourers had a tough life. But it was all relative," Alan told us. "At that time, they thought life was easy."

66

"Farmers must have had difficulties finding and keeping reliable employees," I replied. My thoughts were on similar problems in my own trade when I spoke.

Alan's stories don't have a lot to do with your grocery world, Robbie. You'll just have to allow Alan to tell his tales. You may learn something.

"That was no easy task," Alan sighed.

"What was the problem?"

Alan explained that farm workers in those days were engaged on six-monthly 'terms' (contract). Term times started and ended on 28th May and 28th November. If, for example, a worker wished to move on to another farm, he would have to tell the grieve in advance so that another worker could be 'fee'd' (contracted) for the next six months. If, on the other hand, a grieve decided not to extend a worker's next term time, the worker would have to let it be known to other farmers at the end of a term that he was 'available'.

"If a worker didn't have a good record, it would have been extremely difficult to be 'fee'd' by another farmer for the ensuing six months. It was not an uncommon sight to see farm families moving home by horse and cart on the 29th of May and November. You see, boys – it's much the same today," Alan told us. "Your reputation went before you. That's the message I want to leave with you both."

Alan hadn't set out to give us a lecture, but his stories helped to illustrate to Peem and me how it was important to apply ourselves in our respective work situations. We spoke all the way to Aberdeen about our holidays, tattie picking at Woodside and the hard, uncertain life that farm workers had. I had hoped to pick Alan's brains about fruit and vegetables – especially buying and stock control, and the avoidance of waste – on the return journey, but we seemed to spend more time discussing our recreation fun.

"There was always something to do," Alan said, "whatever the weather."

"That's true," Peem added. "On good days we fed the hens with corn or grass cuttings, and went around the hen houses collecting eggs."

"Aye, getting eggs from under a 'cloaker' was tricky," I remember Alan saying. "You could get a nasty peck from an angry hen. Same wi' lassies," he joked.

"Remember, Peem, when you got a peck on your wrist that went septic. That's when we learned the difference between pink lint and white lint."

"Oh, that's right. Granny put bandages on you, with Epsom salts on pink lint to draw out the poison."

Alan's graphic tales became more amusing when he recounted long stories of how he dealt with catching hens and breaking their necks when it was time for grandad to sell his poultry, followed by tales of him catching pigs when they were being sent off to market and gory accounts of how he caught rats at threshing time.

Alan's in full flight. You're in his hands. It'll help to pass the time, Murray. Just let him enjoy himself.

After a few minutes' gap, while we digested Alan's encounters, Peem added his own recollections.

"Even on wet days we had fun," Peem grinned. "We played on the swing in the tattie shed, or went indoors to play Granny's old '78 records on her table-top record player." This triggered my own memories. Sandy, our cousin who lived close by, was a real music enthusiast. He kept the wind-up portable player going for hours as we each played our own favourite "seventy-eights". My repeated choices at the time were Robert Wilson singing 'Down in the Glen' and another old record was one called 'Beautiful Dreamer'. That song still lives with me to this day. The label, I think, was Paramount, Parlaphone or HMV, and was dark red or crimson in colour. The song was written by Stephen Foster, and the singer then was Nelson Eddy. I have now heard Roy Orbison and Bing Crosby – amongst others – perform it, but I feel they never quite captured Nelson Eddy's style of the time. Strange that a twelve year old should find such a lullaby so repeatable, but still to this day it has, for me, a mesmeric or haunting beauty about it and immediately drops me back into granny's living room with the big black 'fire range', the brass oil lamp hanging on one of the bacon hooks and the record player sitting on granny's big dining table.

"A shame. We must have worn out granny's new records and needles," Peem sighed.

"And probably poor old granny too!" I had to add.

* * *

As Peem and I recalled the day of that long drive and Alan's unstoppable tales, the more I came to realise how helpful it had been.

"Peem, the thing I recall most about that day was Alan telling us how reputation went before workers, and how he advised us to seek to progress."

My brother had told uncle Alan about his work with Tattie Thomson and of his frustration, and I had expressed my worries about my delay. I had reminded Peem of Alan's advice. "What do you mean?" he asked me.

"Well, Alan made the point that it's all very well doing what you're doing, but how long can you keep up that kind of hard work? 'You boys, I hope, will not have to do that.' That's what he told us. 'No, you stick at what you're doing. It'll pay off on the long run'."

That was Alan's message, and it is still strong in my thoughts to this day. "Did he say that?" my brother wondered aloud.

"I remember it exactly, Peem. You know I enjoy my work, but I don't know any more than you about where I'm going in life. We need to make the most of it. So, you will just have to keep trying and not give up. You don't want to be at Tattie Thomson's all your life, do you?

I was using one of mum's old sayings, to me especially, when she encouraged me not to think of working all my life as a shop assistant in the Carnoustie shop. Unwittingly, Peem and I had that quiet resolute way of 'plodding on' in the hope we would progress. Somehow it was built into us.

All of the time spent with uncle Alan that day seemed to drift us away into times past. But looking back, there was a message in all that Alan had told us – somehow he had managed to encourage each of us to find a belief. We had both had a helpful chat, for in a strange way it helped me to get over my disappointment of Mr Munro's news about my delayed move. I told Peem, "You know, my mind still goes back to question behind the real reason for the delay. Is it good news or bad news?" I wanted him to see that I, too, had my concerns.

Uncle Alan's company had been good fun, and we all had a good laugh about our holidays at granny and grandad's croft at Dunninald. It was a diversion away from the worries of work, and possibly from the loss of Uncle Will too. Our chat didn't remove or resolve any problems, but I remember thinking then that what uncle Alan had done was to give both Peem and myself a feeling of family history which emphasised the need to keep working. "To get something out of life you have to put a lot in," he had said. "That's the way for advancement." I realise now that this was my 'built-in' DNA – that unwitting inner strength. Little did he know how much he helped me that day.

At that moment, mum called upstairs to us.

"Come on, you two! I have a 'ticky' more rice pudding to finish off." There was that unique 'ticky' word of mum's again.

"Coming, mum!"

"Thanks for your help Robbie," Peem said.

"No problem, Peem," I told him. "You and uncle Alan probably helped me more."

CHAPTER 6

April 1962:
"Exams and a New Challenge", or
"An Old School Question"

"**W**HAUR'S that wee besom?" I heard a loud voice come from the front shop. I was checking some invoices in the back shop, and Isobel was tidying the fridge.

"That's like wee Mrs Rice's voice," Isobel said with some alarm.

"Come oot here an' eh'll gie ye a skelp on the lug!" The voice was even louder now.

Winnie was serving a customer, but popped her head around the doorway. "You'll better come, Isobel! It's Mrs Rice, and she's up tae high doh!" Winnie whispered loudly.

"My hands are a' greasy," muttered Isobel.

"Whaur's that young laddie?" The volume was continuing to increase. Now she wanted *me*. This was serious, and I urged Isobel to face whatever the trouble was. I followed.

"Puir auld Mr Connors hirpled here tae get his messages, and look what ye gave him!" Mrs Rice held out a wet-looking brown bag in the palm of her hand.

"What is it, Mrs Rice?"

"Whit dae ye think it is? It's your rotten tomatoes, that's whit!"

Isobel hesitated to take hold of the soggy looking bag. "What's wrong with them?"

"Ye've diddled my neighbour! Puir auld Frank."

Isobel looked inside the crumpled bag. "I don't think I gave him tomatoes like that. When was he here?"

"He trauchled here on Monday."

"But this is Thursday now, Mrs Rice."

"Dinna gie me yer haivers! Ye'll replace they rotten things, or ye'll loss *twa* customers."

Isobel looked at me and said, "I didnae sell him tomatoes like that."

"Dinna be a wee clipe now, lass. Are you goin' tae replace them or no'?" she sounded as insistent as ever.

"How many did he buy?" I asked her.

"Half a pund."

Robbie, there's no point in arguing. You don't want to lose customers.

Pausing to think, I said: "Just give Mrs Rice half a pound". Turning to Isobel, I added, "And put in an extra tomato."

"He'll need *twa* extras for a' his trouble!" she persisted.

With some hesitation, I nodded to Isobel. "Sorry about that, Mrs Rice," I said. "Sometimes tomatoes look alright on the outside."

"Ach, dinna gie me yer patter. Ye're aye runnin' aboot like a hen on a hot griddle."

74

I could see Isobel carefully selecting and weighing up the tomatoes and putting in two extras. "There you go, Mrs Rice. Sorry about that. Tell Mr Connors I'm sorry for the trouble."

"A' richt, lass. Jist gie me a half loaf when ah'm here."

Luckily no other customers had witnessed the trouble, and a subdued Mrs Rice had soon gone on her way.

"You did the right thing, Isobel. Now just put the soft tomatoes on the tray." I kept a tray of soft tomatoes for frying on the counter and, as she placed them on the tray, she looked at me.

"Jings, she's a wee toureg!" Isobel exclaimed.

It was another excellent example of how people looked after each other. Mr Connors was lucky he had such a good neighbour.

Our next customer was a lady whose name we didn't know. Winnie was filling shelves in the front shop while Isobel moved forward to serve. In a rather upmarket, 'posh' voice, the customer asked for seven pounds of potatoes, a pound of carrots and then hurriedly – as if she'd suddenly remembered – in a completely unthinking but contrasting voice added, "Oh yes, and a pund o' ingings." What must have been an accidental slip of her real self, the mistake caused me to look up sharply only to see Isobel with her back to me, silently trembling with contained laughter while perched on the stepladder. With true professionalism, we all kept silent until the lady left – when we all doubled up in mirth. After the scathing remarks by Mrs Rice, it was exactly what we needed to regain some sanity.

* * *

Nearly two weeks later Mr Munro made his routine visit to the branch. "I'm sorry about the delay, Robert," he told me. "I have had the most difficult time trying to sort out staff moves."

"It's not a big problem, Mr Munro. It allows time for the part-timer to train with me before I move."

"Good thinking," he agreed.

"My only worry is that I have those exams soon."

"I've been thinking about that. The best plan is to remain here until your exams are past. Then we'll get the stock-take done here on the first Saturday after your exams. You'll then start at Logie Street the following Monday."

Robbie, you can now prepare your space suit!

"That's fine, Mr Munro."

"So, you'll get a clean start with all your studying past."

"I won't have any excuses if I fail my exams though," I said with some trepidation.

"Come on now, Robert. You're not worried about that, are you?

With senior managers, directors and owners of long-established retail businesses in Dundee in the class – not to mention my two senior and experienced company colleagues – I was concerned how I would compare.

"Not really worried," I told Mr Munro, "but obviously I hope to go on to year two."

With a few more issues to discuss, including something about a new company policy relating to Avery scales and Weights and Measures Regulations, Mr Munro was on his way, having left me feeling more secure about the move with a practical plan now in place.

A few days later, not unexpectedly, my friend Alan appeared. "Ah, you're here! I've been to Logie Street – no sign of you there."

"That's because I'm not there yet," I replied jokingly.

I explained the circumstances, and we chatted about a few things – mainly related to Carnoustie. But then he surprised me by saying he may not be around in his van in future.

"I've been thinking, Robbie. You're making good progress – a bigger branch, and so on. But I see no future running around Dundee fixing radios and TV's, so I've applied for a job with NCR."

Realising immediately his situation, I replied, "Not at all surprised, Alan – you've said before the pay's not good, and I knew you were looking for more challenging work. Go for it!"

"The pay's a lot better, and I'll have a lot more interesting work. Apart from that, Dundee seems to be 'on the up' these days – American investment, some news about a new Overgate, and maybe an airport. I don't think running around fixing TVs and radios is going to take me anywhere."

"I hear what you say, Alan. There's a buzz in the city, and I sense it too."

This was quite a turnaround. Only some seven years previously, Alan had seen the glistening new technological world of TV as a bright challenge which had also influenced me to pursue the same course. His low pay did not seem to reflect the engineering qualifications and know-how that he possessed. We chatted about this and, inevitably, Alan's favourite subjects somehow cropped up. "You know, Robbie, my mum told me I'd never get up in time to get on the train to Arbroath High school in the mornings."

I'd heard Alan say this more than a few times. He blamed his lack of advancement into the world of high technology on him not getting a senior education. "But Alan, my mum told me she couldn't 'send' me to Arbroath High because she didn't have money for all of us to go. I just had to accept that."

Each time we met it was inevitable this theme would crop up. It was a fact that Carnoustie, then, was the only town in Angus which did not have a high school. Alan had made this observation repeatedly, and couldn't let go of the fact that by sheer lack of pupils we didn't have a high school on our doorstep. Otherwise he would have been able to walk effortlessly to school. We each had qualified to go to high school, and I shared the same sense of denial and loss of opportunity.

"Bear in mind, Alan, I think there was another agenda," I told him.

"What was that?" he asked, puzzled.

"Well, just think of it. Although we could have, we were never encouraged to go to high school. I was in the top four in the class in the qualifying year when we were twelve years old (the 'quali year'), but nobody spoke to me or my parents about high school. I think I know why.

"Go on."

"Well, there had to be enough pupils with some ability retained to keep classes going in the secondary school in Carnoustie. My guess is that there had to be a numbers game to balance teaching staffing at Arbroath High and at Carnoustie. In fact, Alan, for all we know "Peppie Ness" (our headmaster) had his salary based on the number of pupils he retained at Carnoustie, so he may have had a different plan!"

"I'd never thought about it that way." He seemed genuinely intrigued. Here we were, having this serious conversation about our lack of chances when we were both about to advance in our respective work.

Looking back, this constant feeling of abandonment by the system still hurt us. It always arose in our chats. Underneath it all was the fact that although we each had friends who went on to Arbroath High, Carnoustie was a divided town – broadly, an east and west split. It must have changed sometime shortly after our time, likely after the new High School was built in the 1970s, but in our day it was almost entirely only our friends whose parents were well-off enough to finance their children to senior school who were admitted. Alan and I had spoken about our respective "what if?" scenarios for years.

* * *

My new assistant, Janet, had now commenced work and was doing well. Mr Munro, on his next visit, said that on reflection a full-time assistant to help my replacement was more advisable than engaging the part-timer. I discussed this with Janet, who responded immediately by saying that was what she originally wanted.

Now, Murray... do you need any more evidence that Mr Munro has your interests at heart?

CHAPTER 7

May 1962:
"A Surprise Haircut", or
"New Challenges at Logie Street"

O NE Thursday on my usual lunch-time trip into the city centre I decided to have a haircut and popped into a barber shop in Panmure Street.

"Just have a seat there, sir," said a senior man, wearing a perfectly-starched white coat, indicating one of the big swivel chairs. "This young man will see to you."

I sat down as invited, and looked in the mirror opposite to see – behind me – a well-known Carnoustie face. "Ian McDougall! What a surprise! What are you doing here?"

"I'm here to make a mess of strangers' hair before I'm let loose in Carnoustie," he joked as he pulled a long narrow black comb out of the top pocket of his smart white jacket. He was grinning from ear to ear.

"So, I've come all the way from Carnoustie to be a guinea pig, have I?" I enquired gamely.

"Aye, that's right. Now just keep your head still."

"How long have you been here?"

"This is my second week."

"And are you learning a lot, Ian?" I asked him, forgetting to keep still.

"Yes, such as to ask customers to keep their heads at rest while I'm cutting!" he responded in a mock angry voice.

I got the point, and laughed as much as he did. "Just think, Ian; you'll soon have your own supply of randy *Reveille* newspapers!" I teased.

"Oh yes, but my mum won't be pleased to see risqué newspapers lying around in the shop!" Ian told me he'd decided to take up a hairdressing job as he thought there may be an opportunity to run his own barber shop in Carnoustie someday, but thought it a good idea to train where he didn't know anybody. "There's two things people need, Robbie," he told me: "haircuts and food."

"You're right; clever thinking," I said. "And have you looked at the Dundee Estates printed in *The Courier*?

"No, what's that?"

"Well, I can't believe it myself, but it's legally permitted to print in the press the amount of money people leave in their wills. And guess what? Grocers and wine merchants' names appear alongside lawyers and accountants."

"No barbers?"

"Not until your time comes, Ian!"

"We'll see," he replied modestly. "But I need premises."

"Well, Jimmy Tait started off with his hairdressing business in a caravan. He toured Carnoustie and the countryside, and stopped at various places on set days and evenings. I used to get my hair cut on a piece of waste ground at Westhaven on any Thursday."

"I'll try for a wee rented shop somewhere," Ian assert-ed, indicating his ambitious preference.

Ian completed his apprenticeship and did go to Car-noustie, where he started his own hairdressing and newsagent business. He cut hair for generations of customers – over the course of fifty-five years, in fact – until he retired in December 2018. By then the printed 'estates' practice had stopped, so I may never know how many millions Ian made.

"Aye, hairdressing and grocery shops are long-lasting businesses to be in," Ian had said that day in 1962. He wasn't wrong.

Well-known Carnoustie faces had a habit of appearing for me in Dundee. Bill the banker, Alan the 'tellie' man, Jim the 'bobby' and now Ian the 'snipper'. It somehow helped to make me feel nearer home in the big city.

* * *

During most evenings I did some revision at home for my forthcoming exams. I had no real worries, but I made up my mind that since I had been selected as one of three managers in the company to attend, I had better make a good show of it. I had a high regard for Jim and Tom who were senior, middle-aged managers with a lot more experience and maturi-ty than myself. No pressure, then?

There was no special day or place for the tests. We at-tended our usual class venues on a Monday, and it was all quite low-key. The exams marked the end of the college year for us, and the results – we were informed – would be posted to us and to the company. It must have been about ten days later when I arrived home to find a letter from the course director along with a certificate in a large cardboard-backed envelope telling me that I'd passed all parts of the course.

Say farewell to Planet Brantwood, your first management training base!

Meanwhile, I had taken stock along with Mr Munro at Brantwood, said farewell to my staff, and started in Logie Street on – from memory – I think the second Monday in the May of 1962.

Well done, Robbie. You've now landed safely on Planet Logie.

A period of increased activity and high excitement had come and gone. Brantwood, my nervous first management job since August 1960 now completed, the first year of the Retail Management Principles diploma course which seemed at the start to be quite daunting was complete, and now I was appointed manager to my new branch – another challenge lay ahead.

You see, Murray? There was nothing to worry about. Keep going! If you think you would have done better by attending Arbroath High School, you'd better prove it.

That same week there was welcome news and even more excitement. For when I arrived home, I was told by mum that Peem had received a letter inviting him for an interview at Valentines, the greetings card company on the Kingsway, Dundee.

"He's awfully pleased and he's gone to tell his pals, but he said you could read the letter."

"That's great!" I said, relieved to hear the good news.

"It was in reply to a letter James had sent asking about vacancies. It sounds quite encouraging," mum said as she cheerfully handed me the impressive-looking letter. "At long last, something's going right for James. He's been awfully moody and upset lately. Nothing was going right for him. He'd even started to say that he'd move away to find work."

"It'll all come right eventually," I told her with a smile.

* * *

"How are you getting on in your new branch?" dad asked that same evening as he laid down his copy of *The Courier*.

"All well so far. The staff seem fine and, although it's a bigger and busier branch, it will – I think – be easier to manage."

"That's good," he said. "And how does it compare to the Carnoustie branch?"

"It's similar, dad. It has two windows about nine feet square, and the front shop is about the same dimension with around possibly 800 or so square feet. Maybe more. The back shop is small, only ten feet wide, and when the weekly delivery arrives it's packed solidly with little space to move. It's long and narrow, running the width of the shop, and has toilets and sinks at the far end. There's a walk-in fridge just like the Carnoustie one. I have almost no office space, and there are no chairs. The biggest difference is that I have one till positioned at the exit door and one person deals with every sale."

"Could that be tricky?"

"Yes, it certainly could – if that one person is sick, or on holiday, I need a replacement. But even more worrying is if the regular person isn't honest or good at the job. I could lose a lot of money."

"So, it's a self-service shop?" dad enquired.

"No, the boss calls it a 'self-selection'. Customers pick up a basket at the door and select all their own purchases, and we have two counters where they're served. One is the provisions counter where they're served cooked meats and bacon, and another at the other side of the shop where they ask for fresh fruit and vegetables. There's an assistant at each counter who weighs items and marks the price on the bag."

"Does it work well?"

"It's amazing! I can't think why we didn't do something like that in Carnoustie, but I can see the shop would have had to be re-designed to make it work."

"Is everything pre-packed, then?"

"Yes, all our dried fruits, cereals, spices, baking products and that sort of stock is now delivered to the branch already packed in bags at the warehouse or bought from manufacturers."

Dad seemed curious. "That all sounds good, but surely prices of everything will be higher?"

"Yes, you would think so," I admitted, "but just think of the saving on staff to pre-pack everything like we used to. I used to spend hours making up bags of loose products."

"How many staff do you have, then?"

"Only five. There's May at the till, Harry Greig in charge of provisions assisted by an apprentice, Kathleen responsible for fruit and vegetables, and Bunty who fills shelves and is reserve on the till. And you'll never guess – Kathleen is the wife of John Thomson, who was my boss when he came to manage the Carnoustie branch for a short time. Oh, and there's no message boy – we don't deliver around all the nearby tenements. It's a different way of managing a grocery shop, dad."

Mum had heard the discussion from the kitchen and put her head around the door.

"What do you mean, Robert?"

"Well, in my earlier shops all the staff did pre-packing (remember, sugar came in 2 cwt bags), serving at the counter and handling cash. Now different staff specialise. Harry, for example – after discussion with me – is responsible for ordering all meats and bacon. He also sees that the provisions window display is made ready. He keeps that whole area clean and tidy and, along with the young apprentice, serves at their counter."

"Do you find it easier than counter service?" dad enquired of me.

"Yes, it is – but I worry about losses at the till." I sensed dad's great interest. He hadn't always been so interested in the operation of the Carnoustie shop, but it struck me at the time that he too was witnessing the big changes going on in the world of grocery retailing. "Kathy looks after the fruit and veg counter. I'm very lucky, because she is an experienced assistant. In fact, she suggested to me this morning that it would be a good idea to pre-pack apples in bags. I think John, her husband, must be doing the same. He's a clever manager. The apples are sold at 1/11d per pound, but she has worked out that four apples which are all the same size happen to weigh a pound."

"Will apples and oranges all be pre-packed eventually?" asked mum, who was immediately alert to the changes which would come to herself as a customer someday.

"Yes, mum. Everything will be pre-packed someday, and exact prices put on the packet. The changes are happening quickly."

"What about the lady at the till all the time – will she not get tired?" asked mum, who was beginning to sense the impact of all the changes.

"Mum, I should get you a job in the new grocery trade!" I teased. "You're right, she needs a break and needs to be replaced. But that's a new problem – who do I trust? And if there is a shortage at the end of the day, who is to blame?"

Dad looked thoughtful. "What happens if one of your staff is off sick? Who stands in if they are all specialised now?" he said, posing yet another valid question.

"I think we could open up our own shop, you two!" I joked. "You're right; it's a different kind of problem. I can't afford to have a reserve in every department. I will just have to fill in as best as I can. The young apprentice can be moved about." As I said that, I realised I hadn't yet encountered this problem – but I was certain it would come.

"Do you think you'll get used to it all, Robert?" asked mum, with some concern in her voice.

"Funnily enough, we were discussing this in the college a few weeks ago. It's called division of labour, and it's all about specialising. In some ways it will be easier, because I won't be tied down to serve customers like Mr Stewart, my old manager in the Carnoustie shop. I will supervise the main buying, all the administration and keep an eye on the whole operation. There's one huge advantage now, which is that is all stock has a price label attached. So I know the correct price is being charged. The only worry is at the till, as I said earlier. Remember in days gone by, when goods were not price-marked and I had to keep the price of every product in my head?"

"Goodness me, Robert!" mum exclaimed. "Do you think you'll like all those changes?"

"It's amazing, mum. There's a lot of psychology in the new selling methods now."

"What does that mean?" dad queried with a non-plussed expression.

"Well, Mr Munro was telling me that studies have been done in the USA so that shops are laid out to try and encourage maximum sales. Special offers should be on display, where customers enter the shop to create a 'bargain' atmosphere. Then key items must be situated at places inside the store to make customers have to look for them."

"Fancy that," mum said wonderingly. "What kind of things?"

"The best example is sugar, but also bread, salt, biscuits, or tea."

"That's a shame, Robert, making customers do all that," dad chimed in.

"Not really. When the customer is searching, they'll find other goods they didn't think of buying. Oh, and by the way, it's rumoured that stores someday will sell milk."

"That's clever; more things under one roof," said dad with enthusiasm as he seemed to follow the thinking.

"But there's more. Not only that, but bulky or heavy items will be nearer the checkout."

"Is that more psychology?" quizzed dad with a growing smile.

"Yes, because if a customer puts those bulky items into a basket early in their walk around the shop, they will stop shopping because they will feel they have no more space and too much to carry home."

"Will you remember all this, Robert?" mum asked me with some apprehension.

"The company will provide plans on how best to do things, don't worry," I tried to reassure her. "But here's the biggest piece of psychology." I paused for effect. "Research has shown that customers are most comfortable if, when they enter a store, they turn right and move around clockwise."

"My goodness, that's clever," mum observed. "But do you think that will work?"

"I don't know. Only time will tell. Mr Munro says there's going to be a managers' conference about all this someday. But I had a customer in the shop today who asked where she could get butter off the slab, as she preferred it to the packets. You see, changes aren't good for everybody – more psychology, Dad."

The number and variety of the questions mum and dad had posed made me realise just how fundamental the changes happening were going to be. Not only were staff and managers seeing benefits, but customers were in for a pleasant change in shopping.

When I had stepped into the Logie Street branch on that first day, I could sense the changes. Customers were free to walk around the shop and pick stock from shelves and from a unit with a new name to me – a 'gondola', a double-sided five-shelf display stand which customers had access to – along with large thirty inch-wide diameter wire baskets on stands about three feet high, which contained the 'special offers' shoppers could browse around and pick and choose. A new term for me was a 'tumble display'. Goods were not thrown into display baskets, but they looked like they had been.

The selling techniques had also begun to change. Previously, window displays had the greatest impact on customers, but now new in-store ideas were being used. One example I noticed on my first day at Logie Street was a can of peaches and a can of cream pre-packed in a clear bag. This was an idea to attract a sale. I remember thinking there were likely many other examples for me to experiment with. What about 'a can of prunes and a packet of custard'? The new psychology of grocery shopping had arrived, and I was beginning to get the hang of this new shopping world I had stepped into.

* * *

My move to Brantwood Avenue in 1960 had been an eye-opener. Carnoustie had been busy, but Logie Street had a greater city buzz. One day, while sorting out paperwork in the backshop, I heard great laughter coming from the provisions counter. I looked out to see what was going on and noticed Harry having some merry banter with a tall fit looking man.

"What was all that about, Harry?" I enquired when the customer had left.

"Oh, that was Pat Liney – the Dundee goalie. He's always having jokes. He was asking, since the Dee were now Scottish Champions, if he could get a free extra slice of boiled ham. He comes in a lot, and he's always good fun."

"I've seen him quite often."

Harry then joked, "I was telling him he'd get an extra free slice if they win the Championship again next year, and Pat said: 'That's an awfi lot o' saves for a slice of meat'!"

Pat Liney, a new local hero, had saved a crucial penalty against his 'home town' team St Mirren a week or two earlier at Dens Park, to give the 'Dee the League Championship in Dundee's 2-0 win, and went on to beat St Johnstone to win the Scottish League Championship 1961/62. Pat became a lifetime legend for Dundee FC. An interesting connection for me was that Pat Liney had taken over from Bill Brown, who was a former goalie for Carnoustie Panmure – my home club, which as a boy I supported regularly. I saw him play against

Manchester City (yes, *the* Manchester City) when Westfield Park, Carnoustie, was officially opened. I think it was in 1954.

* * *

A month had passed – the delay in moving to my new branch turned out not to be a problem, as Mr Munro had engineered the timing to fit with my exams as promised. The first year of my college course was successfully behind m,e and the changes in retail grocery which had been discussed were no longer a theoretical issue – I felt very close to them. I remember thinking at the time 'bring on year two'.

New ways of doing things were evident, and I had an inner confidence that I could make something of growing the business. However, I could not remove one nagging fear – the till. Were all goods being registered? How did I know that the prices on all the goods were correctly entered on what was effectively an adding machine? How did I know the correct change was being given?

My shaky feeling was that the wonderful new system of merchandising and serving customers' needs at Logie Street had a big flaw – one till, and one person potentially either making or losing me money. Unlike today, there was no barcode system to automatically register a price on a checkout computer, or to keep a stock record. In those early days there was still a high degree of human involvement. Looking back, it was a period of significant change, but staff honesty was crucially important – even more than it is today.

Come on, Robbie. You must trust people. You'll have to wait and see what the stock results will be.

Today, almost sixty years later, some shops trust customers to do their own checking and paying at 'self-service checkouts'. I imagine managers today may have very similar worries as I did.

CHAPTER 8

June 1962:
"Learning Harsh Realities", or
"Finding My Management Feet"

MR Munro was obviously aware of the limited facilities I had inherited, and asked if I wanted a space for all my papers. This indicates that although progress was being made on shop layout and selling methods, office paperwork and systems were still quite rudimentary.

"You could do with a space to keep all your papers together, Robert," he observed in that calm voice of his.

"Yes, all my cash books and ledgers are in the safe beside the light switches near the fruit window. It would be helpful to have everything in one place."

"Why don't we put up a desk and a few shelves around the safe for you?" Mr Munro suggested.

"That sounds a good idea," I agreed. "Can I get the phone there too?"

"I don't see why not. I'll get all that organised."

I had to give up a half-day, but a joiner came to the branch and did exactly as requested. In the space of a few hours I had an office I could hardly turn around in, but one which had shelves above and below me. The new sloping desk would allow me to draw all my own display tickets, and all my papers were in tidy spaces.

"Do you want a wee wicket door on this?" asked the pro-active joiner.

"I've never thought about that... but what a good idea. It makes it more official."

"I'll put a wee sneck on a half door for you."

It was my own private area. A week after the phone was re-installed, Mr Munro looked in.

"What do you think then, Robert?" he asked me.

"It's a bit tight, but it's a tidy place where I can keep all my papers – and it's near the till."

"Yes, and there's a step up so you have a better view of what's going on all over the shop."

Then it hit me. Mr Munro must have had exactly the same feeling as I did, but he was only able to suggest it. Now I would be nearer the till to see and hear what was going on.

"You'll be more visible now, Robert."

It was a boon – no longer were my little notes left lying around the back shop. As the daily rush went on, I was able to safely toss papers and delivery notes on to my new desk for sorting later.

The only downside was that during very busy spells, I had to jostle through queues of customers to get into my 'office' or to answer the phone.

Robbie, you can't possibly complain about having queues of customers!

What I learned from all of this was that Mr Munro was really thinking of getting me out of the back shop, where traditionally managers were found unless they were serving at the counter. Now they could see and be seen.

Looking back today, I can see this tiny box of an office for me was the embryo of customer service desks and information points we see in the giant supermarkets of today. As for dealing with staff, I just had to use my common sense. My own system of trial and error. And, of course, reminding me to "assert myself" – which, Mr Munro had probably noted, went against my natural timid demeanour.

* * *

My new 'planet' was spinning around well. Looking back, I now see when and how I began to learn the absolute basics of management. No one had ever told me how to manage. I'd never been on a management techniques training course. I had observed Mr Stewart ("Go, go, greasy grocer, go"), of course, and listened to his advice on practical matters. I had managed Brantwood branch and attended a retail management course, but I'd never had any 'sit down and listen about how to manage' chats. Management theory had, so far, not been on the syllabus, but that was something which would be included in my second year.

Being 'hands on' in counter service shops at Brantwood and Carnoustie was different. Now, in this self-selection store, staff were delegated responsibilities and I had an opportunity to stand back, observe, and – in my own way – analyse. It sounds silly today for me to mention such a basic point, but I discovered by accident the art of planning. I started developing checklists for myself. Not only for each section of the business, but a 'to do' management list for the next day. Hitherto, I had been going home each evening with stomach-churning worries, being preoccupied with what seemed like a million things to remember for the next day. Then I started to develop a checklist of 'musts, shoulds and nices' for the next day. Time and priority were of the essence, and I found this released me from going home with nagging questions and started me off with priorities for the next day. I suppose I was simply growing up in the business.

I never had, in any branch, a desk or chair. No pads of paper and no calculator in those days, although Peem had given me a pocket-book 'ready reckoner' as a Christmas gift a couple of years previously. However, I mostly calculated everything by longhand multiplication and division. The company policy, which must have been at the heart of its success, was all about running the branch with minimal expense. It would not have been wise to ask for a desk or chair. All staff, including myself, stood beside or sat on a box at 'tea break' time, and we used our own cups from home. In retrospect, I now realise Carnoustie branch had an excellent small office which was probably part of the original custom-built grocery shop fitting from over fifty years previously.

* * *

Almost all goods were delivered to the branch from the company's central warehouse. However, there were a few exceptions. Biscuits were ordered by me and delivered direct from manufacturers. Additionally, fruit and vegetable suppliers in the city called me each Monday and on two or three other times each week by telephone seeking orders and providing news on price changes. New stock would arrive within a few hours from Dundee wholesalers – Harrison & Reeve, John Smith, or Clark and Sinclair. Compared to the present day, the range of vegetables and salads available to customers was frugal: potatoes, turnip, carrots and onions, along with lettuce and tomatoes, were the only products on offer. There was a reasonable range of apples, pears and oranges, but no exotic fruits and vegetables imported from countries around the world as we enjoy today. Over the years I had become aware of seasonal selling – soups and stews being good winter sellers, and as summer approached salads and cold meats became important.

With no factual evidence of how my total sales were broken down, I just had a feeling of what was selling – or otherwise. By sending my paperwork to head office, I had no information to study. The company's reputation had been built over many years (since 1868) on provisions and fruit and veg, but I noticed that biscuit sales seemed low and the variety limited. I had always been aware that customers (like mum) "liked a wee change", and I set out to invigorate sales.

Ordering goods from Head Office was routine and well organised, but I found no systems in place at Logie Street for reordering goods direct from manufacturers. I set up a comprehensive method of maintaining stock levels for an extensive range of biscuits. Only a few years previously, loose biscuits were handled by staff, but now all biscuits were in packets so it was an easier product to deal with. Biscuits, I knew, were a popular product – rather like sweets in Scotland – and reaped a healthy profit margin. My plan was to set up a stock reorder system of my own, and provide more space on shelves for this good profit-earner.

At a recent branch managers' meeting, the subject of space allocation had been discussed. The directors had visited the United States of America and been shown a film in which the principles of allocating space were explained: this was called the Dylon Study. Basically, if a product produced say 5% of your total turnover, then it should receive 5% of the linear footage in the branch (for example, a ten-foot long gondola with five shelves on each side produced 100 linear feet).

I didn't know what percentage of my sales were in biscuits, but decided to award 50 feet – a complete side of my gondola. Breakdown of my total branch sales was all guesswork, but I did suspect my increased sales came from general trading. Thus 'new' biscuit sales would be a bonus.

Management, I found, was all about making things happen and having a feeling of control over matters. I began to feel comfortable about how events were going, and my self-devised methods of setting up prompts and reminders served me well. As I drove home each evening, I kept repeating "systems not memory". To be honest, on looking back I simply discovered my own management methods. I had no idea how other managers worked, but I felt I had reduced the nervous worries I took home each evening.

Days were long: I'd leave home at 7.30am and return about twelve hours later. As a manager it was nothing new to me, but it emphasised that the retail grocery trade was not conducive to having a fully balanced life.

CHAPTER 9

July 1962:
"The Man in a Long Coat", or
"Missing Grandad's Funeral"

ONE evening I arrived home later than usual. "Hi, mum," I said by way of greeting as I got into the kitchen. "Where's dad?"

"He's on late shift," she replied.

But something else was on my mind that night. "How did Peem get on at his interview?" I asked her.

"Oh dear. He's not saying much, but he's very upset. He's upstairs now and wouldn't have anything to eat."

"I'll eat later mum. I'd better have a word with him."

I had been aware all that Thursday that Peem had his interview at Valentines. But in those days, there was no phone to check on news at home – and in any case, even if there had been, I would never have used the shop phone for a personal call. No mobile phones either; for me, in those days, personal communication had to be face to face.

I headed upstairs. Sure enough, my brother seemed downhearted. "Hi Peem," I said. "Mum tells me it's not so good."

"Ach, it was a waste of time."

"Why was that?"

"They must have known I was a 'painter and drawer' before the interview, but what they really wanted was somebody to work in the production department."

"You never know, Peem. They will have your details for an artist vacancy someday."

Unfortunately that was all I could offer Peem. We spoke about our chat with Uncle Alan, and ended on a more optimistic note about perseverance. My younger brother had gone through the course at college and had pinned his hopes on a future which, in Dundee, perhaps didn't offer a great deal of opportunity.

"I'm going to have to go to Edinburgh or Glasgow – maybe even London – to find a job."

There was despondency, but his last comment indicated a motivation which heartened me. "Come on Peem," I suggested, "let's watch the new comedy on the TV. It's called *Steptoe and Son.*"

Enjoying the antics of Albert, the eccentric father as played by Wilfred Brambell, and the frustrated son Harold portrayed by Harry H. Corbett, we succeeded in taking our minds off the problem. "Gee, I hope I don't end up like them someday," Peem muttered.

"Come on now, Peem. There's a lot of people much worse off than us. I heard, just this afternoon, that another polio victim had been found in Dundee. That brings the total of seriously ill people up to twelve."

You need to keep an eye on Peem, Robbie. Spend more time with him. He needs a bit of help.

* * *

Kathleen came and spoke quietly with me one day while I was compiling a biscuit order at the store. "I've been watching a man doing strange things in the shop," she said.

"Oh? what kind of things?" I asked her.

"He keeps picking up cans and packets and putting them down again."

"Well, maybe he's checking prices and shopping careful-ly." It seemed a plausible enough reason to me.

"I don't think so. Being clever, more like it. I can never see exactly what he does, but I think he puts things in his pocket."

I'd never had a problem like this, and immediately I wondered how long it had been going on. Was it Kathy's im-agination? From where she was positioned, she certainly had a greater chance to see what was happening. May at the till would not be able to see so much, so I decided to speak quiet-ly with Harry and the apprentice about the 'suspected thief'. All I could do was to ask them all to be vigilant and let me know if or when the mystery man returned.

Kathy had told me he had a habit of appearing on busy days, which was another reason why there could be a genuine problem. "Let me know as soon as you see him come in next time, Kathy."

As I drove home that evening, I realised this was an-other negative aspect about security of the new methods of selling. Firstly, no-one had ever mentioned the subject – and secondly, there was no training on how to deal with it. I began to think of how to grapple with the problem. Challenge the suspect at the till, maybe? But then, if I asked him "...and what about the stuff in your pocket?", he could easily just say "Oh sorry, I must have forgotten about that" or "Yes, but I bought that in the Co-op." The worries began to grow. Would I end up being charged with accusing him of being a thief? In addition to that, how many other customers could also be successfully shoplifting? I had never previously been aware of pilfering in the old counter service shops because customers stood in a queue and were attended to, face-to-face, by a sales assistant. Distrusting a customer was a totally foreign concept to me.

A week later, while I was completing my weekly order form for the following week's delivery, Kathy came rushing to the back shop. "Mr Murray! He's in the shop!" she told me urgently. I knew immediately who she meant. Following her to the front shop, she then nodded in the direction of an old man wearing a long, well-worn and grubby raincoat. He certainly didn't look like a typical customer. For the first time in my grocery life, I found myself suspecting a customer of robbing me. I didn't like the feeling, and even less the prospect of challenging the man. It was a busy time, and my staff all had jobs to do. With other customers also moving about, it was extremely difficult to watch his every move. If he was a thief, he must have been good at it. I spoke with Harry and Kathleen, and they had the idea that this problem man had holes in his pocket and was dropping items into the bottom lining.

"You must be joking!" I said, feeling like this was like something out of a thriller... or maybe a comedy film.

"No, honestly. His coat looks like it's bulging," Harry argued.

The man in the long coat – was he a pilferer?

This problem began to take on a humorous side. Suddenly there was some potential drama going on. I could do nothing on that first occasion, but whenever the man came into the shop I was 'tipped off' and basically stood around beside him while he moved about. Eventually he stopped coming in. Was he feeling watched, or was he an innocent shopper who moved on? Had I lost any profit?

The effect of the entire episode was to unnerve me about the constant fear of what today is called "shrinkage", and is an accepted part of self service. Back then it was the emergence of a loss that we had never previously experienced in counter service shops, and it was worrying. It became a constant nagging fear.

Nearing the end of June, my young apprentice – after a week's notice – left to work in a jute factory, where he told me he would have roughly the same pay but fewer weekly hours of work. When I told Mr Munro, he asked me if I had any plans to deal with the situation. I referred him to a young lad who had been a message boy, and whose details I held. He lived somewhere near the Brantwood branch, and had shown an interest in the grocery trade.

Losing staff to better jobs is nothing new, Murray. It's simply a fact of grocery life.

"I'll be around your way tomorrow evening. We'll pop up to his home and speak with him." This was typical of the help which Mr Munro gave me. The next evening, we went to the young lad's house. My boss ascertained the boy was still interested, and offered John the chance to start work in Logie Street in a week's time.

* * *

Young John Allardice started work as an apprentice on the first Monday in July. The following day, Tuesday the 3rd of July 1962, I arrived home at the usual time to be met by mum in an upset state.

"What's wrong, mum? You don't look well."

"It's your Woodside Grandad," she sobbed. "He died early this morning."

"That's terrible, mum," I said. "I'm very sorry to hear that."

My mum and dad never showed any signs of being tactile. In fact, none of us displayed any emotion except perhaps at birthdays or some congratulation when a hug was appropriate. Perhaps it was my new-found adult behaviour, but I put my arms around mum and told her: "Sorry, mum. He was a great man. He had a hard life, but a good life."

We spoke for a while about grandad; how he grew up in the Taylor family at Guthrie, near Arbroath, and went to work near Menmuir, where he met my granny. They were married in the Episcopal Schoolroom, Brechin, on the 11th December 1903. They had eight children, and my mum – who was the younger of twins – was born in 1914.

I knew what was coming next, and I dreaded the thought: "I don't know when the funeral will be Robert, but I expect Friday or Saturday. I'm hoping you can take us in your car?"

"Mum, I've got Harry off on holiday so I'll have to work on the provisions counter along with a new apprentice who can't be left on his own. There's just no way I can get away. They are the two most difficult days in any week for me."

"Oh dear. I wondered about holidays being on just now. Well, don't worry. I think your uncle Jim will manage to take me."

This was the first time in my life I felt I should have done something important to help mum, but had to turn down her request. Missing my grandad's funeral was such a big loss, especially as Peem and I had enjoyed such great holiday experiences on the farm. The croft had been – and still was, then – a hub where, on numerous Sundays, mum and dad had taken us to see our aunties and uncles and our many cousins. Those Sundays were special, and we always enjoyed granny's specially-baked biscuits and cakes.

As I lay in bed that evening, although feeling quite tired physically and emotionally, I inevitably had vivid recall of the day I last saw my grandad. I was...

...sitting on a gently sloping, well-trimmed lawn on a warm, sunny Sunday. I could hear birds chirping happily in the nearby bushes. On any other occasion, I would have leaned back comfortably and rested for a while. A moment to reflect – but not today. This was not a happy day.

Stomach churning, head swirling with troubled thoughts, I felt I wanted to die. I didn't want to be a cheat, but that's what I had to be today – and I detested myself for it.

"Are you feeling better now, Robert?" mum asked with concern.

I didn't want to answer her, for I felt a strange empty sickness... yet couldn't be sick. Eventually, because mum remained beside me, I felt I had to tell her the truth. "It's not fair, mum" I told her. "I just can't go on pretending that he's going to be alright."

"Well, he'll wonder where you are."

"Don't worry. I'll look into see him again," I assured her. "Just give me a few minutes out here."

Stracathro Hospital is in the Angus countryside, and I'd driven mum and dad there to visit my grandad – mum's father. I'd told mum that I was reluctant to go inside the hospital, because the smells of disinfectant and chloroform in wards disagreed with me. But grandad was very ill, and mum had been told his cancer was terminal. In truth, I had not been sure if I could cope with the emotion and gave mum my excuse in advance.

When I'd looked in to see him, he was propped up in bed with the summer sun beaming into the small four-bed ward while a gentle breeze fluttered through the pale blue, floor-length curtains at the open French window. He was smiling, and had the usual twinkle in his eyes.

"Hello, grandad! You're looking good. How are you feeling?"

"Oh, aye. Ah'm fine," he replied. "No' bad for a first time in a place like this."

"How's the food?" I asked him.

"Aye, it's fine, but I'm missing my brose in the mornings." My thoughts went back to the early mornings at grandad's croft when I was there on holiday to pick tatties, and could immediately picture him supping brose from a wooden bowl and using his special bone spoon.

"Oh yes, I'm sure you must miss home cooking and all your favourites."

"Aye, aye. But there's things to get on with at hame. I'll hae my brose some o' these days."

"You'll be missing your work on the croft too," I suggested.

"It's been a guid summer. There's things tae catch up wi'. Never mind; I'll be soon oot o' here," he told me.

"That's good news then, grandad."

That's the moment I deeply regretted – for, although aware of grandad's condition, I'd found myself engaging in a false conversation. I recall going quiet, then made an excuse to sit outside.

Having shown weakness by making my escape, I had sat down to think of earlier times I'd enjoyed on his small farm. I recalled grandad's ruddy complexion, his strong voice, his farmer's gait, his energy and his slightly stooping figure – no doubt brought on after over forty years as grieve at Boddin Farm. He didn't ever say anything unnecessary or make jokes. He was a serious man; never rude, never unkind and entirely engrossed in his toils around the croft, which he had farmed even before he retired from his full-time work and continued to do so well into his seventies. Now here he was, looking thinner and weaker but never-the-less bright, smiling and positive. It was so unfair, and I was showing my inexperience and lack of maturity.

Come on, Murray. Stop being a 'cowardly custard'. Get back in there.

Gathering my thoughts and taking a deep breath while making sure my tears didn't show, I re-entered the ward.

"Just needed a wee bit of fresh air, grandad," I told him. Another lie.

"Aye, aye. It's gey warm in here," he observed.

"We'll need to be getting back to Carnoustie, dad," mum declared softly.

My immediate thoughts were that mum must have an opportunity to share what may well be the last words between her and her dad. There were difficulties finding a way by bus from Carnoustie to Stracathro in those days, and with no phone at home it was never certain when visits could be co-ordinated with family members.

"I'm off then, grandad," I said. "We'll look in and see you again some time. Get well soon."

"Aye, aye. Haste ye back," he responded. It was grandad's stock farewell.

I never saw grandad again. He died aged 79 on the 3rd of July 1962. To this day I still wonder why he could suffer from a cancer given his healthy working and dietary life. Only recently I have learned that many farmworker deaths in those days were caused by cancer arising from handling harmful or untested field sprays and weed killers.

* * *

One day, while I was doing a stock check inside the fridge, Kathleen came to speak with me. "There's a Mr Smith wants to speak to you," she said as she appeared at the door with a bunch of bananas in her hand.

"Mr Smith? I don't think I know a Mr Smith," I pondered. "What does he want, Kathy?" I asked, hoping for some advance clue.

"I think he's selling something," she told me.

"Alright. Just tell him I'll be a minute."

As I walked to the front door area, I immediately recognised the caller. "Norman! Where have you been all these days?"

"Oh, been busy growing my carrots at Monikie," my old friend grinned. "Can I sell you some?"

We chatted for a few minutes, and then I asked, "Let's see what they look like, Norman."

He untied a 28-pound jute bag to reveal good looking unwashed carrots. "I'm not sure about this, Norman," I told him. "We're told to buy all our veg from the wholesalers in the town." He then presented me with a price which was lower than expected and well below my normal buying price. Another decision! I accepted his quote.

I immediately thought about my uncle Alan selling veg from grandad's farm in Montrose. Why not give the small operator a chance? "Okay Norman," I said. "I'll take a bag, but I'll have to tell Mr Munro. He may not agree. I'll take a chance." I didn't like having to dull his enthusiasm, but I had no previous experience of buying outside the prescribed sources. For the first time in my managing life, I had to make a buying decision. But the price was right, and more profit would come. With no calculator, I had to divide to get a buying price per pound then calculate, in this case, a 20% increase to arrive at a selling price.

"I'll tell my boss as soon as I can, and see if I can help to get your carrots into other branches."

"Okay, Robert," Norman said. "Let me know."

After reporting this to Mr Munro, he looked in to speak with me and – not unexpectedly – spotted the carrots as being 'different', as I knew he would. Luckily for me, my boss liked the carrots (perhaps more the profit margin!), and gave Norman the go-ahead to sell to every branch.

When I think back, I never heard the final part of the story and I never saw Norman again. Had he realised that he had under-priced? Did he sell all his crop and exhaust the supply? It was a lesson for me in being single-minded. It suited me to take one bag and make a profit – it also told me to accept a price even if it was to the detriment of the seller. But I also gave Norman an opportunity to sell to all branches in the area. I was getting tough – but, still, it was a good deal for him.

* * *

Normal opening hours were 8.30am until 1pm, and 2.15pm until 6pm. Half-day meant closing at 12 midday on Wednesdays. Saturdays became very busy. Along with my staff, we worked out a system whereby we could remain open, gain more business and still allow a break for the staff members.

Harry was a great organiser, and looked in to see the nearby butcher who shopped with us. Soon he brokered a deal to buy steak on Saturdays. We each cooked our own steak, and took turns of who ate first. Freshly-cooked tender steak became a regular Saturday treat.

Look on the bright side – it's a lot better than 'The Dog and Dish'!

It was an arrangement which worked nicely. We each had a break, and we remained open all Saturday which became popular with customers meaning that sales increased.

CHAPTER 10

July to September 1962:
"Peem Gets an Interview", or
"A Celebration"

PEEM was usually up and away to his temporary job before I left the house, but on this morning there was something different. He was still in the house, and all dressed up in his best clothes.

"I'm off then, Peem!" I called. "All the best!"

He was ready for an interview with DC Thomson in Bank Street, Dundee, at 10am. This was a crucial moment in his life. He'd been disappointed with previous letters and his interview at Valentines. I'd have to wait until I returned home at around 7.30pm in the evening to hear the result.

On my way, I had considered how to handle the situation. If the outcome was bad, I planned to chat with Peem seriously about finding out job prospects elsewhere in Scotland – and, if necessary, England. If it was good news, then a celebration was called for.

"Well?" I asked with some hesitancy when I walked into the living room that night.

"Aye! I got it!" my brother beamed.

At long last, in July 1962, Peem was offered an artist job at DC Thomson, Dundee, and he was going to start in August – on the first Monday after the Dundee holiday fortnight. This would be exactly three years after I had commenced as a manager at Brantwood Avenue. A brilliant piece of news and, though we didn't know it then, he was to be employed there until his early retirement in 1980. If he had known all that, he would not have been nearly so anxious in those uncertain days.

"Peem, you're one year younger than me and now you're going to be in a job that you trained for."

"I never thought it would happen," he admitted.

"But remember granny's old saying: 'Whit's fur ye'll no go past ye'." It was a huge relief. I had never spoken to mum or dad about the serious danger of Peem failing to find a job in the area, but the reality was that to make use of his long training and satisfy his built-in love of art he would have had to move away if he'd wanted to find a suitable post.

"Right then, Peem. A celebration is called for. So after I have a bite to eat, we're off to the 19th Hole for a wee dram."

"We can have a joint party now!" mum happily announced. "Remember, Isobel will be eighteen on the 26th."

Excitement was building up. It was a huge relief for the family.

* * *

Peem's favourite place to meet his friends was the Station Hotel, but I wanted to have a special, quieter time with him to chat so I'd suggested the '19th Hole' instead.

"It's closer to home, Peem," I remarked as we walked. "Mind you, I have a bad memory here."

"Oh? What was that?"

"Willie, my pal, was home on leave from the navy and he bought me my very first 'under-age' pint. I thought it had mouse dirt in it, so I took it back to the barman. 'Dinna be daft, son – that's a hop!' he told me. I felt an idiot, and I've never drunk beer since that day."

We settled down at the bar. "Well, how do you feel now Peem?" I asked him.

"It's like uncle Alan told us," Peem reminded me. "Bide your time and it'll all come right."

"You've done an uncle Will, Peem!"

"What do you mean?" he asked curiously.

"Remember: he left the bothy one day and was a policeman the next."

Then we got on to the subject of holidays. "I haven't had a holiday away for years," Peem bemoaned. "But I'm going to save up for a car and do a tour of Scotland."

"Great idea. I've not had a good holiday for years either. The last one was that disastrous hitch-hike to Pitlochry with my pal Syd."

"Gee, I vaguely remember hearing about that," Peem reflected. "What happened?"

"It's a sad tale, Peem,"

My memory of that holiday is so vivid I can still relate every minute detail to this day...

* * *

"We'll go into the town and get needle and thread in the morning," Syd had suggested to me.

"Do you think we'll manage to stitch it up?" I remember asking him.

"We'll need to make the tent habitable for the rest of the week," he said stoically.

"Or we go home?"

"Don't panic, Robbie!"

We didn't sleep that rainy night. The farmer's cattle had somehow entered our part of the field and, in their curiosity, ripped the tent and trod all over our belongings – and worse still, left their smelly 'marks'. We were left lying under our tent as if it was a soggy blanket with our kit scattered somewhere around us.

"If it rains tomorrow, I think our holiday is over," I said dejectedly.

"Let's see", Syd replied calmingly.

As I lay there with my feet inside my rucksack and my groundsheet over me, I wondered how we, on our first night, came to have yet another piece of bad luck on our adventure. On the evening of our first day we'd met the girls in town, partaken in a few hot orange drinks in the café, had a chat, made our plans to meet the next evening and, rather late, made our way back to the wet field.

Syd and I had camped in the same field with the Boy Scouts earlier in the summer and we had met two nice girls. It was now September, and we had planned to return to Pitlochry for a few days. We went through our checklist with great care. We would get there by hitch-hiking from Carnoustie and wear our Scout uniform along with borrowed kilts as a sign to vehicle drivers that we were 'safe adventurers'. We were experienced enough to know what clothing to take, we borrowed rucksacks, and – more importantly – we were given special use by the Rover Scout leader to take the Rover's two-man tent, provided we looked after it. Syd, being the stronger, offered to carry the tent and poles on his back.

As I tried to bury myself under the meagre cover, it was the ruined Rover's tent which worried me most. What a telling-off we will undoubtedly receive. But this was our second slice of bad luck. Our trip had started off enthusiastically. We walked out of Carnoustie, past Clayholes, and stood at the junction with the Arbroath/Dundee road and immediately started "thumbing" for a lift. Our belief was that drivers would imagine we'd walked many miles. The truth was that after the one-and-a-half miles to the current spot we were already buckling under our loads. But all was not gloom. A lorry driver stopped and offered us a lift. Was he going to Pitlochry? No. Could he take us to Perth? No! "I can tak' you as far as the centre o' Dundee boys. Will that dae ye?"

We jumped at the chance, put our kit on the back and climbed into the cab. We asked advice. Which route was best to hitch? Was it preferable to walk around the four mile long circular Kingsway to join the road to Perth, or walk through Dundee? After discussion we came down to earth and decided to go into the centre of the city and get a bus to Pitlochry.

"We don't need to tell anybody, Robbie!"

"Sure, Syd, but it's the obvious practical answer."

Now we were under a useless tent and a large part of our budget had gone on a bus fare. Dates with girls were lined up for the next evening. The pressure was on.

Having reported our predicament to the farmer, the cattle were now removed and – with our pathetic bundle of downtrodden belongings wrapped up – we set off for a repair kit. No such thing such as heavy-duty Gorilla tape in those days; at least, we didn't know of it, and it was in any case unlikely to be available in Pitlochry. With the toolkit ready, we started work on stitching, but it became obvious we couldn't complete it in one day. We had a choice – leave it half-done and meet the girls in the evening as planned, or get it fixed in one go and, with no phones available, fail to keep the date with the girls and meet them the next evening. Strangely enough, we opted to fix the tent – otherwise we were to be soaked, as rain was still a problem.

"Survival first, romance second," Syd muttered.

"Never thought I'd hear you say that, Syd!"

It rained almost the whole time we were stitching up the tent. The next day we relaxed and tidied up our belongings, then planned to walk into town and meet the girls in the evening. It was then that we discovered our third piece of bad luck in the space of two days. The girls informed us, during a quick doorstep conversation, that they were now – after the summer holidays – back at Breadalbane Academy, and their parents refused to allow them to 'go out' in the evening.

With a dramatic downturn in our fortunes, we had fish and chips and trudged our way back to the leaky tent. On the way, we discussed the situation. Had our failure to turn up the previous evening killed our chances, or was the parent rule genuine? We each agreed rather conceitedly it was more likely a school issue with parents, rather than the usual excuse of "I'm washing my hair tonight".

With rain persisting, our hitch-hiking holiday ended prematurely when we decided to take a bus back to Carnoustie. We hadn't followed our "Be Prepared" motto very well, but we had learned something about hitch-hiking, cattle, how to mend a tent... and girls!

* * *

"What a story, Robbie!" Peem exclaimed.

"Aye, I know. But of course, we did adventurous things in those days. When John Blair, Johnny Robb and I were apprentices in Carnoustie, we had a bike run in one day to and from St Andrews every spring holiday weekend. I can remember when I was a Scout, a few of us did a biking round trip of sixty miles to the Youth Hostel in the Round House, Glenisla."

"It's my own Scouting days that gives me the idea of a tour of the country," Peem told me.

We chatted on, and for the first time ever Peem and I had a good long 'blether'. It was an evening I recall clearly to this day.

On the first Sunday after Isobel's birthday, mum prepared a special meal and made one of her famous 'clootie dumplings'. It was, I remember, a happy day – and somehow, yet again, we each found a silver threepenny wrapped in greaseproof paper. How did mum do it?

* * *

Weeks rolled past and business grew, and I sensed – and fell in tune with – the 'pulse' of the business. My staff worked well together. One aspect which had caught me unawares during the summer was that I hadn't been involved in the early planning stages for staff holidays. After a year's service, everyone was entitled to two weeks holiday: that is, two weeks of six-and-a-half days, so that was thirteen days in total. Appropriate parts of a week applied to those with less than a year's service. It was common practice in the trade then that most employees, including the boss, would take only a maximum of one week at a time, and perhaps other days spread throughout the year. I found I was receiving requests for days here and there, sometimes with short notice.

I made up a chart for all holidays – even odd days – of everyone in the branch as far ahead as possible, and began a new page for all of 1963. I had to avoid two things: one, leaving myself short at busy times (which meant identifying Easter dates and how Christmas and New Year dates would fall), and two, avoiding Mr Munro's obvious question: "Why is he/she away on holiday this week?" In small staff branches it was a larger loss to be one short at critical times.

One day, when I was moving about the store updating my notes of staff holiday plans, Harry and John came to me with a special request. "We both want time off for the same week," Harry told me.

In a serious tone, I responded, "Come on now, lads. You know we can't do that."

"But it's important!" John added with a broad grin.

I suspected Harry was putting John up to some mischief. "What are you two up to?"

"We need to go to the States!"

"We want to go to Mr Munro's niece's funeral."

"What?" I asked, confused by their thinking.

"Yes! Marilyn's!"

Then it twigged to me – they were winding me up about the famous Hollywood actress Marilyn Monroe, who had just passed away unexpectedly as the result of a drugs overdose.

"Well you can't go, boys. Because I'm already booked up to be there!"

It was a comfortable sign for me that we could have that kind of fun. We all worked hard, and a bit of light relief like that was welcome.

You see, Murray? You must have developed a good atmosphere. These guys work hard, but they like a laugh too. It's important they enjoy their work. It's a wee bit o' management theory working in practice.

CHAPTER 11

August 1962:
"Another Break-in", or
"A Mysterious Visit by Directors"

ABOUT a week later, I experienced a nasty shock. In the very early hours of a wet and windy weekday morning – I can't recall exactly which day – at 2.30am there was loud knocking on the outside door. Dad came to my room and woke me to say there was someone to see me. To my great amazement it was Johnny Robb – once my fellow grocery apprentice in Carnoustie, now turned taxi operator.

"Johnny, what on earth do you want at this time of night?" I asked him blearily.

"I've had a phone call from your boss, Mr Munro. He asked me to pick you up and take you to your shop."

This sounded urgent. "What on earth's wrong?"

"There's been a break-in."

"A *what*? Not again!"

Johnny asked why I'd said 'not again', so I had to explain what had happened at the time of my earlier Brantwood break-in. Of course, there was no phone at home and no mobiles in those days, so – when I grasped the urgency of the situation – I realised Mr Munro's clever strategy by phoning a local taxi operator.

While driving there, Johnny and I chatted. I suppose, as a means of diverting my thoughts of what may lie ahead, I reminded him he had always been mad keen on cars and motor scooters.

"Oh yes, I was desperate for a scooter," he chuckled.

"I remember Jock and me having to drag you away from Rossleigh's car showroom window in Crichton Street, Dundee, on our way to night classes."

"Oh, you mean the Lambretta?"

"Yes, the red one in the window," I confirmed. "You kept saying you were going to buy it."

"I saved up, and did eventually get it."

"I thought you would. So, when did you start your taxi business?"

"Well, you remember the tiny wooden office in Station Road?" he asked me. "The one where the old boy ran his fleet of hackney cabs?"

"I do. It was quite a good business."

"Yes, but the cabs were on their last legs... or should I say wheels? And a lot of the summer business was dropping off. So I bought the business for a song about three years ago." Johnny had stuck to his plan, and was now running his own business. "I run only one car now, but it got me started."

I remember thinking on that journey how my pals were advancing – John running his taxi business, Jock in England in the canning world, Bill off to India banking, Jim now a bobby,

Ian working towards his goal to run his hair-dressing business, and here I was up in the middle of the night dealing with a break-in which, I thought at the time, could be costing me big losses.

Dinna panic now, Murray. The thieves may not have got much. Anyway, your cash is in a safe place.

Soon we were approaching the shop, and Johnny braked when I gave him the word. "I'll sit out here in the car," he told me.

It was all quite unreal. Planet Logie was all lit up. All the shop lights were on, and I found Mr Munro in charge in the back shop. The police were there, and so too were joiners who were busy boarding up the rear window.

"They cut and bent back the iron grill and came in through this window," explained my boss. The annoyance was obvious in the tone of Mr Munro's voice. "The police are here to investigate, and we need to know what's been stolen, Robert. Do you see anything obviously disturbed?"

I looked around the front shop. We didn't sell cigarettes or liquor, but I checked the till which was just as I'd left it – open, with no cash in the drawer. To be honest a can or packet of anything could have been taken, but frankly I couldn't tell.

"It'll be money they were after," Mr Munro said. "Where did you put your drawings, Robert?"

The practice in this branch was not to put money in the night safe at the bank, but rather to keep it in the shop (perhaps to save bank charges – I can't recall exactly why.) But now, in all the panic and alarm, I couldn't remember where I had put the box of cash.

"Where did you leave the money, Robert?"

"It's in a biscuit tin," I mumbled, nodding to a large stack of empty biscuit tins against the back shop wall. If I had walked into the shop as usual at 8am, I would have automatically gone to the exact box. But now my mind was blank. No one else knew where I had left the money – only me.

I knew the money was in a 'half tin', but which one? I started to open all the half tins to no avail. It was becoming embarrassing now, with my boss, the police and the joiners all waiting and watching this apparently forgetful 'boy manager' trying to remember where he had left the most important item in the shop. Biscuits were, by then, sold in packets, but the tins had been stored until sent back for a credit.

"Oh yes, here it is!" I said, trying to sound as if I'd known all along. "It's alright! All the money's in here, Mr Munro!"

After the tense wait, all the watchers – who now knew my secret – suddenly decided it was time to go, and I was left with Mr Munro who was still looking a bit bemused by my actions. "Well done, Robert. You just had it too well hidden. We'd better lock up and go. Unknown to the would-be robbers, all that money was only inches away from where they broke in." I then realised that with me resident in Carnoustie, Mr Munro had obviously been named in police files as first key holder and had been called out.

The next morning, I explained to the staff about the disruption in the back shop. Mr Munro phoned to confirm that the would-be thieves must have been disturbed by someone. "I'll get the iron bars all fixed up," he advised me.

It was then I felt the damage: yes, no stock or money stolen, but the cost of a taxi and temporary joinery work – with more to come – added to the iron bars replacement, would all come as an expense against my branch. How many more biscuits did I have to sell to make up that profit loss? I'd had a break in at Brantwood Avenue, I may still have a suspect shop lifter, and now another break-in!

* * *

The second year of the CRMP course beckoned. Without realising it at the time, my life so far had always included an element of day release or evening classes. It was part of my life. My amateur drama days were long past, and now I had no distractions.

From what I recall, the arrangement had been improved for the second year. Now I could close the shop door each Wednesday half-day at 12 noon, finalise all the paperwork, and attend an afternoon at college followed by a two-hour evening class from 7pm to 9pm. There was no denying those days were demanding, but there was no problem with the content of such a long day. I had learned, when chatting with my two company colleagues, that the underlying concern – no, *worry* was a better word – was how things would go on when we were not in the branch. This year was thankfully different. But for a manager to be on holiday was frankly hell. What's going on? Is the deputy doing a good job? Who is pulling the wool over whose eyes? Are the suppliers pushing too much product on a naïve soul and causing me loss? It was always useful to compare such experiences with my two college colleagues from Wm Low, Jim and Tom. They were long-standing, successful managers, and I always had in mind they must have suffered the same nervousness as I did when they started out as branch managers.

In 1962/63, year two of the CRMP course, our subjects to study were Accounts, Human Relations, Training and

Management Theory. I remember thinking that this year the subjects will be more applicable. When I look back now, and keeping in mind the discussions I had with my pal Alan Craigie about our 'loss' in not getting to Arbroath High School, I realise that while I didn't study accounts, maths, history or geography at higher level, I was actually in a demanding job – I needed to know how to manage people, merchandise goods, apply work study and be aware of law and basic accounting.

In fact, I think a good few people then – and perhaps now – don't realise the number of skills and attributes, not least the challenge of handling people, that retail managers must have in order to be appointed in charge of a grocery or supermarket. It requires a unique blend of personal skills that many academics may not have and wouldn't want.

* * *

One day in late September, Kathleen came to me with a friendly warning. "I thought I should let you know, Mr Rettie, Mr Munro and another man are outside."

"Oh?" I asked her, "what are they doing?"

"I don't know. Just looking in the window."

This was a seriously massive shock. Nothing like this had ever happened to me. I nervously peered from the corner of the back shop doorway and, sure enough, saw the three figures staring intently at the fruit window. What was so special? Why were they here?

Why all three?

Calm down, Robbie. It can't be all that serious.

Luckily for me, things were ticking away nicely in the shop with a few customers moving about. Equally important was that I had, that very morning, put on a clean white coat and so felt quite comfortable. But what were they after? What was their mission? Mr Munro hadn't said they were to visit.

As they entered the shop, Mr Munro said "Hello Robert, we're just having a look around. This is Mr Rettie and Mr Conley."

Mr Rettie, the Managing Director of the company, had lived in Carnoustie. As a message boy, I had delivered his weekly groceries. Mr Munro, of course, I knew, but I hadn't met Mr Conley – although I had heard he had a fierce reputation as operations director for devastating any manager whose standards, business or otherwise, fell below his demanding and extremely high benchmarks.

They were a powerful, impressive threesome dressed in serious business suits, and I had no idea why they were in the shop without any prior notice. They looked around the shop and the back shop, checked in the fridge, and generally gave a cursory glance all around the premises while I tried to keep my eyes and ears open from a discreet distance.

Then, with nothing more than a "Thank you, Robert," from Mr Munro, they were gone.

I had never had such a visit, and it was as unnerving as it was mysterious. For the next day or two, my unexpected guests occupied my thoughts. Had they come to see my unusual window display of special offer marmalade, where I had rigged up an electric light bulb under a tumble display of jars? I quickly ruled that idea out.

Dinna be daft, Murray! You know that's a stupid idea, Robbie. They probably make visits to every branch now and again.

Were they checking on me, and the snap visit had been to see if all was in order? Yes, I suppose it could have been an unexpected visit to gain an accurate assessment. Could they have been examining Logie Street as a possible mini self-service store? Until that visit, I hadn't thought about that prospect, but it set my mind in motion. Could such a store be developed? Whatever the reason, it was a clear message about the dynamic heart of the business. It demonstrated to me that the top people were very much in touch, and were probably always mulling around business opportunities and options.

As soon as they had departed, an incident occurred which I had to deal with. A customer had scratched her leg on the corner of a wooden box upon which was a display of bananas. She had ripped her stockings. Kathleen was available in the back shop to help put on a sticky plaster, but the lady was upset. Of course, I had to apologise and give away some more profit by gifting her a packet of biscuits. Out of the event we all learned the customer's name: Mrs Conrad. I had noticed, not having deliveries and credit, that there was yet another downside in that we didn't so readily know customers' names.

"Are you alright, Mrs Conrad?" I asked her.

"Aye, son. I just got a fleg."

Later, I gave the incident some thought, it would probably have been a good example to the bosses that self-selection was really only a 'half-way house', and that the clutter of stock filling spaces was not an entirely safe selling area. Customers' bumps and scratches were possible – even likely.

A light-hearted event happened on the Saturday of that week. The shop was busier than ever. I had survived the mid-week critical examination by the top bosses (at least, I crossed my fingers I had), and when the takings were counted, we discovered that we had broken the £1,000 a week sales figure.

I looked up in amazement at the till and exclaimed "Go, go, greasy grocer, go!" The staff, who were still tidying up, looked at me in amazement. They were unaware of my old boss's chirpy mantra. Of course, it dawned on me. Although, in my head, I lived with my old manager's quirky saying, I had never voiced it.

"Right," I said, "£1,500 a week is the next target!" They all laughed. From that day on, everyone gradually started using the chant I had first picked up years before from my Carnoustie manager.

"Go, go, greasy grocer, go!" I chanted all the way home that evening.

CHAPTER 12

October 1962:
"Taking the Plunge", or
"Realising My World is Changing"

OCTOBER began with a one-week holiday... well, strictly speaking, my honeymoon! This was not a business honeymoon, such as starting my management experience at Brantwood Avenue, for it was the real thing. Yes, I married my fiancée Gail on 6th October 1962. With all the trials and tribulations involved in my management role, it might seem strange to think that I had any time in my life for romance. But if something is important enough, you always find a way to make the time!

Of course, I did spend several moments at my West-haven 'thinking place' before I took the plunge. My thoughts were focused on how to weld together my two worlds – marriage on the one hand and the demands of being a retail manager on the other, with all the unknowns such as call-outs for break-ins, Sunday working in preparation for Christmas trading, stocktaking weekends and unexpected long hours.

Come on, Murray! You'll wait forever to be certain of having no problems. You'll just have to go for it. This is your living; it's how you will pay your mortgage for the £1,000 one-bedroom cottage you've bought in Kinloch Street, Carnoustie.

My life had changed quite considerably in the last two years. Long gone were the nights of dancing at the "Palais" and "JM Ballroom" at Dundee, solely because all my friends had scattered. These days I worked long hours, and had very little time for relaxation. And now I was a house owner. The thrill of buying a wee cottage – it was a big step.

* * *

One day, while I was placing a tray of Canadian Mackintosh red apples into the fruit window, I glanced up to see a bobby sitting on a pushbike parked outside. It was Jim! I motioned him to come in and, after propping his bike on the kerb, he wandered into the shop. It was near my ten minute break time, and – with it being a relatively quieter morning – I offered him a cuppa. If Mr Munro were to appear, I would genuinely be able to say I was asking if any further news had been gathered about the break-in thieves.

"Aye, there's a gang running about causing a nuisance," Jim said in a matter-of-fact way as he removed his hat and scratched his head.

"Are they likely to break in again?" I asked him with concern.

"They'd be awfi' daft tae, 'cos they're being watched now. Difficult to prove they did the job here, though."

"Ah. I understand."

"And how's your mum and dad doing these days?" Jim enquired, changing the subject.

"They're fine. Dad's got his garden up and running well, with a good crop of strawberries and vegetables this past year. And mum's finding the house a lot easier than the flat at Westhaven. Gone are the days of washing and scrubbing in the old wash house!"

"What great days, Robbie – and not so long ago. Look what's happened to us since the days of fishing off the rocks for dargies and poddlies."

It wasn't long before Jim and I were reminiscing about our gloriously happy childhood days at Westhaven. "The greatest fun was when you looked after the fisherman's boats and you rowed Peem, Coffee, Ollie and me half a mile out to sea," I recalled with some nostalgia.

"Aye you all had a 'fricht' when the porpoises leaped around the boat," Jim laughed. When I think of it now, fifteen year old Jim took four of us, aged between 11 and 13, out to sea in a boat owned by a fisher. Only Jim rowed. It was most definitely a risky thing to do, but in those days we seemed to take all those adventures in our stride.

"Do you remember the time the tide went back so far we saw bright yellow seaweed that looked like corn growing amongst the rocks? It was weird," I reflected.

"Aye. We saw that only once, Robbie. Nobody else will ever believe us. I've never heard anybody say they'd seen that."

"And of course, Jim, you saved a life out there on the rocks."

"Oh, aye," he said, recalling the moment. "That was the day Ollie fell in and was nearly sucked under by his wellies."

"Poor Ollie. We told him to tell his mum he got stuck in deep mud and lost them."

"That still didn't explain why he arrived home soaked to the skin," Jim remarked with a chuckle.

"And how is wee Ollie these days? Do you ever hear about him?"

"No, I never see him now."

"He was always in a state of terror. Remember, he stood on a 'flook' (flounder) and thought it was a conger eel. He jumped about three feet in the air."

"Oh, by the way Robbie – do you remember the bobby who chased us when we did our annual prank and set the marram grass on fire?"

"Aye, I do – Colin somebody."

"Well, he's my boss now!"

What a small world. "Does he tell you not to be too tough on the youngsters?" I asked.

"He does. By the way, did you set 'torrocks', Robbie?" Jim reminded me of how, when the tide was far back, I set a long line of baited hooks weighted down by big rocks stretched across the channel at the harbour, then waited hours for the tide to come in then go out. I had to calculate the tide times to make sure I was there when the line was exposed again.

"Yes, I did – once or twice. But one day near Christmas, I remember I checked my line when the tide went back and found a three-pound cod."

"Did you do it regularly?"

"No, because the day I caught that cod one of the fishers accused me of taking it off his torrock line. So, I was always scared he would think I was stealing his fish."

"Aye, you had to be careful, Robbie. Mind you, the Ha'en will no' be the same withoot our cheeky gang. We had a'thing in those days – bonfires, rounders and catching fish and partons" – by which he meant edible crabs. "Aye, and playing cricket and fitba' wi' Donald Ford!"

It was time to glance at my watch. "By the way, Jim, I hear Donald is doing well these days. My uncle Tom who lives in Edinburgh told me when he visited us last week that Donald's been playing for Vale of Avon, and moved on to Bo'ness United. He describes him as a 'clever wee footballer'."

"Aye, but will he ever mak' the big time though, Robbie?" Jim wondered.

I grinned in response. "It'd be great to say someday that we played with a Scottish Internationalist on the ballaster!"

"I'll pay ye a quid, Robbie, if he ever does!"

"You're on!" I agreed.

"Oh, that reminds me – another bit of news. The Council are saying they're going to level off the ballaster."

What saddening news. "What a shame," I said. "That grassy hollow where we played will never be the same."

At that point, John put his head around the edge of the doorway. "Excuse me, Mr Murray. Mrs McGlynn wants to know when the Danish Blue cheese will be in again," he said.

"Tell her the middle of next week."

Jim raised an eyebrow. "You've gone up in the world, Robbie. So it's Mr Murray noo!"

"Well, I don't know what it is behind my back," I joked. Then, hearing an approaching sound I had come to know so well, I added, "Oh, here's a fruit delivery, Jim. I'll need to get a move on."

"Aye, well, I'm off. Give your boss the update aboot the thieves. Oh, and tell yer mum I'm asking for her – and say I'm still missing her braw toffee apples she used to mak'!"

"Sure will, Jim."

"But dinna tell her aboot the copy of the *Health and Efficiency* magazine we found in the hedge up Carlogie Road!" he mentioned jokingly.

"She found it in my cupboard a few years ago and she gave me a right telling off for looking at nudes," I told him, "but I told her it was your magazine."

"What?!"

"Only joking, Jim."

* * *

One evening in October I'd been listening intently to the radio until well after ten o'clock. This was a seriously tense time, when John F. Kennedy had called on Khrushchev – the Soviet leader – to turn back his vessels which were en-route to deliver missiles to Cuba. Previously, a US spy plane had identified missile launch sites on Cuban soil. The big question was, would the Russians listen to Kennedy and turn back the ships? Radio reports were giving almost minute-by-minute updates – would Kennedy's warning be heeded, and the convoy be ordered to return? Eventually word came through that the Russian leader had turned the ships back. The tense moment had passed, and the world seemed to relax again.

Sometime after switching off the radio at the end of the news report, and with the delicate situation still uppermost in my mind, I nearly jumped out of my skin when a tray which had been propped up in the kitchen slipped with a loud crash. There was a real sense then of the tension between Russia and the USA, and I'm certain my own nervousness at the time was not isolated.

A few evenings later, when I reached home after work, I discovered that Alastair McCallum had called in at mum and dad's house hoping to speak with me and find out where I was now living.

"He would like you to go to his house at Tennis Road," mum told me. After tea I drove to his home.

"Hello, Robbie," he greeted me with a smile. "How are you? Come in."

"All well, Alastair. Extremely busy these days. I've been moved to a bigger branch at Logie Street."

He seemed pleased to hear my news. "I saw your wedding picture in the newspaper. By chance I met your dad at church last week and asked how you were."

We spoke for some time about our days on the stage, and some of the laughs we'd had – like the time our unusually nervous producer Steve had erroneously delivered the line "Yes, I heard a shot," when in fact the victim had been strangled. And the time when George, to play his part on stage, had removed his specs... then proceeded to pour a jug of water into a set of glasses which had been wrongly left upside down on the table on stage. Then, on another occasion, our friend John had wrongly exited "left" instead of "right" – where the only door on the set was located – and had to wander back on stage as if he'd walked through a wall.

"Yes, we all made our mistakes at some or another," I laughed. "I remember hearing my cue when I was in the dressing room. My apologies to those on stage, left wondering what to say, were never adequate." Steve had not been happy on that occasion.

"Robbie, I want to invite you to join Round Table," Alastair told me. "Somebody told me you were over twenty-one years of age."

"Yes. In fact, I'll be twenty-two quite soon."

Alastair outlined the routine; members gathered at 7pm in the Station Hotel in Carnoustie, and monthly meetings started at half-past seven. "We have a programme of speakers all through the year," he explained.

"Sometimes I'm not home until after 7.30 or later."

"Ah, but you won't have to eat at home – we all eat our meal at the hotel." Many Carnoustie people I knew were members, and I certainly welcomed the invitation.

"I would have to work out something special to leave Logie Street by 6.30-ish. Can I give it some thought and come back to you, please?"

You do far too much, Robbie Murray. You have no time to yourself, and all you have are your studies. Try and find a way of getting to meetings. You'll be able to keep in touch with your friends This could be your only outlet.

My staff were all usually, except for Fridays and Saturdays, able to be tidied up and away home within thirty minutes of closing time. Along with May, I worked out a way that – on Round Table Tuesdays – she would start counting takings before six o'clock closing time, enter the figures in the book and put the cash in the bag (ready to go in to the famous elusive biscuit tin!). We could then use a new float, and regard any late sales as Wednesday drawings.

After a few trials we found we could be tidied up around 6.15pm on most evenings. May was delighted with an earlier finish, and I called to speak with Alastair a week later.

"Excellent news, Robbie. See you at the next meeting."

"Thanks Alastair," I replied. "I'll look forward to seeing you." Another portion of luck in my life!

Following that piece of good fortune there was more to come, for the speaker at my first meeting was Robin – a young entrepreneur (although I didn't know that term at the time) who had partially trained as an architect, and was now a designer of self-service shop interiors.

I couldn't believe it; Robin's talk covered shop layouts, an explanation of the various types of fittings (I was already aware of gondolas) and moveable sales aids such as display tubs, wall fixtures, specialised cabinets, etc. A later part of his talk was about the developing designs of the best shopping baskets and trolleys. This was new technology, and he was at the leading edge. He already had a manufacturing agent producing trolleys and baskets by the thousands, and he was the selling agent. I was witnessing someone who was already doing brisk business in the new world of retail grocery. I was enthralled.

It became clear that Robin's clients were mainly small shopkeepers who were thinking of minimising or removing counter service, though I had more than an inkling that he would dearly love to secure some huge contracts with the likes of Wm Low. I couldn't enter any discussions with him, for I was certain my company would be energetically and independently assessing their options.

Robin's clever approach was to construct a 'plan' drawing of his prospective customer's proposed shop layout, complete with every fitting and all costed. Although I followed every piece of his concepts and enterprise, I had to be content in the knowledge that Wm Low had already embarked on the new retailing technology. Having enjoyed a fully engrossing talk, my feeling was that even small shops were going to catch up – the race was on, and I was beginning to realise the massive changes that were beginning to emerge.

As I said to Alastair at the end of the evening, "What an opportune first meeting for me – and we can all see how much life is going to change for retailers and shoppers." I could never have dreamt then of the giant supermarkets – the Morrisons, Waitroses, Asdas and Tescos that we know today – complete with 'message laddies' delivering customers' on-line shopping orders in custom-built vans.

My introduction to Round Table was amazing. First it brought me back in touch with my Carnoustie roots, but it also gave me – through the monthly meetings – an insight into the modern world. Other meetings came along which I enjoyed, but one stands out as being particularly interesting. A speaker came along to talk about the possibility of oil exploration in the North Sea. The thrust of the talk was all about prospective drilling for oil. Then, it seemed like an unreal scenario for Scotland. Drilling for oil in Scottish waters? No, surely not. "That's only the stuff of Hollywood films," the chairman had said when he introduced the speaker. For some reason, probably because I was a 'new boy', I was invited to give the vote of thanks that evening – a new experience for me. That's another reason why I remember that evening so well.

Alastair's encouragement to join Round Table provided me with another interesting evening talk when I learned for the first time something about the origins of Carnoustie. The speaker was a Mr David Lowson, whose ancestor Thomas Lowson (Tammas Lousen, as he was called in the 18th century) was the founder of the town. Evidently, Tammas – a loom wright by trade, who lived at Barry village – discovered on a walk home from Inverpeffer, near Easthaven, a most desirable spot on the grassy waste dunes, where he rested and proclaimed he would build a house on the very spot. In time he developed a garden there and placed a dibble stick at the end of a row of cabbage plants. The stick surprisingly took root and grew, thereafter becoming a tree now known in the town as 'The Dibble Tree'.

In the space of only two months I'd learned about supermarket planning, oil exploration in the North Sea, and something about the heritage of my hometown. It was the first time in my working life I had made time to enjoy myself outside constraints of a shop.

* * *

It was approaching 7.30pm one evening after a busy Monday when I opened the back door of Shamrock Street to be greeted with a rendering of "Happy Birthday to you"! We had been invited to Shamrock Street for a meal, and the family had waited for my arrival. Isobel, now eighteen years of age, had been Gail's bridesmaid, and 'Baby' Jean would be nine in November with 'Best Man' Peem's birthday later that month too.

I'd had such a frantic day, I had forgotten all about my twenty-second birthday party until I arrived at my new address in Kinloch Street and found no one there. Only then did I realise my mistake. It was late, and the family had taken their meal. Eventually we all enjoyed mum's big 'clootie dumpling', complete with her safely-wrapped silver threepenny pieces – each carefully dispersed. Yet again, by some magic mum had managed to place a coin for each of us. A great evening, but another example of how long working hours in the trade could be disruptive to family life.

You are a lucky boy, Murray – getting your favourite grub... and a silver threepenny from your mum at the age of twenty-two!

Mr Munro's monthly quarto piece of paper issued to managers in his area in November relating to October results showed Logie Street had another excellent percentage increase over the previous year. I knew for each week in that month the branch had clocked up sales of over £1,000. That was a first for Logie Street.

The next Wednesday afternoon, when popping into the Carnoustie branch, Ian Stewart remarked – as he dashed past me in his usual hectic style – "So, a 16% increase?" He had a broad grin on his face as he said it.

"I think you'll find it was 26%", I quickly corrected him with good humour.

"Naw, Mr Munro's just typed in a '2' by mistake," Ian teased me.

This was the gentle rivalry which we had developed. Ian had been successfully running Carnoustie branch for all the years since before I was his message laddie, which meant he had a greater difficulty in achieving high percentage increases whereas I think I had more scope to see improvements.

I hoped my former boss was secretly jumping with joy, as he could rightly say he had trained me. "The wee greasy grocer's top o' the league again," he beamed later.

My reply was always the same: "Still trying to reach your high standards."

CHAPTER 13

November to December 1962: "Problems and Prospects", or "Catching Up with Jock"

ONE Wednesday afternoon in November – it must have been after four o'clock, after visiting my former colleagues at Carnoustie branch – I was walking along the High Street when who should I meet but my former school science teacher, Miss Fleming.

"Hello, Miss Fleming!" I greeted her cheerfully.

She obviously didn't expect to meet me and hesitated and stared at me. "Who are...?" she started to say.

"Robert Murray, miss," I added quickly.

"Oh, Robert Taylor Murray. Yes, you used to work in the shop along the street, didn't you?"

"Yes, miss, I did. But I work in Dundee now." I briefly told her my news. "You were my first customer when I was an apprentice," I explained.

"Was I?"

"I'm sure you can't have forgotten my fumbling efforts." I'd never in my life had a chat like this with Miss Fleming.

"I don't recall that at all!"

"You will no doubt remember I had my most embarrassing moment when I didn't know what vermicelli was," I reflected, reminiscing with some embarrassment on the incident.

"Oh dear," she said. "I can't remember that."

I was so relieved, for I had been certain for years she must have thought me a real idiot behind the counter. "Counter service is dying out now, miss," I mentioned. "Customers just pick products off shelves these days. It's a lot easier."

"Oh yes, I believe so. But is that progress?" she pondered with some degree of sad resignation.

Sensing her doubtful reaction, I didn't pursue the subject further. We didn't say much more, but then I had another thought. Self-service is seen by shopkeepers, like me, as a step forward. But here was Miss Fleming, now surely close to retirement age, thinking otherwise. It was a thought I took on board: my elderly customers may not see the new shopping methods so favourably.

Something to think about, Robbie. Keep that in mind when you're dealing with your customers.

* * *

The usual Scottish winter soon crept in. Days shortened, and icy roads became the norm. More welcome birthday dumplings appeared for the celebrations of Peem and Jean's special days. Always good fun: mum kept those traditions going. By now my bags of sand were firmly loaded into my car boot, and hopefully keeping me safe. It was just a normal part of life.

News came to me via mum that Jock Brown was home on holiday from England. It was a good example of how mum picked up this gossip which spread along the small-town High Street of Carnoustie. Realising he would probably be making a 'flying visit' to his company's factory at Forfar, I decided to act promptly.

Later that evening, after my meal, I walked to Jock's house. We had been in the same class at school, and as message boys had a great friendly rivalry. His customers were mainly from the east end of the town – known locally as the 'posh end' – whereas my message boy duties took me all over the town and into country areas too. We had jested with each other for years about our respective products, Jock seriously believing his products were far superior to mine – especially because Wm Low's butter was sold off a slab, and I was never allowed to forget that his sugar was West Indian cane while Wm Low's was merely beet sugar from Cupar, Fife. In those message boy days I didn't believe him, but now – a few years on – I did agree that his customers were probably wealthy enough to buy higher-quality teas, sugars, cooked hams and bacon. As I approached Jock's parents' home, I realised he had probably been correct all this time, but I cheekily planned to keep up the rivalry anyway.

"Hi Robbie! Good to see you," he said, grinning as he answered the door. "Come in!"

"Jock, you've returned from the deep south! How are you?" I asked.

Jock guided me to the lounge, where Mr Brown was reading the *Evening Telegraph* and Mrs Brown was darning a sock. They both greeted me kindly, and we chatted for a few minutes. "Jock, we don't need to disturb your folks," I said eventually. "We can go out for a drink somewhere."

"Good idea," he agreed. "There was a time only a few years ago we would have gone to Tom Swan's cafe for a hot orange," Jock reminded me.

"That's true," I said, "but we grew out of 'Swannies' hot orange drinks and tried different flavours."

"What kind of flavours?"

"Well... alcoholic flavours," I admitted with a laugh.

"I haven't been up here for a long time. Let's taste what the Station Hotel bar can serve up," Jock suggested as he held the door of the pub open for me.

'Mine host' Arthur's welcoming remarks were: "Well, well... if it's no' the twa grocery laddies!"

We all laughed, and Jock added, "We've come back to take over your hotel – and then the town."

"You can have it wi' pleasure, wi' customers like you twa!" he joked. Arthur expertly ran the Hotel at a high standard, and was a good example of how to 'put your customers' first'.

"How do you manage to get time off at this time of the year then, Jock?" I asked him once we were seated.

"The canning industry has got all the seasonal produce dealt with for the year, so I have a little gap." Jock had left Bradburn's retail grocery store around 1959 and joined East County preserves as a trainee production manager, eventually becoming production supervisor.

"How's it going then, Jock? Canning the highest quality products in the universe?" I teased him.

"It's not easy, Robbie. I was promoted to production foreman earlier this year with Worcester Foods, but the competition in the canning business is fierce and the demands on staff are high." This was not the Jock I had known. He gave me some idea of the tonnage he had canned and how difficult the market place was for his products.

You see, Murray? You're not the only one with worries. There's no such thing as a job with no problems.

We exchanged some of our recent work history, and soon were reminiscing about the 'old days'. "We have quite a lot in common, Jock. We both played golf while at school, but you progressed to the final of the School Trophy Cup competition. And we were both on stage with Newton Panbride drama club – well, once – in *The Happiest Days of Your Life.*"

"We didn't know it then, but we were actually enjoying our own 'happiest days'," Jock said in an uncharacteristically serious tone. "Has that got anything to do with being in the grocery trade? Two show-offs?" he wondered aloud.

"Don't know, but we both did a lot in the technical class at school – does that prove anything? I remember you made a golf caddy car, and then a bathroom cabinet... in walnut, no less! I tackled a card table and a standard lamp."

"I wonder how old 'Pop' Lindsay is doing these days? He was a tough master. I'll never forget we had to queue up to get our 'teckie-drawing' homework marks, and that meant we were inadvertently sniffing the bubbling glue in the pots on his bench."

"I've always wondered if he did that deliberately to calm us down a bit."

"Or perhaps the opposite – though it would be a bit risky getting us 'wobbly' on it!"

"Maybe he needed it himself when dealing with us lot." Looking back from today's point of view, we didn't then know about glue sniffing and all its dangers.

"When he got really upset, he used to throw chisels at some of us," Jock added. "Maybe he was 'on the glue', as they say!" We both laughed, knowing that we had been spared that danger.

"Jock, there's one experience which stands out hugely for me, and that's the time you took me on your journeys around the Angus countryside in Bradburn's travelling shop."

"Oh yes," he said, remembering the occasion. "You had broken your wrist when you had your motor bike accident and you sat in the van with me."

"I didn't interfere; I just sat in the cab and listened to your velvety patter with all the ladies. You were lost in the grocery trade, you know," I ribbed him.

"You know, we just seemed to teach ourselves all that counter service patter," Jock added. "Back to being 'would be' actors. Remember how, on our way to evening classes, we dreamt of being food sales reps with big cars?"

"That's true," I admitted, "but as an apprentice I began to see how the glamour disappeared."

"I saw the same – how a line of reps would stand, for up to an hour in the shop, waiting to speak to the manager… who was busy seeing to his greater priority of serving customers."

"These guys wore immaculate suits, carried upmarket professional bulging brief cases and always tried to keep a smile."

"Not the way I'd like to spend my day."

"Nor me! But you know, Jock, it's changing fast. Almost all goods now all come through our warehouse, and reps are a dying breed. After all those years I'm now selling what you used to tease me about."

"What's that, Robbie?"

"You joked with me that my products were cheap and nasty, while you sold everything top quality and in packets. But now *all* my products are in packets."

"You see, Robbie?" he chuckled. "I was just a few years ahead of you."

That was more like my old friend. We shared a laugh and, after planning to meet up again sometime in future, began our walk home. "So, the pubs still close at 9.30 here in Scotland?" Jock asked, seeming amazed.

"They've been talking for a while about opening until 10pm, but nothing's happened yet," I told him.

"I can be in a pub up to 10.30 in England, and in some places I can walk across the county boundary to drink until 11pm if I wanted to."

"It's all getting easier. Remember in the old days, when we had to travel three miles to get a drink in a pub?"

"Oh yes, the old rule about having to be a 'Bona Fide' traveller. Happy to say it didn't bother me, Robbie."

We were both right, though; the times were changing. "Well that was a good blether, Jock," I said. "Plenty to talk about."

"Aye, we've had some interesting times," he reflected. "I was just thinking the other day of our Saturday evenings when we were bored teenagers."

"You mean when we went to the 'pictures'?"

"Yes, followed by a walk to Tommy Swan's café to buy a quarter of Sharp's toffees."

"And then our big moment – to pay 9d to go upstairs at the YMCA to watch the dancing."

"We thought that was our big night out!" Jock laughed.

"Once we plucked up courage to dance, we discovered it was safer upstairs."

"You're talking about the night when the Dundee 'Teddy Boys' terrorised you for dancing with one of their girls, Robbie?

"That's right! I was rescued by Terry, then driven home in a police car!"

"Well, we survived it all."

Jock is as close a pal as you can get, Robbie – school classmate, fellow grocery apprentices, night classes. You must keep in touch with him whenever you can.

CHAPTER 14

Christmas 1962 to January 1963: "An Old Pal Arrives from India", or "A Mysterious Interview"

MY day release and evening classes continued, and I found each week more enjoyable than the last. Whilst accounting was an interesting subject, it was geared towards double entry book-keeping, profit and loss accounts and balance sheets, none of which were of direct interest to me. The training and human relations subjects, on the other hand, were of great value. While training was of interest, strangely enough it had the effect of telling me how little – if any – I and the company had done on a formal basis. While the course highlighted training as an essential element in business, it didn't help me to create a plan to aid me and my staff. All I had to work on was the need to ensure staff were given what I could call "planned experience", but in my small world it seemed like a limited target for me. Human relations, however, was a deeper matter. That subject allowed examination of human behaviour and how control and management – especially communications – were interlinked. Management theory introduced me to organisational structures and span of control – helpful, but of no day-to-day practicality for me.

An unforeseen aspect of my day at college was that I shared time with my two senior company colleagues while we had a bite to eat prior to the evening session. While I gained considerable knowledge on how they each operated their respective branches, I also picked up many negative vibes on certain issues. Yet again, I was hit by a feeling of being out of touch with what was going on. In truth, it wasn't a feeling – it was a reality. I could never convince myself one way or the other – should I develop chats with other managers? If so, with which one or ones? Is it a sign of weakness to feel the need to share problems? Would Mr Munro be told by some unthinking, even well-intentioned manager about my calls? If other managers began giving me negatives, it would be all too easy to be drawn into revealing my own worries and misgivings.

An example of a negative was that, on one evening, I was told me that a new shop had been opened in High Street, Arbroath – a new store in addition to a small counter service branch in Keptie Street (where I had once been sent to assist when the manager was on holiday). At first I was pleased to hear that the company was seeing fit to grow, as the new store was self-service, but Jim then introduced the downside: that the shop had three checkouts, and that the manager was thinking of leaving as he had too many worries about cash control at the tills.

Looking back, it was something my boss would probably never have imagined could have happened. My question was then, and still applies to this day: is it a good idea to allow a young eager manager to get the drift of all the downsides and negatives from two older managers?

Come on, Robbie. Try not to get too despondent about it. Stick with your own aims and ambitions.

* * *

Christmas and New Year trading beckoned. As always, how demanding it was going to be depended upon when the Christmas and New Year dates fell. It was always a most testing time, with great effort put in to determine delivery days for the general order from HQ as well as from other suppliers. Calculating the extra stock required equally careful planning – or guessing!

Each year merely brought a variation of the problems. The underlying success depended on the availability of all staff plus seasonal part-timers – especially part-timers who were willing to extend their hours. Shop closing (and consequently staff holidays) in those days was one day at Christmas and two days at New Year. On checking, I see Christmas Day in 1962 fell on a Tuesday. This certainly would have made for exceptional sales on the preceding Saturday the 22nd and on Monday the 24th. Without doubt I and a few others would have been to work on Sunday the 23rd to fill shelves and restock units. A similar pattern would also have applied for New Year trading, but with added effort required for increased sales before and after a two-day closure.

With no credit sales and no message boy deliveries, the operation was hectic but less complicated. Because of the antisocial aspects related to these and other holiday periods, such as Easter and public Monday holidays, it was difficult to recruit staff and then find that they left after short service.

There was a core of reliable long-serving staff, but in those days it was easier for employees to pick and choose jobs – and the more attractive working conditions – available in US-based companies, such as NCR, on the "Kingsway Rim" in Dundee. This made staff retention doubly difficult. I'd already lost another one young apprentice in the previous six months.

When I stopped to think of the anti-social influences the retail grocery trade had on recruitment, I began to dwell on the impact my working life was having on my own personal life. Not that it mattered greatly, but I frequently picked up from the staff – especially the young ones – references to films and the world of pop music. In a nutshell, my awareness of current films, theatre and recent music was... nil. Although I overheard them refer to the successes of Cliff Richard and Elvis Presley, I was devoid of any relaxing time to enjoy their music. I was, quite frankly, over-worked and far too serious.

It's not the end of the world if you never hear Return to Sender *or* Bachelor Boy, *Robbie. So don't get too worked up about it.*

* * *

Another catch-up with a former school pal came along when Bill McGregor called at my house without notice one evening. "It's too hot in India, so I'm having a break at this time of the year," he explained to me.

With my seasonal period of exceptionally long working hours already upon me, I spoke briefly with Bill and fixed up a meeting early in January. My 'stress-driving' was already reaching dangerously high levels when I was finding myself practically doing entire journeys to and from work on 'auto-pilot'. After my exhausting festive period – during which time

Bill had probably, in contrast, enjoyed a totally relaxed time – we met up.

"Happy New Year, Bill!"

"Aye, and the same to you, Robbie. A bit more civi-lised than the ones we used to celebrate though."

He wasn't wrong. "Remember those Hogmanay nights when we met at the Cross in Carnoustie, then seemed to wander all over the place carrying a bottle of booze?" I couldn't help but laugh. "We must have been mad. So, you've escaped the heat, Bill, and come to freezing Carnoustie to re-lax? It can't be that bad in India, surely?"

"Oh, you must be joking," he replied. "It's the flies, and even the cooler early morning and late evening working hours don't help. I'm just glad to breathe fresh air, even if it is freez-ing. Anyway, what's all your news around here?"

"What news would you like, Bill?"

"Anything," he replied. But where did I start?

"Well, apart from the tension between the Americans and the Russians these days – not to mention the race to the Moon – we've have a real mish-mash of news. We've just had the 'night of the long knives', with half the Cabinet being sacked."

"Yes, I heard. But what about Dundee news?"

"There's news of the old and news of the new. Trams in Glasgow and Dundee have been withdrawn. The Royal Arch in Dundee, the one built to welcome Queen Victoria off her ship, has been demolished."

"Didn't do any good anyway, did it?" he suggested.

"The news about the future is that Dundee Corpora-tion is to spend £40m to modernise the city centre. There are to be new roads, new car parks, and £2m on a new Overgate development. There's a big outcry by motorists about reduced parking spaces in the centre."

"You can't please everybody in the march to modernise," Bill grinned.

So much was happening. "Some old tenements in Dundee city centre are being pulled down as part of the progress," I informed him.

"Much needed, too," he said. "It'll be goodbye to all the 'pletties', the 'backies' and the 'greenie poles'."

"Of course, if you decide to return to Carnoustie you could always buy a Mk.1 Ford Cortina for £573 – a snip for a returning colonial," I joked.

"Get away with you, Robbie!" laughed Bill.

"Apart from that, it's just all new music nowadays. Cliff and Elvis."

"I don't hear a lot of that in India, thank goodness."

"To be honest, I don't have time to listen to it here – I'm too busy. Boring, isn't it?" *But enough about popular culture*, I thought. "Changing the subject, have you caught up with any other pals?"

"Only Richard so far."

"How is he these days? Remember we used to visit him at Noranside when he had his TB?"

"He's fine. That's right; he spent six months in a small log cabin with doors and windows open in all weathers."

"What about David?"

"He's away to sea now, but I went round to see how his mum and dad are keeping."

Bill was referring to a pal who had joined the Merchant Navy. His older brother Willie, our mutual friend, had died only eighteen months previously from Hodgkin's Disease – a form of cancer. It was a huge loss to his parents and to us, as we had been close friends. This was another negative aspect for me – my retail work prevented me visiting his parents, In fact, it had also restricted my visits to Willie before he passed away; something I have always felt bad about.

"Alan Craigie is still around. He's moved on to work at NCR. He looked in to see me at my branch recently. I can give you his new address," I told Bill.

"Thanks, Robbie."

"Jock Brown is home from England at the moment. He may still be about if you want to catch up." As I said this, I remembered my own great disappointment of knocking on the door of a cottage rented by Harry Reid – another of my friends who had also joined the Merchant Navy. My mum had heard (High Street gossip again!) that he was home on leave, and I went immediately to see him. Alas, no answer – Harry and his Japanese wife had left only the day before. "This is the problem, Bill. There's no easy way of keeping in touch with what's going on."

In retrospect, I can see clearly how difficult it was knowing who was doing what and where. Connections were not easily kept. Nowadays, mobile phones, e-mails, social media and whatever can make it so much easier. How marvellous it would have been to have kept in touch with all our friends, especially those who sailed the world or moved about a lot.

"Of course, the other problem was when people were called up to do National Service. They seemed to just disappear, never to be seen again." It was true. We had lost contact with so many acquaintances of years past.

"And what's the social life like in India, Bill?"

"You could say it's a bit different from what I left here," he told me. I realised Bill was probably really saying there was no comparison.

"What, so no JM Ballroom or Palais like we frequented in Dundee, or the Marine Ballroom in Arbroath? With a few drams at 'The Skate' before we created havoc on the dance floor?"

"No, nothing so exciting," Bill guffawed loudly as he spoke.

"So, only quiet nights in over there?" I was fishing.

"No, we have our own social club and bar, so we arrange our own entertainment."

"That sounds a lot better than walking home from dancing at Arbroath or Dundee!"

"Gee, in those days we had to get a Dundee Corporation bus to the city boundary at Monifieth, then walk about eight miles to Carnoustie!" Bill added.

"And arrive home about one in the morning!"

Our reminiscing ranged from work to studies and earnings. "What are your work plans then, Robbie?" Bill asked me.

"Don't know. Any plans are not in my own hands," I admitted. We didn't use the term 'career' in those days. "I have progressed twice, which is fine, and now I'm managing a shop which is nearly self-service. That's the way things are going now." I didn't go into details of the negatives of shop management, but in conversation I picked up the fact my annual salary compared well with Bill's as I was now earning around £1,200 p.a. – with hopefully some bonus payments to come. "Are you still studying Bill?" I asked him.

"Yes, I have to keep up with company procedures and policies. And you?"

"Yes, the company has put me on a management course. It's been helpful."

As we chatted, I became aware that my own progress was entirely in the hands of my boss. I supposed at the time that was all I could expect. Bill may have had similar concerns about how to plan his future, but we didn't go into all that.

It was always a pleasure to compare notes with Bill, but I didn't know that evening when I would meet him again, if or when he returned to the banking world in Scotland. Another e-mail or mobile phone gap!

* * *

With 1962 now behind me, I sat in my car at Westhaven and mulled over what the past year had brought me. What could the New Year usher in?

Come on now, Robbie. You're a married man now; what are you worrying about? Despite your worries, your time at Brantwood went well and you moved to a bigger branch. You're in control of your staff, and they all work well for you as a team. You have been left to organise your administration and buying, and your sales have gone up and stayed up. The course you thought was going to be difficult is perfectly alright, and you are doing as well as Jim and Tom. Hearing them be so negative may indicate their own worries, so you are not alone. So what's your problem? Shop-lifting, break-ins and mainly the one checkout. You are not the only one with such problems. It's how you deal with it that matters. Wait and see what your next stocktake tells you.

Throwing up every concern was fine. It was my usual way to analyse how things stood. The only way to gauge my performance is by a stocktake. *Just hang in there – if there's a problem, it won't be your fault. Back to uncle Alan's advice*, I told myself.

A stocktake took place in mid-January and, at the end of the month, Mr Munro revealed to me a good result. The sales were known to be growing steadily and now the tell-tale statistic – the average 16% gross average margin – had been achieved. In other words, there was no worrying sign of shrinkage, either in stock or in cash margins. Mr Munro said my bonus would be paid at the end of February.

You see, Murray? You're a hopeless case. What were you worrying about?

1963 was going extremely well, and at the start of February, I had an enormous shock. Mr Munro phoned the branch to say, "Robert, can you make arrangements to look after the shop next Tuesday? You are requested to attend an interview at head office at 2pm."

I can't remember my exact words, but it was something like, "What for?"

Whatever I said, it didn't seem to cause my boss a problem. He simply added, "This is extremely confidential, Robert. I can't tell you anymore."

Oh no, I thought. *What's happening now?*

Right then, Robbie – check your space suit. You may be needing it.

CHAPTER 15

February 1963:
"Interviewed by the Managing Director", or "Backwards to Go Forwards"

"COME in Robert, and have a seat here." Mr Rettie, the Managing Director, stood behind his big desk and waved his left arm in the direction of a vacant chair situated at the long glass-topped conference table adjacent to his workspace.

What on earth was going on? *Am I in trouble?* Surely not, as my stock result had been satisfactory, and my sales were increasing... BUT, that being said, my move to Logie Street had been surprisingly delayed and I'd experienced that mysterious visit by the top three directors of the company. Another moment to sit and ponder at the ballaster?

Okay, Robbie – this is big. But for goodness' sake, you'll have to start being a bit more realistic and confident about yourself. Get your stage presence into gear.

Mr Munro, who had entered the boardroom with me, sat two seats away on my left while across the table Mr Stewart – the very same gentleman whose weekly groceries I, as a boy, had delivered to his home in Barry, Carnoustie, sat with a small notepad and a posh fountain pen in front of him. The sparsely furnished room, complete with the whiff of fresh furniture polish, added to the formality and the presence which those most senior people in the company tended to ex-ude. Sitting up straight, I tried to look at ease with my hands resting on the table in front of me.

Robbie, this is the table where big decisions are made. Make sure you don't show your nervousness. Seven years ago, you were a message laddie – now, for whatever reason, you're sitting at the board table. YES, the board table. Just relax now and look confident.

My nerves were tingling.

"Robert, thank you joining us today," said Mr Rettie. "Mr Munro has told you how confidential this meeting is. Are you aware of this?"

"Yes, I am," I replied.

"Good. You see, we are interviewing for the post of Fruit and Vegetable Buyer – based here at head office – and we are hoping to make this an internal appointment, so..." he touched the right side of his nose with his index finger to em-phasise secrecy, "...this is very confidential."

You see, Robbie – you were worrying about nothing again. You are not in trouble. In fact, this could be good news.

There had been, to my knowledge, at least two outside holders of the job previously. But I was only vaguely aware of who they were, and when they had been employed. As I sat there, I was quite certain that I was not qualified to be a candidate as I had never had to buy any fruit and vegetables. Those decisions had already been made for all managers. My thoughts were immediately negative. I had never had to decide which oranges, apples, pears or bananas to buy – only how much to buy. Similarly, all vegetables I had purchased had been through Dundee wholesalers. Again, only decisions on quantity were needed. Fruit and vegetables were never, as a subject, included in my Grocers' Institute studies during my apprenticeship. Something I had never had to think about.

Murray, this is going to be a tough interview.

"What variety of apples are you aware of, Robert?"

"Oh... Cox's Pippin, Worcester Permain, Granny Smith and Macintosh Reds." I recall that I knew more, but couldn't quite reel off the names quickly enough.

Then more testing questions arose.

"When would you buy Permains? And Macintosh Reds? Golden Delicious? The list seemed to go on for an agonising time, especially as I managed to correctly answer only one or two. As plain as day, I can still recall my feeling of total embarrassment and ineptitude – trying to answer questions I'd never had to consider. All the thinking on the subject had been done for me; all I had been doing was selling the fruit.

Then I had a repeat of the torture with pears: similar results. Cooking apples, oranges and especially Seville marmalade oranges were high spots for me in an otherwise poor performance. To this day I regard this experience as my worst – in fact, what I consider to be my only bad interview. Looking back, even if I had been given notice of the purpose of the meeting and had the intelligence to think through the likely questions, there was no-one I knew with whom I could speak confidentially. I did have a friend in a fruit and veg wholesaler's office, but it would have been out of the question to ask and explain why I needed to know. The Internet didn't exist back then to get 'clued up' on subjects.

The simple reality was that even if I had 'spruced up' some accurate answers, I did not have the insight and background to tackle the job. Looking back today, of course, I question why I would have to known when to buy – for example – 'x, y or z' type of pear, because I could only have purchased what importers and wholesalers had to offer at any given time.

Eventually some comfort. "And how are you enjoying Logie Street, Robert?" I was asked. I could immediately sense the reason behind the switch in the questions. I had failed.

"Fine, Mr Rettie. Just had a good stock result, so it's going well."

"Yes, I know. Well done."

I didn't reveal my worries about one checkout and control of cash. I'd had a good result: *Why be worried about nothing* is what I'd have been told.

"Good, Robert. We'll let you know."

On the way out, Mr Munro walked downstairs with me. I was fully expecting some awkward questions about my lack of knowledge. I was only partially correct.

"How did you feel about that, Robert?"

"Terrible," I replied.

"Oh, really?

"Yes, I didn't do very well."

"Not too bad," he reassured me. "You have never had to think about those things." His confirmation of my own troublesome thoughts said it all. My interview was not a success. "I wouldn't worry about it, Robert. Don't dwell on it," were his parting words.

Robbie, time for a re-think. Looks like you won't be needing your space suit after all!

Making my way to my car parked in the street I took a deep breath and grimaced. After starting the engine, I sat staring out in front.

You see, Murray? You're not as clever as you thought. If you think you were bright enough to go to Arbroath High School, you would have found a way to study fruit on your own. You surely must have seen the pattern of which apples and pears were on the market at various times in the year.

As I pondered on all the negatives and my failure at the interview, I reflected on something which gave me a tip for the future. Prior to meeting the directors, Mr Munro had said, "Let's freshen up before we go in." He had guided me to the executive toilet and, looking in the mirror, washed then dried his hands, tightened his tie and combed his hair. I followed suit. Not only did his actions emphasise the importance of the meeting, but it also taught me that even Mr Munro felt the need to present himself in a tidy and professional way. So even my boss seemed to need a few minutes to steel himself before meeting his bosses. It was something I learned at that interview that I practice to this day – first impressions count!

* * *

That was it. What else could I do? Just get back to the known world of my branch and get on with things. However, that hope was dashed for, when I arrived, a customer was in full flight with a complaint.

"Eh paid a lot o' money for that an' it's no fair!" the visitor exclaimed.

"Sorry, Mrs McCleary. It's just been a mistake," said John in a placatory tone. It seemed that it was he who had been on the receiving end of the problem. As I passed, I felt I couldn't ignore the unhappy situation.

"What's the problem?" I asked.

"It's Mrs McCleary, Mr Murray. She's brought back her streaky bacon because she doesn't like the fatty bits."

"Oh, that's the supplier," I told her calmingly. "They're always trying sell us fat."

"Well? What are you goin' to dae aboot it? My bairns'll think I'm glaikit if I gie them that!"

I turned to my junior colleague. "John, take back the pieces and give Mrs McCleary better slices. And give her an extra free slice," I advised him.

John did the needful and tidied up the half-pound of bacon, along with adding a free slice, and repacked everything in fresh parchment and bag. "There you are, Mrs McCleary. Sorry about that," he said as he handed over the package.

"Aye, yer a wee scunner son. It's no' the first time that's happened. Dae ye think am doze'nt?"

Mrs McCleary continued her way around the shop and picked up a packet of biscuits. Once she'd gone, John said, "Sorry, Mr Murray."

"Don't worry; she'll shop with us again. We have to get rid of these fatty pieces, so I know what you were trying to do. You'll just have to watch out for Mrs McCleary next time."

It was part of the job for John and Harry to get rid of all the fat that we had paid for, and my way of dealing with it was to 'work away' little pieces to each customer. The way

we did it was to sell the streaky slices from a tray and, in between the layers of good slices, we popped in the fatty slices.
I'd learned that back in my apprenticeship days.

*Jings, Robbie. It's nothing new; fatty streaky's always
been a problem. You must sell it.*

When I reached the back shop, Harry was standing in
the fridge sorting out stock. "I heard all that," he told me.
"She gave me a 'roasting' because I gave her bad slices just a
week or two ago, and I thought I'd better keep out of the
way."

In a strange way, the episode took me out of my self-
pity for the bad interview experience – which I couldn't share
with anyone – and perhaps helped to cover up my unusual
absence.

I didn't say anything about my day when I reached
home. But after tea, I took time to drive to my 'thinking place'
at Westhaven to ponder on the issues. Would my poor performance damage my future? Should I have learned more
about fruit over the years? I wonder if very competent managers like Jim and Tom had been interviewed. Perhaps they
were candidates under consideration too? And had they put
in more effort to research? Come to think of it, should I have
been bold enough to ask Mr Munro what the meeting was to
be about?

*Yes, Robbie, but he would probably have said it was
confidential.*

On further analysis, I convinced myself Mr Rettie's
questions were not entirely essential: if only Conference pears
are available then only Conference pears are available! However, I did have to acknowledge the questions cleverly exposed my lack of depth.

Mum, I remembered always had a saying: "It'll be a nine-day wonder." And I do recall it took me at least that long to rid my nagging annoyance. Even as I write this today, I feel the emotion of being so inadequate at that interview.

* * *

Running my branch was uppermost in my mind, and I consoled myself that my promotion to Logie Street must have been because I'd impressed Mr Munro by my Brantwood results. About two weeks after my dismal interview, Mr Munro arrived at the shop and – after he cast his critical eye over my window displays, the ticketing and the general presentation within the store and back shop – he asked if he could have a quiet word.

He guided me along to the far end of the back shop and, once he had glanced around to ensure privacy, delivered an amazing statement. "Robert, I have a proposition for you. How would you like to manage the Perth Road branch?"

What my face looked like when he delivered the question, only Mr Munro would know. I'm sure I must have staggered back in disbelief. "Perth Road? That's counter service, isn't it?" In an instant I knew this was a downgrading.

"It is, but not for long," he told me. "Work has started to clear the site almost next door to the shop, and we're building a 2,000 square-foot supermarket. It'll be totally self-service, with six checkouts and back shops upstairs and downstairs."

"But why is the manager there not taking on the new store?" I asked.

"Because he's been promoted to Fruit and Veg Buyer!" Mr Munro explained.

What felt like a thousand questions swamped me: Had the buyer's job interview also been an interview for the new supermarket? If I had been better at the interview, would the current manager stayed put? Who is the current manager? Why had my college course colleagues never mentioned the new forthcoming supermarket? Or had they, and I had simply paid little attention? Was I never really a candidate for the buyer's job, and had Mr Rettie and Mr Stewart been looking to find the best solution to fill two posts?

"Who is the manager at Perth Road?" I managed to enquire.

"Alec Millar."

"Ah, yes." Of course, I had heard the name, but I didn't know much about him – although I would probably recognise him, having seen him at managers' meetings. My immediate thought was that Mr Millar was a mature man with a serious-minded appearance, and I felt quite comforted that I had been chosen to follow him.

"When will the supermarket be ready, Mr Munro?"

"No exact date, but sometime mid next year."

"Do you think Mr Rettie and Mr Stewart were looking for a Perth Road manager as well as a buyer?"

"They wanted both appointments from within the company, so one option was if Alec became buyer, they would need a replacement at Perth Road."

This had all come as such a surprise. "When will the move take place?" I asked.

"As soon after you say you'll take on Perth Road. They want a buyer in situ as soon as possible."

"It's a big challenge." As I said that, I felt the trust being placed in me and the higher profile of the new job being offered – as well as the quiet confidence that after only two and a half years of managing two small shops, this responsible job was mine.

"Well, Robert? What do you think?"

"Yes, okay," I answered him. "I'll do it."

"That's what I like to hear! There's no point in you seeing Perth Road until Alec takes stock. You'll be there for only fifteen or eighteen months. Just keep all this quiet until it's announced," he advised me.

Things are moving fast, Robbie. You should get that space suit ready now.

"Will I be taking stock again here soon?"

"You've just taken stock, so I think we can waive that. I'll report this to Mr Rettie today, and you'll see the announcement soon." The disappointment about my buying job interview performance, which had given me so many sleepless nights, was now over. I was going to do something I knew about.

You see, Robbie? Why did you worry so much? You must get out of this bad habit. The directors' unannounced visit may have been to check you out for Perth Road. Maybe Mr Conley disagreed. "What? He's only twenty-two years old! He can't manage the Perth Road branch. Let me see him and his shop!"

It was that strange thing called luck again.

CHAPTER 16

March to May 1963: "A Bright Future in the Top League", or "Visits to Self-Service Stores"

I T took some time to absorb the impact of Mr Munro's surprise invitation. But that was it: one of the biggest decisions of my life, made in minutes during a back shop discussion. I remember thinking that I'd be meeting my two senior colleagues at college the next day, but this would all be under wraps. Quite a bit of news to tell them eventually, and I wondered what negative comments I would receive about the experience to come.

March saw the end of what felt like one of the longest winters I'd ever experienced, and to this day I can still recall the raw damp cold which seemed endless. It was recorded as the worst winter since 1947, with no frost-free days from mid-December until March with a serious snowfall in February.

At long last spring days were with us, and so on a bright sunny morning I remember thinking the gloom of winter and the dejection of my humbling and bumbling Head Office performance were now behind me.

Now will you believe in yourself, Murray? You would not – repeat, not – have been offered Perth Road if the company didn't think it was right. A new supermarket is a big investment, not to be risked.

The announcement was made through the company 'News Sheet', and Mr Munro phoned and asked me to look in anytime to see Jim at his branch, which was already a fully-fledged supermarket, and also to pop in to the Broughty Ferry store which was in the final stages of development and would be open soon. It took a little time for me to realise I was now in the company of managers with vastly more experience than myself. Arrangements were made for me to visit Perth Road along with Mr Munro. When we arrived, Mr Millar was busy serving at the counter and acknowledged Mr Munro's wave as we entered.

You've arrived on Planet Perth Road – time to recce and check the atmosphere, Robbie.

Perth Road was the worst example of a branch within the company that I, so far, had worked in. With double windows and a frontage similar in size to both Carnoustie and Logie Street branches, initially I was suitably impressed. This was short lived, however, for when I walked into the space to look at the back shop... I discovered that there wasn't one. All there was to see was a large casement window, through which I could glimpse the River Tay – a welcome view compared to previous locations. Yes, welcome, but one I thought immediately I would never have time to look at. This was the only uplifting feature for, positioned at the window, there was a large sink in the style of what we would today describe as a 'Belfast', with a gas hot water geyser positioned on the left-hand wall. The floor area was approximately four feet by four feet, with a large ring fitted to a trap door which took up almost the entire area of the floor. Standing at the sink and washing meat trays was a ginger-haired lady.

"Oh, can we go down, Florence, please?" asked my boss, who stood behind me. The assistant had to pull up the trap door then brush past us to step back into the front shop. "The back shop's down here, Robert," Mr Munro explained to me. "Just go down, but watch your head – and the steps are steep." He certainly wasn't wrong.

When I arrived at the bottom of the stairs, I found myself in a 'back shop' – or perhaps I should say 'undershop' – with an area which appeared to equate with the shop upstairs. It was very tidy, with pallets on the floor around the perimeter apart from a section where I could see toilet doors. Pallets were also laid in lines along the length of the floor, with spaces in-between. Stacked on pallets were cans of product such as soups, vegetables and fruits. In the corner there was a large, strong-looking door which I imagined led to a side street adjacent to Perth Road. (I later learned it opened onto Taylor's Lane.) It was immediately obvious that goods came in there and were moved about by a 'pallet-mover' device which I saw nearby. Stock had to be stored in such a way to avoid two rows of pillars. My assessment was that although it was instantly clear to see the nuisance of the steep stairs, the arrangement of stock in the spacious storeroom was impressive and stock handling appeared well thought out.

"It's not ideal, Robert. There's some dampness down here, so we keep stock off the floor on pallets. But it's easy to find stock."

Two smartly-dressed young apprentices were busy moving stock about, and Mr Munro approached them. "Everything all right down here then, boys?" he asked sociably.

"Yes," they replied, almost in unison.

I was still taking in my surroundings. "Getting back upstairs must be a problem if somebody's working at the sink," I said in what must have sounded a rather negative tone.

"All you have to do is knock on the floor and, if anyone is there, they'll step aside and pick up the ring," Mr Munro explained. "Or you can push the floor up." To this day I still remember thinking that, although a cleverly devised arrangement, it must have been a constant frustration in the day-to-day activities, rushing around the shop to find stock to efficiently serve customers.

While Mr Munro walked towards the back door to show me what – I presumed – was the unloading area outside, flashes of disappointment went through my thoughts. Had this been a permanent situation for me, I would not have relished moving to such a badly-designed shop. Also, quickly filling my mind was the fact that – now having seen four company shop layouts – all of them, except Carnoustie (which was probably designed to order when it was built in 1894 to the company's specification), were quite badly designed for efficient running. In fact, I realised for the first time that my company must have, over the years, purchased or rented properties which were ill-suited to the purpose of running a grocery shop – and Perth Road was the worst I'd seen. In fact, shops then, I concluded, had not been designed with any particular trade or business in mind. However, I rationalised that this was not a relevant issue for me – and in any case, the business had probably outgrown the properties.

"Ah! Here you are, Alec," said Mr Munro as Mr Millar approached nimbly at speed down the stairs. Before any introductions could be made, Mr Millar barked out: "One of you boys – upstairs, quickly!" As soon as his order had been issued, the tall, freckly-faced one immediately dashed away.

"Not easy to see what's going on upstairs or downstairs", I ventured, having observed the problem.

"Yes, it works both ways," Alec said with some despondency, which I took to mean that he as a manager couldn't supervise upstairs and downstairs simultaneously.

* * *

During the next week or so, I visited both Dundee and Broughty Ferry supermarkets. Jim gave me an informed tour of the entire store. It was impressive, and I gained a huge amount of knowledge not only about the layout of both selling and storage areas but also about the fact that provisions remained as 'over the counter' products. There was clearly no manufacturer 'out there' yet which was pre-packing cold meats and bacon. Clearly that was a marketing opportunity. The areas of greatest concern I thought were not really surprising: the handling, prepping and the critical pricing of all products prior to packing on shelves; the new skill of managing specialised tasks (the division of labour) and the supervision of that; security on the shop floor, shoplifting, and goods 'going out' at the back door; and my constant fear – control of cash at the checkout.

"What are your biggest worries, Jim?" I asked.

"The constant supervision of front shop stock replenishment," he replied, "but mainly making sure stock is carefully checked and signed for on arrival."

"Why the back door?"

"It's just that I've never had to deal with such large volumes before."

"Anything else?" I enquired of him.

"Yes, the checkouts. By far. Is stuff going out to pals free or at half-price? Have we got the goods properly priced? Of course, most customers are honest, but if we have a leakage there we could be in big trouble."

"I've always had that feeling with only one crucial checkout at Logie Street," I told him. Jim nodded in response. Looking back, I'm amazed such a huge risk was taken. There were no barcodes to scan then to control prices. Equally, the checkouts were not able to keep track of stock levels to assist re-ordering. All re-ordering had to be gauged or 'professionally guessed' by the manager.

When I visited Broughty Ferry store on a Wednesday afternoon (the word 'shop' was gradually being replaced) I found, as I had read in the company news, that Jack was the manager. He was a highly experienced and respected manager, having overseen the busiest counter service shop in Mr Munro's area – 33 Overgate, Dundee. He gave me almost identical opinions as Jim about areas for concern. In fact, when I arrived at the store I had to wait inside the door until Jack was freed from operating at a checkout. I asked him about that. "I like to be on the till," he told me, 'and then I'm certain everything is paid for." Clearly, I wasn't the only one with these worries. I made a mental note that Jack had used the old-fashioned term 'till' rather than checkout. I was reassured that the biggest problem I could face at Perth Road would be exactly that: the checkouts. Six of them!

Jack's approach emphasised that, historically, a manager in a Willie Low's branch was not confined to an office all day

– the culture was to be 'out there' serving customers and filling shelves when necessary. The reason I could visit that afternoon was due to the fact that Wednesday half-days did not apply there. There was a growing move for stores to remain open six days a week.

As I had expected, Jim and Tom gave me much advice when we had our evening bite between college classes. With the prospect of moving up a step in the store (branch) managerial hierarchy – into the company's top league of managers – I found it easier and more relevant to chat with each. As I had predicted, although there were many positive attributes in the stores the company was now building, there were many negatives as well. Jim and Tom were sometimes full of doubt and concern about profit margins and bonuses. Checkouts were singled out as the big worry by all three of us. When I related I'd seen Jack working on the checkout at Broughty Ferry, both Jim and Tom said immediately, "Yes, but Munro gave him a real blasting for doing that."

"How do you know that?" I asked, genuinely curious.

"Every manager in the area knows! Munro was so annoyed that Jack had tied himself down to the checkout, meaning he wasn't able to supervise what was going on in the rest of the shop." It was a tough one for Jack. He was a manager of the 'old guard' and wanted to control the checkout, but Mr Munro would be looking at the future running of supermarkets. As a spectator I was learning.

Take notice, Robbie. Mr Munro is looking to change the thinking. He's looking for managers who are going to manage in a different way.

What shook me was the fact that all the managers apparently knew of the story and I, because I never contacted other managers, knew nothing of it. There was a world of connections going on out there of which I knew nothing: I began to think perhaps I should join the gossipers. There was also the possibility that Jack had told the entire 'world' of his worries about control at checkouts.

Another moment to pause and ask a question about the policy back then of the company spending sizeable sums of money on those large supermarkets on the same sites as their original branch. All the supermarkets were bigger and attracting many more customers to buy increased amounts of items, but being in the same streets meant that the emerging need for shopping by car to supermarkets couldn't happen unless new greenfield out-of-town sites were built. Perhaps that intermediary step was not required? Should the company have gone first into out-of-town sites without developing large supermarkets which had insufficient car parking? Easy in hindsight, I suppose, and I reflected on the news item I had once read out of *The Courier and Advertiser* to mum – namely that "The new Overgate shopping centre will allow housewives to buy everything under one roof..." With city centre tenement blocks being demolished almost daily, how were carless housewives going to carry large shopping bags home? Parking spaces, I had read, were being drastically reduced in the city centre which would exacerbate the problem. Looking back, it appears there was little or no consultation between town planners, architects and traders.

Later that evening when I had time to think about my day, I began to realise that in a place like Dundee supermarkets would likely prosper at the expense of small 'specialist' shops such as butchers, bakers, and fruit and vegetable outlets. Perhaps Carnoustie's one-man grocery shops would not be so seriously affected, but realistically they would never manage to offer an extensive range of product – nor at such keen prices as supermarkets.

CHAPTER 17

June 1963:
"Football Rivalry", or "Not Clever at a Managers' Meeting"

O N one of his regular visits, I asked Mr Munro about something which had been concerning me. "Is there any chance that Harry and John can move with me to Perth Road when the time comes?"

"Oh, I can't be certain about that," he informed me. "You may get one of them." I was aware the boss had to secure his on-going business, but equally I was keen to take with me people who I trusted. "I can see your point, Robert. I'll be able to help somehow; you won't be left in the lurch."

"I would also ask for Kathleen," I suggested, "but she probably wouldn't want to travel all that way."

"Don't worry. We'll have things all sorted for you."

Football managers, when they move on to a new club, tend to take their management team with them. With this move ahead of me, I could see clearly see the merits of their thinking.

Dinna worry, Robbie. You can trust Mr Munro to look after you.

I then had to ask a question about a date to move to Perth Road. "Like last year, Mr Munro, can we fix a date for my move to tie in with my exams?"

A date was set, and with no stocktake required it was agreed I'd move to Perth Road in April with my exams taking place afterwards. This would release Mr Millar to his new buying job at the earliest opportunity. In due course I did carry out a 'handing-over stocktake' along with Alec. We had not had any opportunity to chat about our respective moves. We never referred to our interviews. I'm not sure if he would have enjoyed hearing that a youngster like me had even been considered along with him as a candidate for the Fruit and Vegetable Buyer job.

"I wish you all the best at Head Office, Alec. I'll be looking for better profits on my fruit and vegetables now!" I joked.

"Wait and see," he smiled, "but all the best here at Perth Road."

Welcome to planet Perth Road! Unfortunately a temporary reverse step.

It was then I sensed his caution about his future role possibly as much as I did about my impending move.

* * *

Luckily happening on a Sunday, my car suddenly came to an unexpected grinding halt. It was eventually towed to the nearest garage in Dundee, and was going to cost a large sum to repair. It's taken many years for me to think about what on earth caused such an untimely end to my car and the reason, as opposed to an excuse, as to what caused the problem. In addition to my general neglect, I can only think I was so wrapped up in everything going on at work that I forgot to maintain the correct oil and radiator water levels. To be accurate, it's only now that I have been able to confess being such a careless owner, and it's a weak reason to say I was too busy – but sadly, that was true.

What perplexed me more than anything was that when I was eighteen years old, I had taken great care of my first car – my Wolseley 14. Having paid £27 for it, I sold it around eighteen months later for £32. Maintaining my cars was something I felt strongly about, but there had been the long and severe winter and that, combined with my carelessness, must have been the cause. It was going to be embarrassing to report my car problem to dad. He had shown Peem and me every detail of looking after our bikes over many years. Clean wheel rims with Vaseline to stop rust, oil chains and other moving parts, keep tyres pumped up, and take out batteries in summer months. It had been a rigorous regime, and now I felt I had seemingly thrown all my disciplines away. Stupid me!

I say 'luckily' that it happened on a Sunday because, had the car come to an instant halt (as it did) on a weekday, the repercussions would have been serious. Again, it's another example of not having a mobile phone in those days. Mr Munro's telephone number was not with me for the simple reason that I never knew his number and never had to call him. In those days I would have had to find a red telephone box. Not having his number with me was obviously an omission on my part, but it indicates we moved about in those days without any thought of needing to contact one another – it was the norm to live with no telephone.

The train became my new form of transport from Golf Street Halt at Carnoustie to Dundee Tay Bridge station, and then a bus journey along Perth Road to my branch (not yet a 'store'). One immediate problem I had was that I was never going to get to Round Table meetings in Carnoustie by 7pm. Luckily my friend Alastair agreed to leave his office on the Kingsway, make a detour to Perth Road and stop off at the shop.

My friend Bill McGregor had gone back to India and, when we last spoke, he said he was unsure when he would be able to return on leave to Carnoustie. Once again, those connections were difficult to maintain. The truth of the matter was that I had precious little time to write letters. With my move to Perth Road, my concern was that Alan Craigie – who had told me he was moving on to work with NCR – would have no idea where I had gone. Perhaps he would enquire in the Logie Street shop?

Another friend lost at this time was Jim, my boyhood hero. The last I ever saw of Jim was the time he had looked in to see me shortly after the Logie Street break-in. He too wouldn't know where I had gone. Those connections were valuable to me, but in those days it seemed quite normal not to write down addresses and keep any changes up to date. In a period of a few months I'd lost contact with them all.

* * *

My two young apprentices, Frank and Tommy, were proving to be very efficient young lads. They worked well together, keeping the 'under-shop' clean and tidy. Sometimes I had the impression they liked working down there too much, preferring it to serving customers. However, one Wednesday morning while I was in the fridge checking stock with Florence – who was in charge of cooked meats and bacon – I overheard them having quite a loud argument.

"What's going then, lads?" I asked them.

"It's nothin', Mr Murray," Tommy said sheepishly. "It's just that Frank's tryin' to tell me Dundee's a better team than Celtic."

"Listen, boys. If Dundee do well, both teams will be the best two in Scotland. So whichever one gets a European title first, I'll give the winner £1."

"You're on, boss!" they both said, grinning from ear to ear.

I realised straightaway what the situation was. Dundee Football Club, by winning the Scottish League Cup, had qualified to play in the European Cup. They were drawn to play the German team Cologne in the first leg at Dens Park. My friendly customer at Logie Street, Pat Liney, would be looking forward to being in his element in such high-profile European games. Excitement in the city was at fever pitch, and while the rivalry between the two young boys was understandable, it had become a bit too serious.

They're good workers, Robbie. Keep them both happy. Humour's best.

College exams came and went and, despite the excitement around my work obligations, I felt I had dealt with the subjects satisfactorily. The move to Perth Road – and the news, now around the company, that I was to be the manager of the Perth Road supermarket – presented me with a strange mixture of feelings. On the one hand I felt and appreciated the trust that was being put in me, and that since I was the youngest manager in the company it was a source of pride for me to be in the group of managers who were leading the way within the Dundee and Angus area. Linked with that was a feeling of great reservation, for I fully recognised I was going into the unknown. In the world of retail grocery there was no room for complacency – no room to let any of it go to my head. From my earliest Brantwood experience I always took the view that I was only as good, or safe, as my last quarterly stock result.

Around the end of May, the customary letter from the college arrived. With huge relief I discovered that I had passed all of my exams. The relief wasn't so much about the passing, but more to do with the fact that I had no other 'distractions' to muddy the waters for my launch into a new and bigger world of grocery management that lay ahead.

In early June there was a meeting of all managers in Mr Munro's area. It was held in 'Mather's Hotel' (a temperance hotel in those days), nowadays the trendy Malmaison in Union Street, Dundee. Meetings had been held previously which I had attended, and I had begun to recognise faces of managers and put names to them. It was also now a more relaxed experience for me, as I had closer contact with Jim and Tom and, more recently, Jack at Broughty Ferry.

During coffee prior to commencement of the meeting, managers – on greeting each other – chatted animatedly. "What's this I hear about the wee greasy grocer, then?" The words came from behind me. It was no surprise when I turned around to find Ian Stewart, my old boss, with a wide grin on his face.

"Oh hello, Ian!" I said, my own tone matching his cheerful greeting. What surprised me was that for the first time ever I had called him by his first name.

"You're fairly jumping about these days, are you not?" he said good-naturedly.

"Being found out too often," I joked. "I'm looking forward to even bigger sales increases on the boss's league table."

"It's a big move," he declared. "All the best. Go, go, greasy grocer, go!"

My Wednesday afternoon visits to Carnoustie branch had almost ceased by this point; I was now spending some half-days doing DIY in my little cottage, and I missed my visits. I knew Ian's sense of humour from my Carnoustie days, and he had always been supportive, but as I settled into my seat I couldn't help thinking that during the past three years I had moved through three branches, advancing each time. Admittedly they were all smaller than the Carnoustie branch, but now I was probably about to overtake Ian and it seemed unfair that he, with a grown-up family, would likely be earning less than me. That's when I remembered my own dictat – 'you're only as good as your last stock' – and Ian had seen many. I wasn't there yet.

After the business meeting, when company policies and procedures had been outlined, there was usually a period when a few managers would give their updates on their business experiences and their respective successes. Both Jim and Jack gave their views on the plusses and minuses of their 'new world' self-service operation, following which there were opportunities for questions. Mr Munro then reported on the plan for Perth Road and a likely opening date of next summer. Heads turned around to me sitting at the back when he announced my appointment. My feelings were mixed: pride on one hand, and controlled fear at the thought of my report on the Perth Road self-service successes – or otherwise – sometime after the end of the first year ahead.

It was time for lunch. The managers who had known each other for years and who knew – I guessed – the best stories and jokes to tell all made moves to sit together in relaxed groups. It was at times such as those that I was reminded that managers probably did have a network of pals within which they regularly communicated. I had never been part of the network – I think mainly because I regarded myself as a young person with nothing much to contribute, and also because I felt that I was still a new boy on the block.

I found myself with no obvious seat and, just as I looked around, Mr Munro said in a quiet voice, "Come over here with me." Then, immediately, I heard Mr Rettie's distinctive voice. "Over here, Robert! Join us here."

I saw the already-seated Mr Stewart, the director, and Mr Munro positioned beside him. It was something I instantly knew I didn't want: not because I didn't want their company, but because it probably looked like I was exposed to the group of managers as being politically astute or, as they say in Scotland, "sookin' up". The last thing I needed was to be seen like this. Those older managers probably made sure they quickly sorted out their seating rather than be 'caught' and sucked into the director's table. Nevertheless, it felt as though there had been a plan to include me.

No mention was made about the buying job, but Mr Rettie did say he was pleased I had accepted the Perth Road challenge. "It's the next important step in the company's plans for the future," he told me. "We are going to develop a lot more of such stores all over Scotland."

As soon as he said that, I got the sense of the thinking at head office. Messrs Rettie, Stewart and Conley were the brains behind the future. Did Mr Munro and other area managers get involved too?

"Robert, you've done very well," added Mr Stewart. "And I hear you have completed your college course. How do you think that helped you?"

Were they assessing the course for others to come along after me? Did they genuinely have a plan for others? My first reaction was to think very carefully. Was I really in a situation of helping to define the company's future training and development policy? "I think it helped me to understand the various aspects of management, but there were parts which were not relevant to a Wm Low manager."

"Oh? Such as?"

"I don't think a manager needs to know about final accounts, and the administration part didn't help me. Economics wasn't a great help, except with laws of supply and demand and price-setting. But merchandising was too wide a subject, as it tried to cover all types of retail businesses."

"What was most useful, Robert?" asked Mr Rettie.

"Without doubt work study, human relations, training, and some law."

"Very interesting," he said thoughtfully. "What should we as a company be doing, then?"

This was becoming quite tense. These were valid, serious questions, and I was now convinced a deliberate plan had been made to capture some views from me about the course. But now about the company, too?

Perhaps I took too long to think about the answer, or perhaps I supped some more soup to give me time to think. Maybe it was both. "I was in Thurso recently, and I was asking my friends about what grocery shops were available to them. Only a Co-op, they told me. So, I think there must be more scope to open branches in places like that."

"How would we get stock there?"

Here was my MD asking me, the youngest manager in the company, serious questions.

Yes, Murray. You are being tested. So don't say anything silly – if you don't know, say so.

"By rail," I ventured. There was a rail link all the way to Thurso then.

Just then, Mr James Miller – the company accountant – passed by the table. "James, how would you like to open a new branch in Thurso?" Mr Rettie asked with an impish tinge to his cultured voice.

"Not on your life!" was the professional but cheeky reply.

"You see, Robert? We could expand, but we must do so in a gradual way which is cost effective. Building routes as we go."

As soon as I had that answer, I realised how thoughtless my response had been. Of course, you would not overstretch the distance travelled until it was worthwhile.

"Economics, Robert," Mr Rettie said as he leant back in his chair. My earlier view about economics was now in danger too.

"Yes, I understand," I told him.

"But you're right. We need to expand."

Looking back, that was the exact moment – if I had thought of it then – to suggest "Why not go straight to 'out of town' sites and build supermarkets and car parks, because the bigger shops in old high street sites are going to be out of date in the near future?"

That, I think, may have been a valid topic for Mr Rettie to take to the boardroom. But you see, Robbie, you're not as good as you think.

I went home that evening and tried to unravel my performance. I convinced myself that I hadn't impressed Mr Rettie too well recently.

CHAPTER 18

July 1963: "Disloyalty", or "A Massive Decision About My Future?"

A SUNDAY game of golf at Pitlochry was a welcome break in July. A golf outing was, evidently, an annual event for Carnoustie Round Table, and I welcomed the chance to meet up with my new-found fellow members. The fact I hadn't played golf for several years became obvious, but it was nevertheless a pleasant distraction from all that was going on. A meal and a chance to chat and catch up with my friends was a luxury, and decidedly more enjoyable than trying to rub the rust off my golfing ability.

Recalling that day, the big topic of conversation was football and – amongst the business members who journeyed occasionally to London and England – the subject was air travel from Dundee, which was then the largest British city without an air service. Meanwhile, Dundee's modest airstrip was to be enhanced with an all-round security fence and a terminal building constructed, while the gent's toilet at River-side Park, to the great mirth of some members, was to be converted into a control tower. One can only imagine the jokes 'flying around' after a few beers on that topic. Another piece of news which captured the interest of the 'high-flying' business members was that the Air Ministry had evidently turned down a plan for an application to use RAF Leuchars for civilian flights from Dundee.

On the entertainment front, I learned that the Dundee 'Rep' Theatre – having been made homeless after a fire in Nicol Street – was to possibly move to a church building in Lochee Road. The highest decibels recorded that day were around the bar, when football was again the excitable topic. Glasgow Rangers had regained the top place in Division 1, while at national level Scotland had defeated England, Wales and Northern Ireland during the previous season. Glory days!

When I went home that evening, I wasn't sure when I would play golf again. It led me to think that the working hours of a grocery manager limited the amount of time for relaxation. However, having tasted a rare moment of freedom I sat down in peace and quiet and took stock of my myself for a change.

It was 1963, and at twenty-three I was poised to take over one of the company's biggest stores. Without pressing my boss for advancement, it had come my way. Since my nervous start at Brantwood, results in two branches had been consistently good. Money was not a problem and, with bonuses, my earnings – I knew from chatting – were very good. Hours were long and tiring, but I felt comfortable in the company's style of operating. My college experience had invigorated my brain, and I had coped as well as my senior colleagues. My summary was that things couldn't be better, and I had a clear challenge ahead. Life was hectic, but good.

Come on now, Robbie. You can't start feeling sorry for yourself. These Round Tablers seem to enjoy themselves in a different world from you, but you're in no position to change things.

The missing ingredient was leisure time, and a lack of opportunity to engage with the world outside my realm of work. Today I look back and realise the huge gaps I have in my knowledge of films, TV programmes, pop music and general news events in the early 1960s. The cause was simply long working days, no real weekends and almost no free time. Above all, the animated chat about football, air transport and theatre brought home to me just how out of touch I was, and emphasised the fact that I was working too long and too hard in a vacuum.

Following that one carefree day on the golf course, a massive shock was to come my way. It was so big that I initially didn't quite comprehend how great it was. To this day it is one of the most life-changing moments I think I have ever had. One of my in-laws had seen an unpretentious-looking but apparently relevant job advertisement within the employment pages of the local *Courier & Advertiser*, and passed on the word to me. When I eventually saw the advertisement, I couldn't quite reconcile the impact of the modest-looking item and the potential effect it could have on my life. It was so insignificant it could easily have been missed, and to this day I conjure up all imagined paths my life and work could have taken had it never come to my notice.

The post advertised was for a "Lecturer in Distributive Trades Subjects" at Dundee Commercial College. Applicants must be a Member of the Grocers' Institute and hold the Certificate in Retail Management Principles (CRMP)." A salary scale would apply, and applications in writing must be lodged by a date (from memory, sometime in early August) to Mr D.G. Robertson, Assistant Director of Education, Dundee.

Robbie, my boy, this is mind-blowing. Think carefully.

Reading this had an impact so vast that I reeled back in total disbelief. The advert could only apply to me. Nobody with the Grocers' Institute qualification, at least in the Dundee area, had so far also achieved the Certificate in Retail Management (CRMP), for it was a new course and I knew the people on it. There may well have been others in the country with the qualifications, but the CRMP was new and this was unlikely. My colleagues Tom and Jim had done the course, but did not hold the Grocers' Institute qualification.

Before even considering a response, I had to sit down and examine a nerve-wracking list of possible advantages and disadvantages. Having made such good progress within Wm Low & Co., how could I seriously disown Mr Munro, Mr Rettie and the company in which I had grown up since I was twelve years old? Those managers and directors had included me as a prospect for the future. They had guided me and steered me to the valued position I now held. I felt I had a future within the company. How could I possibly contemplate leaving my 'grocery' environment?

Now, potentially, here was a totally different world beckoning. What differences could it bring? Possibly a working day of 9am to 4.30pm. No Saturday working. No Sunday prepping days at busy times. A working week of perhaps 35 hours compared to my present 60 hours. No worrying checkouts. No concerning stock losses via the back door. Worries of shoplifters gone. Would there be regular performance checks? Probably not. Two weeks holiday at Christmas and New

Year. Six weeks holiday in the summer. No pressures about staffing. This was a serious question. As I write this today, I still feel the stress and intense emotion – the prospect of leaving my working 'homeland', and the possibility of stepping into the unknown. The prospect of telling my bosses: "Thank you very much for all your trust, expenses in training and consideration shown, but no thanks. I'm off!"

But what other reasons could there possibly be for me to leave? The probability was that my boss, Mr Munro, would be the area manager for years to come. How many? perhaps twenty or more before I could hope to step away from day-to-day store management. And what would life be like as an Area Manager? Mr Munro seemed to be available within the business seven days a week! Even then, there would be no guarantees that I could expect promotion. Did I want to remain a store manager for all those years with limited time for family and leisure activities? (I thought back to my mum's careful words in 1960: "Do you want to be a grocer's assistant all your life?") And what about uncle Alan? What advice would he offer? The realities expressed by Tom and Jim came flooding back too. And Jack's worries about his checkouts.

No doubt about it – this little advertisement had created a deeply troubling dilemma. Whatever decision I made would affect my entire life. This was a 'cross-roads' if ever there was one.

Peem was around, and I decided I must have a chat with him sometime soon. I spoke with Gail, then went to see mum and dad so that I would have the chance to talk with my brother.

"I have a big problem," I told him. "I need your help." I brought the matter up as soon as I had a private moment for, as it happened, I hadn't yet told mum or dad about the 'incendiary bomb' landing.

"Gee, not another break-in?" he asked, alarmed.

"No, it's worse than that."

"Jings! Alright, what?"

We agreed to have a walk along the beach to Westhaven. "Have a look at this," I said, showing him the newspaper cutting which he read entirely without comment.

Peem looked puzzled. "What's the problem?" he enquired innocently.

"Well, I have all the qualifications to apply. But can I even think of leaving Willie Lows after all they have done for me?"

"You haven't even got the job yet!"

"I know, but I haven't told you yet – I'm being promoted again. This time to another branch which will soon be a supermarket."

"Gee whiz," he exclaimed.

After pointing out to Peem the many advantages I would probably find in a teaching job and listing my worries in my present job, there was only one remaining straight forward question: "Do I apply for the job?"

"I've heard what you say about the huge change in the work environment, and there's no doubt it's got to be worth applying for. Remember what uncle Alan told us about the bothy lads – the farm workers who were throwing heavy baskets of potatoes up onto a cart? He said you had to progress in the world. There's no sense in killing yourself, you know. You mustn't work yourself into an early grave," he had advised me.

"Maybe I'm just running away from a difficult job?" I suggested. "You know I'm a worrier."

"But remember, Alan also told us about uncle Will – and what he did was probably more of a culture shock than your situation. He left a bothy one day and was a policeman the next. It must have taken guts to do that."

"But Peem, I suspect I may not get more money if I move. Uncle Will probably doubled his pay."

"Yes, but it's not all about money, Robbie."

"I don't mean to boast, Peem, but when I look back, I always wanted to be involved – I don't just mean being a boss, just to feel in the thick of things. Remember the Sunday Young Worshippers League? As soon as Harry Reid left high school and stopped stamping the children's attendance cards, I was first at the church door because I'd made up my mind I was to be his successor."

"I remember," Peem told me.

"Then I was desperate to be a patrol Leader in the Scouts."

"Yes, you were."

"Being competitive, I think, is what it was – not just being a manager."

"Maybe it was both. But I remember you saying you didn't want to leave school because you said you wanted to learn more. This job may help you to do that."

"You're right, Peem. But how do I know if this college job will aid me in doing that?

"You don't," he said, "and that's why you need to apply and find out."

It was the first time I had shared a serious problem with Peem, but I knew he was talking sense. I wrote my letter of application detailing my qualifications and work history the next evening. This was the start of a colossal feeling of guilt to have my boss firmly believing I was on the path to managing a new custom-built supermarket, yet behind his back applying for a post which was probably poles apart in scope and range. This feeling of guilt was to live with me for a long time, and it is not an exaggeration to say it still lives with me to this day.

Within two or three days I received a reply from Mr Robertson (with a lot of initials after his name) to attend an interview the following week at his City Centre Education Department office at 2pm. Another deceitful moment, for I'd have to tell a fib about taking an unusual lunch break.

My first 'inside' brush with the education world was to walk along what seemed like a never-ending office corridor bearing names of some senior persons with high-ranking job titles. To this day I recall the warm centrally-heated building in July, and the 'office' smell of warm paper and ink and the noise of typewriters from behind opaque glass doors. A feeling of comfort and 'no expense spared'. It was my initial glimpse of the Council's administration world, and my first instinct was to imagine the 'no profit' culture which I imagined lay behind each door. My feelings of inadequacy also started here, when I had to realistically accept my low level of academic achievement – namely a Scottish Leaving Certificate. How could a 'wee fifteen year old school leaver' seriously contemplate being a lecturer? It felt unreal. This was only the second proper interview I'd had in my life.

Now waken up, Murray! Make a better impression than your last disaster.

I was greeted in a most friendly fashion and, after answering some basic background questions, I was asked to talk about my vocational qualifications. My school record, to my amazement, wasn't mentioned at all. Mr Robertson was only interested in my studies since leaving school and the fact that I had been a manager for three years. On reflection he didn't ask me why I wanted to leave my current job, nor did he explore my work history. He didn't ask about my stock and profit results either, nor did he allude to any means of performance assessments I had been subject to.

"Mr Murray, we have a new college session starting near the end of August. How soon could you start?"

Being referred to as Mr Murray seemed hugely impressive to me, coming from this top official. The question of notice period hadn't occurred to me, for I had never had a contract of employment (apart from my indentured apprentice agreement) during my entire employment with Willie Lows.

"Not sure about notice period, Mr Robertson. I have no contract."

"Could it be one week or two?"

My tension was now at fever pitch.

Robbie, do you know what you are doing? This is not a dream or a nightmare. This is happening. "Leave?" "Notice?" *What are you doing? What are you saying? Are you sure you really want to be here?*

My feelings heightened. There was a world outside of Wm Low, and the fact that whatever I had done in the past had now – after many years of hard work – brought me something like a win on the football pools. It suddenly dawned on me that I hadn't appreciated the true value of just what work and study experience I had been acquiring.

"A week would be too short," I said after some consideration. "My manager would need time to find my replacement."

"Alright, Mr Murray. Please take this application form, complete it and drop it back to me along with a note of your required notice. Oh, and take this away with you too – it's our salary scales."

After further pleasantries, which I can't recall exactly, I found myself standing in Dundee City Square totally bewildered and wondering what on earth was happening to me. There was no word of my application being considered or any other candidates. Not even a "We'll let you know." It seemed as if the appointment was a foregone conclusion based on a discussion and my letter of application.

"When can you start?"

Robbie, he probably says that to all applicants. Yes, based on the letter he could have said "Thank you for your application, and I'll be in touch". But no, he gave you a form to fill in and send back – that's probably for education procedure purposes.

To say it was unreal was an understatement. I remember trembling with a mixture of excitement, guilt, pride – and yes, fear – at the incredible unknown world which seemed to be at my fingertips. I tucked my innocent-looking envelope, containing what I felt was the greatest and most potentially damaging piece of evidence to my entire future, under my arm and headed back 'lunchless' to Perth Road.

As I walked into the shop, I wondered if anyone would read the guilt on my face. But luckily there was a diversion.

"That's downright annoying. I'm not having it," I overheard. It was a stern, cultured military voice, adding something to a conversation which had obviously started before my arrival.

"I'm very sorry," I heard Flo say.

"Well, madam, what are you going to do about it?" said the gentleman as he held out a section of papier mache egg carton to Flo, upon which lay what looked like the raw yolks from at least two eggs accompanied by a few pieces of eggshell.

"I can give you another two eggs."

"No, I'm afraid I'm not having that. This is not the first time I 've been sold rotten eggs here."

My readiness to engage in the discussion was not required when I heard Flo say, "I'm very sorry. I'll give you another six."

Being dressed in my 'street' clothes, I was able to blend into the scene, and while Flo prepared another six eggs onto a new piece of carton the customer kept up a running commentary which included: "I know one of the directors of your company, you know. I shall jolly well report this."

With the customer now gone, I was able to get to the trap door. Before disappearing down the stairs, I gave Flo some encouragement. "Well done, Flo," I said. "Do we know his name?

"Well, madam, what are you going to do about it?"

"No," she replied.

"That's one of the disadvantages of not doing deliveries." As I said that, I realised when self-service was introduced more widely it would probably never be easy to know customers' names. "We'll call him 'the Colonel'."

The egg issue had happily masked any unease by my late arrival. My determination now was to get home and examine the application form and salary information, then chat with Gail and Peem.

Where do you go from here now, Robbie boy?

CHAPTER 19

July 1963:
"I Tell Mr Munro I'm Leaving", or
"A Trip to See the Queen"

"**I**T'S entirely up to you, but being given an application form sounds like an education department procedure is being put in place." My school-teacher wife listened to my account of the interview. She made no case for me to stay in the grocery trade, or to enter the world of education.

The job was not mine yet, though Mr Robertson had given a most positive signal by asking when I could I commence. I rationalised that was an obvious concern of his, as he would be seeking to fill a post at the start of the session and so it was perhaps of less significance than I first thought.

"The salary may be an issue," I explained.

Peem had been so grateful for my help in his difficult times, and I was aware of how much he wanted to reciprocate. We planned a walk to Westhaven to find time and the privacy to chat.

"Well, how did it go?" Peem asked as soon as we met.

"Very well. I got the impression there was not a stack of applications. Salary is a problem, though." I outlined to Peem how the interview had gone, with an emphasis on a starting time. We chatted for an hour or so, and concluded that the merits and demerits were quite clear. It was a very tempting situation, but my long-term allegiance to my company and especially the trust put in me to manage a new store with the latest technology and operational ideas was a huge barrier. I was at the leading edge of the grocery retailing of the day. Why jump off the ship?

"It's all about loyalty, Peem. What a way to treat my company."

"It comes back to salary."

"Yes, I know. I would immediately drop from a basic income of £1,200 p.a. to about £900 with no bonuses."

"How would your salary increase?"

"It rises with each year of service, but it's a slow progression," I said as I passed over the document to Peem. "But I could improve my salary immediately with higher qualifications."

"You could do that over time, couldn't you?"

"Yes, I suppose. I should have asked."

It became obvious. Yes, the work would be less demanding and worrying and the salary was an immediate drop, but there was a route to improve that. "It's a monumentally risky step to take – from near-certain development within the company, or a step into the theoretically more comfortable unknown."

We talked around the entire scenario for an hour or so. In fact, we watched the tide make steady progress across the rocks occasionally, giving us an opportunity to reminisce about our happy and uncomplicated days spent on our boyhood playground.

"I never thought I'd have to return to this idyllic, untroubled spot and its history of simplicity with a quandary like this," I mused as I gazed out at the encroaching waves.

"Remember uncle Alan's wise words, Robbie – if you see an opportunity to progress from a hard existence, don't be slow to adopt a better life."

"Is that what this is, Peem?

"Exactly," he replied, "it's precisely his advice."

"I understand, but I'm not convinced."

* * *

Sleep did not come easy for two nights, and I was aware of being pressed for time to give my reply. The simple equation was a long hard road with good money, albeit with no guarantee of further advancement in Wm Low, or a risky, potentially suicidal step into a more secure world with less money but with scope to rebuild my salary.

That was it. Some instinct – perhaps even survival – filled my thoughts. I completed the form, adding a letter saying I estimated a notice period of two or three weeks, and put it through the Education Department letterbox in City Square. Then I held my breath.

That's it, Robbie Murray. You've done it now.

Three or so days later I received an offer of employment commencing on the lowest salary grade of £900 p.a., and asking if I would please report to Mr Newlands – the Principal of Commercial College in Cowgate, Dundee. I was also requested to confirm the earliest starting date possible. Time was not on my side, and I decided not to wait until Mr Munro next appeared on his routine visit. I knew that I would have to phone him, which I did as soon as the staff had left just after six o clock.

"Oh my goodness, Robert! Do you know what you are doing?" was his first reaction.

Sensing his obvious disappointment, I found myself outlining all the pros and cons which Peem and I had teased out. Mr Munro knew my wife was a schoolteacher, and I guessed his understanding of the situation. I'd never ever imagined having this conversation with my boss, but he seemed to take my news in an understanding way, and we talked about my notice period.

"There's no hard and fast rule, Robert. If they want you early, we'll just have to finish up as soon as we can. I'll let you know tomorrow." After some reflection, he added, "Finish up on Saturday 31st August. There's no need to take stock; you've only been there a month."

Looking back, Mr Munro was a complete gentleman about the situation. He had known me since I was a message boy, had secured for me an indentured apprentice agreement, allowed me time off to attend night-classes and nurtured my entrance into management. As a young person I could not have asked for more. I'll never know what he and Mr Rettie said behind the scenes, but I don't think I could have blamed them if they had cursed me or not. Or was it all just in my mind? Why should I think so much of myself?

Looking back today, I liken my situation then as being rather like that of a young football player who has been nurtured in the game within a secure environment, provided with the basics to go further and given every chance to succeed in the profession, only to turn his back on his team and deny them the benefits of his coaching, then say to his manager, coaches and friends: 'Farewell, and thanks'.

All that then remains is to disappear off to a life in another club. Except in my case, there were no extra millions of pounds or an upmarket, sound and reliable future with a well-known club.

* * *

Mr Munro looked in a week later and we chatted. To this day I don't know if he harboured any unhappiness with me, or indeed any anger. Presumably he had told Mr Rettie and the news was out.

Now just think about, this Robbie. Some of your management colleagues may be saying, "Lucky so and so", so there's two sides to this.

There was an arrangement for Mr Munro to pick up the keys on my last Saturday evening. When he did, there was no grand farewell, no dwelling on the past or any emotion about my time with the company. To this day I am left wondering what the real attitude was towards me, and I try to recall whether I had correctly expressed my gratitude for my training and opportunities presented to me from the day I was offered my first branch. Should I have written a letter of resignation outlining my thanks for the care given to my development? Analysing it now as I write, I still feel the eerie silence which I interpreted as disappointment and anger, and I dearly wish I could ask someone. But there's no-one left to discuss the situation.

It's not only goodbye Planet Perth Road – it's farewell Universe Willie Low.

Jim or Tom didn't phone me, and I didn't call them either. I'm left trying to analyse that too. It was a highly emotional time for me, more than for anyone else, and because I felt that intense guilt the lack of response was all the more vivid.

* * *

Dad had progressed from his long-serving and well-maintained Raleigh pushbike to an unreliable two-stroke 75cc Excelsior motorbike and now, after many tough years of frustrating and wet journeys, had finally managed to buy a little black Austin car. My parents had planned to drive us in their new acquisition to Crathie Church, Balmoral, as mum wanted to see the Queen. They invited Gail and me to join them, and so on Sunday the 1st of September, with my mind in turmoil, I sat nearly all day in dad's car saying little.

To this day I can't remember much about the drive to Balmoral except that, thankfully, during the drive various topics of the time were discussed. The fact I recall the topics discussed serves to indicate the deep imprint that situation had on me. It was as if I'd jumped off a high precipice without a parachute. Dad, I remember, talked a lot about Ian Ure – the Dundee Football Club player who had recently signed for Arsenal. What appealed to dad was the fact that evidently, after nearly three hours of discussion in a lawyer's office in Reform Street, Dundee, Ian set off with Billy Wright for a flight to London to play in a match that same evening. Dad was quite taken with the ability to finalise discussions in Dundee and have Ian Ure on the pitch in London that evening. This led to some chat about Logan Air commencing an air service from Riverside air strip in Dundee to Turnhouse Airport at Edinburgh. I vividly recall during that journey my unusual inability to join in the chat, which I think prompted mum to say, "I still miss our little news chats on Wednesday afternoons, Robert."

"Yes, mum. It was always a good time to keep each other up to date." I think that was all I said, for I wasn't in a comfortable frame of mind. My thoughts were so taken up with my situation – and, looking back, I can only imagine I didn't want to reveal my intense nervousness to them. It was then, I think, in an attempt to say something relevant that mum mentioned she'd seen a piece n *The Courier* newspaper in which it was reported that a 'new' Commercial College was not to be built in the Perth Road area after all, but near Constitution Road, Dundee. Nothing in her statement gave me any comfort – I simply had no identity or loyalty with the college: my new employer. The 'Great Train Robbery' had been carried out a few weeks earlier, and I was grateful when the 'car-chat' moved on to that event instead.

Mum had always been sensitive to my work situations. "You're very quiet Robert. Are you alright?" she asked. "Are you worrying about tomorrow?"

"No, Mum. I'm fine." But it must have been the biggest lie of my life.

Robbie, what are you doing? Are you mad? You were happy with your life – why are you doing this? Now you're upsetting mum and dad.

Of course, my little decision was nothing compared to moments when national leaders decide to go to war, fight to win a general election, or when a sports person breaks a world record. But for me, in my little world, it was seismic. Events had moved so swiftly – Brantwood Avenue to Logie Street, then to Perth Road. The sudden appearance of a tantalising advertisement and now, here I was. I had jumped, and was now in a limbo weekend with an unknown future. It was truly a scary step into darkness for, although I had discussed the post in general terms, the salary and the hours with a senior educational administrative figure, I had no idea of the people I would work with – nor indeed the students I would teach. Looking back, I realise I had made some huge assumptions and with no clear picture on how I intended to work my way up the salary scale. Everything is easy in hindsight, but I could have – or should have – asked to visit the college and speak to someone who could tell me what the job would entail.

What were you thinking, Robbie? You should have asked more questions and visited the college. Then you would have got a feel for the job, the students, the environment and your colleagues. You're not very good at interviews, are you?

Well, Murray, you've done it now. It's too late. Or is it? On the other hand, the Director of Education didn't offer much time to think about things. It's probably how the education system works, but it's a risky policy as 'new starters' could leave after a short time. The world of teaching in schools, I was told, is how that worked – obviously not in Further Education. Compared to the rigours of the grocery world, you're now on an easier route with less money.

You had better stick with it now, Robbie. Luck has always gone your way, but have you stepped into your first bad luck scenario? Stop worrying – get on with it!

CHAPTER 20

September 1963:
"Do I or Don't I?", or
"A New Door Opens"

THE historic Monday morning finally dawned. "I should be home about half past five," I said to Gail, which as it turned out was to be the first of a series of unreal experiences on that momentous day.

It was one of the most daunting moments in my life – far more so than my first management experience at Brant-wood. Here I was on the packed platform at Carnoustie's 'Golf Street Halt' railway station at about 8.20am. My thoughts were with my staff at Perth Road, who would be preparing the bacon and cooked meats window display and making ready to pull up the blinds at 8.30. What was I doing here?

Looking around my fellow passengers, I could distin-guish all age groups. Some people I recognised – office work-ers, students, teachers and managers. Realising they were to be my fellow daily commuters, it felt as though I was on another planet – another 'world' which existed in my own hometown, but hitherto unknown by me. It felt to me that morning as though I had been on a rocket to Mars and now, suddenly, I was on a balloon to the moon.

The train arrived at Dundee Tay Bridge station, and the mass of travellers sped off in hurried, purposeful and confident steps in different directions. How I wished I could feel that same sense of confidence. The last time, only about four years previously, I had made my way to Commercial College at Cowgate had been as a student. Now I was walking towards it as a lecturer – but a lecturer of what, exactly?

As I walked to the Cowgate I had strange, comforting thoughts – happy goodbyes to Mrs Cruickshanks and "Spot", Mrs Rice and the rotten tomatoes, the scary shoplifter, Mrs McCleary and the fatty streaky, and then my most recent problem – 'the Colonel'. But then I had conflicting feelings that they were all real, genuine people that deep down I liked as customers, and part of my safe grocery world that I had suddenly left. It was almost, I imagined, like leaving a family.

The first advantage of fewer daily working hours experienced in my 'new life' came to mind when, at about five minutes to nine, I approached the front door of the college. Quite suddenly I was like a fish swimming in the tide with a shoal of students and teachers.

Here you go, Murray! For better or for worse, and certainly for poorer.

If someone had said to me at that moment, 'Turn back to the safety of Perth Road branch and get on with it,' I may well have done. My first impression was of a busy, noisy commotion as chattering students made their way to appointed classrooms. From my earlier experience, I knew the principal's office and administration office were on the first floor. With 'jelly-like' legs and my heart pumping, I approached and was grateful to meet an office lady, later known to me as the principal's secretary.

Robbie, do you know what you are doing? Do you really want to do this? There's still time to turn back. Mr Munro won't have made a final decision for your replacement. Start thinking. Are you Robert Murray or Mr Murray? How do you introduce yourself?

"Good morning," I said. "My name is Murray, and I have to report to Mr Newlands this morning."

Welcome to Planet Cowgate, Murray. You're a wee apprentice again, so beware – you may find a different force of gravity here.

"Oh, I'll let Mr Newlands know. Just have a seat, please."

This was not a doctor's waiting room, nor a dentist's – not even Mr Rettie's office. This was a crucial first meeting with a man who was to be my new boss, and I knew absolutely nothing about him. I wondered what little he would know about me.

After some ten or fifteen minutes, a suited, slim, business-like, bespectacled gentleman – looking perhaps fifty plus years old and sporting a 'university type tie' – appeared in the room. "Sorry to keep you waiting Mr Murray," he said. "Busy time of the day. Please, after you." As he ushered me into his large, high-ceilinged office – which I took immediately to be a converted classroom, divided into his large office and a smaller area for his secretary – he shook my hand and welcomed me to Commercial College. Once seated behind his paper-filled desk, I began to mentally conjure him into the persona of a quietly efficient bank manager or lawyer. This was not the grocery world now. I immediately sensed the academic culture – my new domain. He was not a fearful figure, but one who exhibited a calm, benign nature. There was no sense of a tough tyrant lurking within, but the gently demonstrated power was there. I didn't think he would be the type to give "six of the best", but I guessed he could devastate with his intellect if forced to.

"This is the main part of the college," he told me. "We are a converted primary school. There are other buildings we occupy in the city, such as St John's and South Tay Street primaries." It was then that I suddenly recalled seeing this man many years before, when he once visited a classroom during the time I was a young apprentice student in Mr Leitch's class.

He won't have the faintest idea of that, Murray.

Following a general, brief history of the college, some parts of which I had been aware as a student, he added some details of the courses available. "We offer an increasing array of courses. New ones each year. Mainly secretarial, shorthand typing, typing, clerical, bookkeeping. Of course, the retail courses are growing too, and that's why you are here."

My application form wasn't visible on his desk, and I began to wonder just how the wheels of education worked. Did he simply receive the candidate who was interviewed by the Deputy Director of Education, or had he some say in my appointment?

"I believe you have your Grocers' Institute membership and completed your Certificate in Retail Management. Where did you study that?" How did he come to know that?

"Here in Cowgate for the grocery exams, then Dundee College of Technology."

"Ah, yes!"

Perhaps he has seen my application after all. Not much more was said, but I was now anxious to find out about my students and what I had to teach. Will I have daily contact with this gentleman? I already began to realise the word 'boss' probably didn't fit in this educational world. As if by telepathy, Mr Newlands gave me my first inkling. "I'm going to call upon the gentleman who is in day-to-day charge of our retail courses. He'll give you all the background, and will explain the work you will be involved in." This was getting close to finding out if my assumptions about classes and students were accurate. I couldn't believe at that moment I would, in the past, have managed a shop without first seeing it. How stupid had I been?

My immaculately efficient new leader pressed a button on the telephone control device on his desk and said in a quiet, almost timid voice, "Would you ask Mr Ferguson to come to my office, please?" This was not a trading or business organisation, nor profit making. It was, for me, a new world of a different kind of authority and power – quietly powerful within its own unique environment. There was no small talk. No enquiries about the business world I had just departed. No word about having to adjust to my new situation. I wondered if he had any concept of the world I had just exited. There appeared to be no shred of understanding the sheer terror which had my insides turning somersaults. Does he see any fear in my eyes, my voice or my body language? Has he ever taught students himself? If so, he probably reads me very well – but he didn't comfort me. It wasn't hostile, but I took it to mean that in this environment big things happened without showing emotion.

A loud, confident knock could be heard on the opaque glass door.

"Come," said the cool, quiet, almost clinical figure opposite me.

"Good morning, Mr Newlands," said the newcomer. "You wanted to see me."

"Yes, Mr Ferguson. This is your new member of staff, Mr Murray."

All very formally polite. I stood up and shook the unsmiling Mr Ferguson's extended hand.

"Will you take care of Mr Murray?" asked Mr Newlands. There was no explanation of when or if I had to report back anything to Mr Newlands. No best wishes for a happy career in education. It began to feel rather like remote management. In a strange way, it became clear that Mr Newlands had seemed to have just greeted someone 'off the street', all based on an interview in which he had taken no part. Then this thought was followed by an even more unreal situation; Mr Ferguson, of whom I knew nothing, equally had been handed a person he knew nothing about.

So this is how it works, Robbie. It's all about qualifications. The personal chemistry and the 'fit' or 'feel' of an employee does not come into it – it must be the education department's hands-off responsibility for the quality or otherwise of the product, produced inside the building.

"Thank you, Mr Murray," I was told. "Mr Ferguson will show you around." Mr Ferguson showed no emotion, nor indeed any kind of collegiate attitude towards his boss. He simply had to take what he was delivered – that, in fact, was the case.

Once out of the office, Mr Ferguson went off at great speed along the corridor and bounded up a flight of stone stairs. For all the world it was like the "Go, go, greasy grocer, go!" initiation again.

He opened a door marked 'Staff' and, turning to me, said, "After you!"

CHAPTER 21

September 1963: "A Box of Homework", or "Meet the Students"

MR Ferguson was a fast talker and mover. He seemed like a 'ball of fire', and my first impression was that he must certainly be a 'retailing' man.

Not so bad now, Robbie. You should feel some rapport with this man – he must once have been recruited just like you.

Once inside the staffroom, he said, "Classes have started, so this room is quieter right now," and then – in a raised, mocking voice – added, "but these gents here are resting!" And with a huge grin, he theatrically stretched out his arms to indicate the gesture – 'relax'. To this tongue-in-cheek comment there was an all-round derisory reaction of "Watch it!", "Come on Fergie", and hearty high-pitched "Oooooohs!" It was immediately obvious that the swarthy, Latin-looking 'thirty-something' Mr Ferguson enjoyed winding up his older colleagues with what I detected was his Glaswegian humour.

"This is Mr Murray, gentlemen," he informed them. "We've doubled the size of my department today."

"Only a section, Fergie!" was the chorus, which indicated to me some technical distinction.

Another burst of jolly derision, including the voice from a figure I instantly recognised – Mr Leitch, my old night class teacher! At that moment my mind went into a spin – me, now a colleague of my old teacher! He obviously hadn't retired, but why do they need me?

"What's your first name?" Mr Ferguson asked me. "Are you a Robert, a Bobby, or Bob?"

I'd not thought of this choice coming. For twelve years I'd been a "Robert" in Wm Lows, but in an instant I couldn't see "Robert" fitting into this new world. "Robbie" and "Bobby" then both sounded too boyish. Without any delay, I blurted out: "Bob".

"Right, Bob. This is Fred Leitch," Mr Ferguson said by way of introduction.

"Hello, Mr Leitch, how are you?"

"Fine, Bobby."

Mr Ferguson presented each of the others in order.

"And John Buchan."

"Hello," he said cheerfully. "How do you do?"

"And George Brown."

"Hello," he replied in a serious voice. "Pleased to meet you."

"And I'm John," Mr Ferguson added at the end of the process.

It must have then been about 9.30, and I was already acquainted with four colleagues. I'd had a 'behind the scenes' glimpse, witnessing three well-dressed, cool, calm, comfortably relaxed men in a cosy staffroom.

Gee whiz, Robbie! This looks like a holiday camp compared to a Willie Low back shop!

After the introductions I had time to glance around the long, narrow room. An odd selection of non-matching and decidedly grubby second-hand, well-worn easy chairs lined both long walls, with a sink and cups and saucers stored on the draining board at the narrow end. An oblong-shaped coffee table sat in the centre area. The drab furniture was out of place for, although the school building was probably many decades older than the dowdy chairs, it was uniformly bright and clean. Up to shoulder level was a dado clad in vertical wooden strips painted in pale green, and above the dado a pale cream paint with white ceilings.

"We all come here at tea breaks and lunch times, or for free periods," said John, my new boss.

"Or to prepare for our next class!" chipped in John Buchan, a remark which was received with a gentle giggle from around the room which I took to mean he was talking theory.

"Right, Bob. Come and grab some books," John said briskly. He dashed out of the room and leapt sprightly up a flight of stone steps to the next level, to what I recognised immediately as the top of the building where I had attended my three years of Grocers' Institute classes ending in 1959. And here I was, in shock and unexpectedly back as a teacher – amazingly, without ever having had any ambition to do so. The building obviously had seen better days, and yet it had worn well for probably over seventy or eighty years. Many hundreds of children must have passed through this school and here I was, not a teacher and with scant educational qualifications, being let loose into the educational world. It seemed to me I was something of a charlatan.

John went along a row of cupboards fitted into the wall and, one by one, pulled out books. "You'll need this. You'll need that. And that one." A moment later: "Take these two. Better take those as well."

As he said this, he was literally throwing them onto a table. As he did so, it looked quite brusque and impersonal, and I remember feeling as if he enjoyed delegating a lot of material he no longer required – as if he'd done it all and didn't need the books. *Over to you*, was the signal he was giving. In all, there must have been around a dozen books of varying sizes and on various topics – grocery, drapery, retailing and distribution. My heart sank when I caught glimpses of particular books – all about weft and warps.

Remember, Robbie: you'll be teaching students from all sectors of the retail world.

"Did you bring a brief case with you?"

"No," I replied, keeping quiet that I didn't have one but making a mental note that I must rectify that as soon as possible.

"Right, we'll get a box for you. But now we need to have a look at your timetable. Let's go in here." Leaving the small towers of books on the table in the corridor, I followed John into my old classroom.

"Now this is your week's programme for every week. Two periods in each half-day, separated by a fifteen minute break." The quarto paper was designed with four boxes for each day. "Boxes with lines across them indicate free periods," he explained.

So there you are, Robbie. Why be so negative? They do exist, and there's a few during the week.

"The other boxes show which classes you will have," John told me. The page looked simple enough, but the initials inside the various boxes meant nothing until John explained further. "FT means our full-time class, and you will be the register teacher for them. That means you mark them in or absent every morning." I could see a sprinkling of FT's across the week. "RD1 means year one of the Retail Distribution City and Guilds class – that's a national certificate class with its own syllabus. RD2 means year two of the same, but it's a higher level. NRDC is the highest, year three, of the National Retail Distribution Certificate. Co-op means students who are from Co-operative Society shops, and who are following the Co-op's own national syllabus. On Wednesday you will see GS. That means garage storekeepers; we make up our own syllabus for them."

John had explained it all very clearly. Then he added, "Now, that fifth small box at the bottom of Monday, Tuesday and Thursday is for Grocers' Institute night classes. Prelim on Mondays, Associateship on Tuesdays, and Master members on Thursdays."

I recognised those evenings from my early night class days (though the Thursday evening was a new departure), but I was immediately puzzled why Mr Leitch would not take these classes. (Or would he?) Quickly absorbing the entire page, it all looked straightforward enough – some free (or prep) time, a balanced level of work and some night classes. The thought did occur to me whether the subjects were of a similar level, bearing in mind my salary scale, but I decided to ask later. With interest I noted the three evening classes, which would mean extra pay. All of this was relevant to my reduction in salary. Of equally important interest to me was the syllabus for each level of work and, just as I was about to ask a question, John looked at his watch and said, "In five minutes, the bell will sound. We must go to the ground floor and supervise your register class."

What's coming now? I wondered.

He raced off at great speed and I followed closely behind him. We entered a classroom devoid of desks and blackboards, its door labelled 'Common Room'. A few students were taking trays of sweets and biscuits out of a tall, wide cupboard and placing them on a large counter.

"Now, this is Mr Murray," John said, addressing the students. "He's your new register teacher, and he'll be in charge." The students looked at me but were otherwise preoccupied: it didn't seem the correct time for the introduction, but it wasn't a serious point.

The common room filled rapidly with students, and a queue formed at the counter.

"Everything alright?" John asked one of the students.

"Yes, Mr Ferguson," came the reply.

"It's tea break time, Bob," he said. "Let's have a quick cuppa."

We set off upstairs to the staffroom, where I found the original three members of staff now numerically swamped by a line of teachers already flooding into the room. "It gets pretty packed in here at tea breaks," John explained as we squeezed in. He wasn't kidding; it was quite hectic. Earlier occupants were starting to move out, while new arrivals – both male and female – made for the teapot. John tried his best to introduce me to names, and some of my new colleagues introduced themselves. It was not the calmest setting to meet people and remember names, but at least I was spotted as a 'new boy' and received a friendly welcome.

Soon the bell was ringing again, and several staff members rushed out while some remained. Everyone knew exactly what they had to do and where to go. When the dust had settled, only Mr Leitch remained – sitting exactly where he had been when I first saw him.

"Excuse me, Mr Leitch – is there a toilet I can use?"

"Of course. There's one at the end of the corridor." He opened the staffroom door and indicated a door marked 'Staff'. Never in my life did I expect to find myself someday writing about a toilet, but this college staffroom facility was something to behold.

The room was probably about six feet wide and around twenty feet long. The ceiling was as high as the classrooms, and the colour scheme was in the exact same tones as the corridor and classrooms. The splendid feature, which I was now gazing upon, took my breath away – for the toilet bowl was indeed a 'throne'. It was on a raised platform some nine inches high. I'd heard jokes about 'thrones' before, but here was a classic 19th century facility in all its glory with the added feature of a scrubbed-clean wooden seat. Every piece of brass fitting in the room was highly polished, and the period wash-hand basin and towel rail were in pristine condition. I gazed around the relative opulence of a facility that had probably been in use for over a hundred years and must have been luxurious in its day. In fact, it was still in immaculate form. My thoughts went immediately back to my shop experiences, and I could not help thinking this facility alone signalled the new world I now inhabited. If it could have been reconstructed in some museum, it would have be a wonderful example of a classic antique of 19th century Dundee school architecture.

On returning to the staffroom, without remarking on the magnificence I had just encountered, John reminded me of the next chore. "Right, Bob. Let's check the stock situation."

Back in the common room, John checked the money counted by the students, supervised the stock going back in the cupboard and then locked it. "Just go back to your classroom again – we'll be with you shortly," he advised the students. John explained they had been left in their classroom to read books while he had been dealing with me. "Your register class will always be with you before morning break, so I need you to always allow the students five minutes before the bell to set up the tuck shop."

We retreated to the room on the top floor and John talked me through the syllabus for each class. Prior to the lunch time bell sounding, John took me to my class and introduced each student by name. They were young – fifteen or sixteen year olds, boys and girls, including an overseas student, Amos, from Nigeria who had left school in Africa and opted for a year at Commercial College to study retailing. "You won't see them until the last period today, when you can find out what they have been doing."

When we made our way to the staffroom, John asked me, "What are you doing for lunch?"

"No plans," I replied.

"Do you want to walk with me to Wallacetown and get a school lunch?"

"That sounds good. Thanks."

As I said that, rather bad memories of school lunches at Barry School in Carnoustie came flooding back, and I wondered if I had made a hasty decision.

The lunch room, located in a corrugated walled and roofed building which I learned was nicknamed 'The Tinny' –

which looked more like a Colonial bungalow – housed two classrooms and the dining hall. Facing south, it looked across the road to the substantial, tall Wallacetown primary school which I was told was now closed. As we arrived, John introduced me to Ron – also based at Cowgate – who had come for lunch.

The dining room was well filled when we arrived, and I was informed we were the only teachers who used the facility; the others were 'mature students'. When I enquired about that term, John told me they were people who had left work and returned to temporary full-time education to gain academic qualifications with a view to better employment prospects or university entrance.

John, in his brisk style, introduced me to a kitchen staff member: "New customer today, May. This is Mr Murray."

"Welcome to 'The Tinny'," said the cheery and stout white-coated server behind the counter.

Despite the friendly atmosphere, the quality of the main course was barely 'one-star'... but the sweet course soared to a 'three', with jam sponge and custard. I made a mental note to see if my star ratings improved.

Ugh! Dear me, Robbie. As mum would have said, "There's a downside to everything."

Ron joined us on the walk back. He was a very jovial man who taught history and geography, and happened to be the college representative of the SSA (Scottish Schoolmasters Association, in reality a Trade Union). It didn't take him long to try to enlist me as a member. "I was once a member of USDAW (Union of Shop, Distributive and Allied Workers) in Carnoustie, and at my first meeting the entire evening was utilised to discuss the problem of a 60W lightbulb in the Carnoustie Co-op grocery department, so I never went back," I told Ron.

He seemed unfazed. "Well, it's important in our world to be a member for your own protection. The other union is EIS (Educational Institute of Scotland), but it largely has primary and secondary school teacher members and no Further Education representation."

"Thanks, Ron. I'll think about that."

* * *

My register class had a period of English during the first part of the afternoon, so I enjoyed my first free period during which time I found a cardboard box and packed in my homework – the serious-looking stack of books. Taking a few moments, I cautiously looked inside a few of the covers. I remember thinking that the way in which John had tossed the books at me in a 'machine-gun' salvo indicated either some relief that he was happily passing over some less-than-favourite topics, or that he was trying to impress upon me the need for a good deal of research and homework on my part.

I'll never forget the moment when the bell rang after that afternoon interval and I walked alone into the classroom to meet my first class, already seated and waiting – presumably with baited breath – to hear how this new teacher, surprisingly allocated to them, was going to perform and be rated for discussion at the first opportunity.

Come on now, Robbie. It's not as bad as stepping on to the stage in a Dramatic Club play.

The first point I realised was that they were not school children, but school leavers who had made a vocational choice to be here. It wouldn't be so much 'teaching' but rather discussing practice and principles. It was a relatively easy time for me, and all seven students gave me their ideas and hopes for their future which helped me considerably. I didn't feel any threat of disciplinary problems, which was my first fear.

During that first encounter I heard a gentle knock on my classroom door and, on opening it, found Mr Newlands. He made no move to enter, but merely whispered, "How are you getting on, Mr Murray?"

"Fine thanks, Mr Newlands," I replied.

"Good." Then he added, "Just look them in the eye!" He said this in a gentle, friendly fashion – almost like a genial uncle.

"Yes, of course."

So far that was the only advice I had received on how to deal with students. John hadn't advanced any help, but my immediate thought was how much my drama experiences had

"Look them in the eye, Mr Murray."

aided me.

Thank you, Newton Panbride Amateur Dramatic Club. You provided me with some confidence.

Standing up in front of the class was not a problem, and I sensed the best way was that I must be clever enough to keep their interest and adopt a friendly, courteous attitude while relating to their aspirations in life.

It's going to be up to you, Murray. Do it your way.

The bell rang at 4.40pm and, complete with my box of books and syllabuses, I made my way home on a busy train to Carnoustie.

As I sat on the train clutching my immediate future contained in a cardboard box, I couldn't help thinking that a working day had passed with no rush, no hustle and bustle, and no stress. Enjoying the second obvious advantage of leaving Wm Low, I was home at 5.30pm.

After an earlier meal, which was more relaxed than normal, I chatted with Gail about the college, the staff and the students. I described Fergie and his handing over of the textbooks. Amazingly, she reminded me of a strange happening some four years previously at a coffee evening with dramatic club friends, when we had played the Ouija Board game.

"Do you remember what the 'spirit of the glass' said to you that evening?" she encouraged me to recall.

"Didn't take much notice," I admitted.

"The glass spelled out 'Beware Swarthy'."

This confused me. "So... what do you mean?"

"Well, you described Mr Ferguson as 'swarthy'."

"That was just a game! I don't believe in things like that."

* * *

Later, as requested, I set off to give mum, dad and Peem my first impressions as they had requested. The reactions were as I had expected. Mum's cautious words were, "Do you think you'll like it, Robert?" Peem suggested, "That'll be an easier day for you," while dad added a practical, "Not so much stress now."

It was only later, when I was at home, that I tried to summarise and make sense of my introduction into the world of education. My day had been interspersed with thoughts of what was happening back at my Perth Road branch. Who is the new manager? I still harboured some guilt at feeling as though I had 'abandoned ship' in some way. I pondered on what Jim in the city, Tom at St Andrews and Jack in Broughty Ferry would be thinking. Did they wonder if I had 'run away scared', or would they be thinking, 'Wish that was me'? What would Mr Munro think of me tinkering with a minute tray of biscuits and chocolates? A tuck shop! *"What on earth are you doing Robbie? Playing at Shoppies!"* he'd probably have said.

All my retail grocery experience, in one insecure step, seemed to have disappeared. Yet that's why I was there – to impart my knowledge. Even so, it didn't feel comfortable. Thinking back to the moment of the melee when teachers crowded into the staffroom, I began to realise the huge difference in the work culture. There were no 'teams' – each teacher was a single unit responsible for his or her own work, effort and results. The staffroom was filled with individuals all doing their own thing. The nearest to a team would be me and Fergie, but even so we simply did our jobs individually. The only common denominator was the employer – not the head of department, not Mr Newlands, but the Education Department of Dundee City Council.

Those same colleagues were like myself – I wouldn't dream of asking their background or what they were doing with their students or their qualifications. Apart from John, there was no need to discuss anything related to work. Those colleagues were, in fact, no more than acquaintances I would meet at tea breaks – although I was aware that they were probably graduates teaching top-grade subjects like English, history, geography and maths at Scottish "Higher" level. Within my grocery world, there was a clear and common target with a team to deliver a result. In my new college life there appeared to be no collective team with no defined common goal. The comment I'd heard about 'mature students' interested me. Could I be part of that? That's exactly what I would need if I were to try and improve my qualifications.

How do I sum up the most important person in my new world of work – John Ferguson? No doubt he was a teaser, one who liked to wickedly wind people up, especially making wisecracks about academics not being like he was (or had been) "in the real world". There was nothing to beware about 'swarthy' John.

Mind you, you didn't like the way he 'threw' books in your direction.

And Mr Leitch? What exactly is going on there, and where do I fit in with him?

My usual physical tiredness at the end of the day had disappeared and made me realise that my new world was to be more cerebral. There was a lot to think about that evening, but I tried to sum up my future – mistake or not? My conclusion was that yes, it was achievable, but I have a huge and entirely new personal challenge on my plate. I may not be working long hours, but I could be studying long hours. Is that all I had opted for... and for less money?

BUT, gone were my worries about stocktakes, sales, staffing, pilfering, break-ins, check-outs and the frustrations with the likes of Mrs McCleary and 'the Colonel'! And perhaps, no longer would I be required to test my mental fitness and level of fatigue by walking along the 'straight line' kerb on my way home at the end of a busy Willie Low Saturday.

CHAPTER 22

September 1963:
"College Life", or
"The Mr Leitch Mystery"

"**G**OOD morning, John."

"Morning, Bob," he replied cheerfully.

Oh yes, of course – you're a Bob now. You'll have to get used to that, Robbie.

During the first free period Mr Ferguson – John – ran through a few more introductory points. "You will also take classes at Tay Street for the part-time students such as the RD1s and RD2s," he told me.

"Oh, I see," I replied. "Isn't that at the other end of the city centre?"

"Yes, Tay Street is another redundant primary school in the centre. That's also where most of the mature students' classes are based. Your register class will also have some periods there, as there's no room for all their classes here at Cowgate."

"So they have to move about between buildings?"

"Exactly. And you'll have to chaperone them to and from."

A picture of my new job was beginning to take shape, and I wasn't sure about it. Imagine if Mr Rettie or Mr Munro were to see me from their car, escorting what looked like a bunch of seven school kids. "What on earth has Robert done to himself?" they would be asking themselves. "How can he possibly be enjoying that? He must be mad."

"Don't worry, Bob. A routine will soon develop," John reassured me, having perhaps detected my silent nervousness.

* * *

Day two of my bewildering new world had dawned. I had again travelled on a diesel-powered train on my way to Commercial College, Dundee – a far cry from my first journey to Cowgate when, on a steam-powered locomotive to Dundee East Railway Station, I first walked to the same building for evening classes just seven eventful years previously.

On this occasion one or two fellow passengers nodded towards me – merely, I guessed, in vague recognition. I didn't know them, but it gave me a feeling of belonging to this new office/professional 'herd-like' commuter world I had entered.

At work John continued his advice, which shook me. "Next point is that courses start in a week's time, and I can now tell you which subjects the RD1s and RD2s will study." He then reeled off the curriculum for each class. Subjects included retail distribution, calculations and accounts, salesmanship and business communications.

"So you have a week to prepare," he concluded almost casually. Did I detect some mild glee from the swarthy one by dropping me in the deep end?

"A week!" I exclaimed, trying – and possibly not entirely succeeding – to mask my nervous alarm.

John began to explain. "I take all the salesmanship subjects, and business communications – otherwise known as 'English' – will be taken by some of our graduate academic colleagues. You'll be taking the retail distribution and calculations and accounts classes."

"How will I know what ground to cover with them?"

"Don't worry. You just need to swat up this lot," he told me as he passed over several pages of typed notes. "These are the syllabuses for each subject at each level." Was that more glee I sensed?

Taking the notes, I squinted through the papers and could tell immediately that there were clear guides of the ground to be covered at each level. Instinctively I knew that I would have to carve up the syllabus into smaller, more digestible bites. The only question I had was how to digest it myself before next week. "A lot of homework here," I mentioned to John with some concern.

"Remember: you only have to be one step ahead of your students."

"Ah, yes," I responded with obvious relief. Suddenly it felt like the cavalry had come over the hill. John was obviously talking from his own experiences, which gave me some comfort. He then passed over the syllabuses for the Co-op students and the Grocers' Institute subjects. The term 'logistics' was not in vocabulary back in those days, but I immediately saw that John's main job was to plan timetables – so he had to work out which classes met where, and were being taught by whom. How did he know which classrooms were available over two different buildings?

"The only unknown at present is how many students we'll have in each class," he said. "Some companies respond to the adverts in the local press about forthcoming courses, but others don't. So, we won't know numbers until I've been round the shops and done some more recruiting."

"Oh, so you have to go out and sell the courses too?"

"Yes. In fact, today I'm visiting DM Brown's, Justice's, Draffen's and GL Wilson's to try and finalise numbers."

The picture became even clearer now. Not only did the college present the courses to the trade, but the college also had to go out and about to recruit students. This was an aspect I had never considered, and I immediately saw that the employment security of myself and John depended on him getting students into classes.

You see, Murray? You did no homework about the hows and the wheres!

"What about grocery classes?" I asked him.

"Numbers seem okay."

"Any from Wm Low?"

"No, we don't seem to get any names from them," he told me.

This startled me, and I wondered why this was the case. "Have you gone out to Lows to recruit, John?"

"Yes I have, but we don't get any students."

This seemed very odd. I'd never been aware of the college (or indeed John) having visited branches. "Did you go to head office, John?" I enquired.

"Yes, but I never seemed to get anywhere."

My heart sank, not because of the lack of Low's support but because I hadn't made any enquiry within Low's about students from the company. It was then I realised my dogged determination to go through all three stages of the Grocers' Institute programme was entirely of my own volition. And when I look back, I realise in all the years I had attended night classes there was never another Wm Low employee in any of my classes. When I thought about it, it seemed such a fundamental missed observation on my part.

This piece of information sent me into a deeper level of questioning about the blunder I had made. Why had I not had the sense to explore the teaching prospect in greater detail? My rationalisation was that the haste of a new session commencing had forced Mr D.G. Robertson to seek an early start.

Here's a test question for you, Murray. If you met Mr Munro in the street tomorrow and he hadn't filled your job in Perth Road, what would you say to him?

I couldn't help but wonder: *Have I been a real fool?* Seriously, this slender link between shops and college was at first glance quite frail, and I began to ask myself if the College of Technology had also gone out to recruit students like me to attend the CRMP course. A picture began to form in my mind that this may all be about colleges enlarging their own portfolio of courses. Perhaps Mr Newlands did have a budget, and was paid on the number of students he had filling his classrooms? My whole future depended on students, and if it was going to prove difficult to recruit then there was likely to be a clear problem.

Then another thought occurred – had I been recruited to try to gain student numbers from Wm Low? If I had, John, so far at least, had not made any effort to seek my help to recruit students to courses.

* * *

"Will you be lunching with us at Wallacetown again?" John asked me.

"Yes."

"Good. We'll walk over to Tay Street after lunch."

The prospect of lunch did not seem so palatable that day. Did my quieter demeanour show? Perhaps a phone call to Mr Munro may not be so far away as I thought.

After the interval I was back with my full-time students. With a syllabus but no time to prepare, I had to make do with invented material, and I vaguely recall talking through the syllabus with them.

I met up with John later, and we walked again to Wallacetown lunch room. The lunches were just about at acceptable level, but I paid a very low student price so it suited. It also gave me the chance to have some off-duty time with John. Ron joined us at the table and, in conversation, I found that although he sometimes taught at Cowgate, he was based at Tay Street and we all made our way through the city centre to the old school building. This seemed all very well, but I began to think of how this long walk would work in the depths of winter.

The journey was made interesting by seeing something of the huge redevelopment work going on to construct a new Overgate complex of shops, offices and hotel. The old and original street named 'The Overgate' had been demolished, and a modern layout was expected. As we walked along a temporary wooden makeshift pavement, we could see a large crater was being excavated – presumably to start building the extensive foundations. What we didn't know then was that the entire complex would be demolished only twenty years later to create an indoor shopping mall. It was all due to changing customer demands creating new thinking in retailing which were beginning to take effect.

Once we got to Tay Street, John gave me a guided tour. First impressions were that it was, in fact, based in South Tay Street – but this, I found, was the 'label' put on it by college staff. There was no obvious date on the building, but I guessed it must have been established around the end of the 19th century. The stone was weathered, drab and black from many decades of Dundee's industrial and commercial past. In its day it was probably a farsighted design, with its tall and spacious windows. It looked like a two-storey building with windows in the roof. The building was supported by substantial stone pillars, providing a covered area of play-ground directly below the building.

Welcome to Planet Tay Street!

Entry was by stone steps within the covered area on each side of the building. There were half landings, and the staircase zig-zagged its way to the top of the building. The staffroom was on the first-floor level, and could be entered from stairs on either side. Like Cowgate, the furniture looked worse than poor second-hand: in fact, it was downright shabby, with an odd assortment of upright dining table-style chairs and two well-worn brown two-seater settees with saggy seats and a couple of easy chairs. Nothing matched, and the colours were dull. This refuge for staff during non-teaching periods looked decidedly like a poor quality 'past sell-by-date' furniture saleroom.

It seemed to me that full-time Further Education in Dundee city was in its infancy. The policy was obviously 'no expense' on the development until a new college is built. I re-called mum's reference to the siting of a new college. It's only now I can draw a parallel with the changes going on in the world then: supermarkets and Further Education were both in early stages of growth.

There was a desk upon which tatty old newspapers and magazines were spread, and I discovered later this was where the janitor placed the trays of cups (no saucers) and large pots of tea. There were two grey metal filing cabinets, and alongside was a multi-hook wooden coat stand that reminded me of red deer antlers. Another antique item. Despite the dusty-looking furniture, the building throughout was warm and clean, as was the staffroom.

After my visit to Cowgate the previous day, it was not difficult to see the education department's policy on how to create a Commercial College – use old primary schools with minimum running cost. The problem was they were located as history had dictated: in distinct areas of population throughout the old city.

"Do you think there will someday be a central college for Further Education?" I asked John as we walked around. I recalled mum's earlier observation about a plan to construct a custom-built college near Constitution Road, or "the Conshie" as Dundonians referred to it.

"It's been talked about and reported in the press," he replied, "but I've no idea how or when that will ever happen."

Classrooms were on both levels and, as we moved about, John pointed out the rooms I'd be using. At the top of the building, in what looked more like roof space, was the art department. John knocked on a door and entered. "Just showing Bob around the building," John explained to the room's occupant. "Bob, this is Mr Laird – Gordon, this is Bob: my newly-recruited colleague."

"Welcome to the mad house!" said Gordon with an infectious grin and obvious humour.

Now there's a likeable, fresh-faced colleague. Cheer up, Robbie!

Eventually we were back on the first level and John, dashing on at his usual brisk pace, opened a classroom door to reveal an area the size of two rooms. "This is where your grocery classes will be held," he told me.

The door was positioned midway between the two rooms, and there was a dividing, glazed concertina-type partition wall which was partly folded to create one room. The rooms were decorated in the same pale green and cream colours, and were quite spacious despite being laid out with lines of desks and chairs. Near the door on a bench was a familiar-looking item which I had last seen some years before: the coffee roasting machine. The same one I had used in preparation for my practical exams in London in 1959.

My immediate thought was that this is simply a relic of the past, as by chance I had met Mr Leitch about two years previously when he told me the Institute had discontinued product knowledge from the curriculum. As a result tea-tasting and coffee-roasting were practical skills now dropped from the syllabus.

"Ah! I recognise that, John."

"It just sits there now – never used," he explained. "Except when Mrs Cameron, one of our colleagues, occasionally asks Fred to do a special roast of her purchased beans."

John and I returned to the staffroom, where I was introduced to Dave McLaggan, the janitor. My only prior experience of a school 'Janny' was at Carnoustie School, where the janitor kept an eye on us all at playtimes, replaced light bulbs amongst other duties, and worked in the boiler house but otherwise kept out of sight. Dave, this 'janny', was a jovial, chatty man with an air of practical authority about him. He was a smallish, plump man, balding and with an expressive face. In his dark navy-blue uniform, he was no shrinking violet and had a loud hearty voice. It didn't take long for me to gauge that he was the source of all news going on not only in Tay Street but around the entire college. His bright, alert mind was more in evidence when, at the afternoon tea-break, he remained in the staffroom and joined in all the general chit-chat, gossip and repartee going on around him.

As teachers began to arrive in the staffroom there was immediate rapport between them, and Dave joined in as if he too was on the staff. It was clear he was the fountain of all news and views, and was adept at giving his tuppence-ha'penny's worth.

Every tea break is like a stage comedy show. Start to enjoy it, Robbie, Bob, Bobby. Things will come right.

Unlike Cowgate, this larger staffroom was full of noisy, wildly jocular and hugely humorous members of staff. It had the feeling of being almost a separate college, and I realised that there was no hierarchy here. Apart from Gordon Laird, I gathered there were no heads of department present, so the feeling was one of "when the cat's away". There were wisecracks every few minutes, followed by gales of laughter. Cowgate, with the principal and heads inside the building, could never be as free as this – it felt as though this staffroom was more like a meeting place for gentlemen club members or rebellious sixth formers. There were a few ladies present, and one or two were also able to take part in whatever gossip was the 'highlight of the day'. I didn't see any prep work being carried out, and when the bell rang for the end of the break my new boisterous colleagues were still finishing off jokes and stories as they set off to teach. My boss, John, mixed in with the humour, and I noticed again his 'impish fun poking' at the academics whom he classified as 'not in the real world' – and were probably Conservatives to boot, in contrast to his obvious 'leftist' tendencies. My sheltered life in the grocery trade had not prepared me to join in with the exchanges, and I became aware of my lack of personal communication skills. I was the audience.

With the staff room packed full of people there was no chance to be introduced. "You'll catch up with names and people as time goes on," John advised me. "I'll introduce you as and when I get the chance."

John set off to visit department stores in the city centre, and I went to my classroom to read up the paperwork given to me. When I went back upstairs to the staff room at tea-break I found, to my surprise, Mr Leitch sitting in a lounge chair near the door. He was peeling an apple and chatting happily with Dave the 'Janny'. "Fred has come to join us," Dave mentioned in a friendly fashion.

"Yes, I'm here to keep an eye on you all," Fred joked.

"Hello, Mr Leitch. This is a busier place than Cowgate. Plenty to see here."

It seemed a silly thing for me to say, but I was really trying to declare: *You won't be so bored here.*

The saddest part for me, and I guessed for all the staff here in the thriving Tay Street staffroom, was that Mr Leitch turned up for work every day immaculately dressed in a smart three-piece suit, polished shoes and always well-groomed. He was, I gauged, about sixty years of age, a well-built, proud man who had served in Burma during the Second World War. He had been my teacher, and I couldn't get out of my mind why he was being kept around with such mystery surrounding him. Why should that be?

* * *

At home that evening I tried to capture the situation as it now stood. I now had the syllabus content for all my classes; I just needed to meet my classes. There would be a need to work at both Cowgate and Tay Street for my register class. Ron would likely again pursue me to join the union. (As for how should I deal with that, I decided I must ask John.) My colleagues refer to John as 'Fergie', but for me it would have to be John. The hilarity in the staff room seems mostly to be generated by bright graduates teaching academic subjects. Jokes and quickwitted fun have never been present in my previous work situations – at least in such abundance. Everybody so far has been friendly and courteous, but my limited experience makes me more of a spectator than a participant. I feel my lack of academic education.

It was still early days. I'd have to see how things work out. As I write this today, I find it amazing that I didn't panic more than I did, for there was no doubt I had put myself out on a limb. Fergie, or my other new colleagues, would likely have no idea what torture I was going through. I was weighing up every one of the pros and cons. Mentally, every minute I was trying to decide whether I should pick up the phone and call Mr Munro.

Is this not a sign, Robbie, that you had 'run away' from something rather than running towards a new world? The fault is your own, Murray, you stupid boy – not enough research in the first place. But could you go back to managing

Perth Road after having seen inside the world of Further Education?

Today, as I write this account of my college life at the age of twenty-three years, I am sobered to realise all the personalities of those long-ago days have now passed away except Gordon Laird – the exceptionally gifted artist, who is now in his nineties and is the only one left for me, now in my eightieth year, to reminisce with about those long-ago, frightening but halcyon days.

On my first Saturday, I went out and purchased what I called my 'toy' briefcase. I'd noticed my colleagues had rather upmarket, serious-looking cases... but when I saw the prices, I decided to buy a bottom of the range, simple effort instead. It was to serve me well.

CHAPTER 23

September 1963 to March 1964: "A Letter from Mr Rettie", or "My First Christmas Holiday"

ON arriving home one evening, I found an item of mail waiting for me. Ominously, it had the Wm Low company logo stamped on the envelope. What could this be? A problem I'd left behind? A bonus I was due? An innocent enquiry to see how I was getting on? With some trepidation, I opened it to find – to my astonishment – that it was a typed letter signed by none other than Mr Rettie!

Dear Robert, it went on to say, *How are you? I trust is all going well with you?* Then the crunch: *I sincerely hope you will put some life into the grocery classes in that college, for it has been seriously disappointing over the years...*

It was not an unpleasant letter to me personally, but it was critical of the college and what a poor impression he, Mr Rettie, had of the grocery classes in the belief that they were outdated. Mr Leitch, constantly sitting sadly in the same chair and only ever peeling an apple immediately came to mind. Had Mr Rettie been complaining about him, and was he also having a swipe at the Grocers' Institute and its outdated syllabus? Had Mr Rettie, a major retail businessman in the city, had the influence to sideline Fred, or on the need to recruit another member of staff. Perhaps both? If so, I thought it may have come back to bite him – and possibly me.

Could this now explain my nagging question: why was Mr Leitch left sitting in the staffroom day after day doing nothing? Mr Newlands had not mentioned any of this on my arrival. What was the real background? For Mr Leitch, it must have been an embarrassment. What did his colleagues know or think about his situation? And did Mrs Leitch have any idea what was (or was not) going on? I decided not to pursue the matter with John, for he also had been strangely and consistently silent about the odd situation.

Mr Rettie's letter, however, did set me thinking. Had he written to give me an opportunity to understand his views about the college, and was he trying to give me an opportunity to see through his eyes what perhaps he guessed was going on in my mind? Had Mr Rettie given me time to conclude I'd made a mistake, and was offering a chance to return to the fold? Could there even be a possibility that my job was still available, and Mr Rettie was giving me an opportunity to respond. Of course, it's only in hindsight I have those thoughts. To my shame, I couldn't find the correct way to reply and I never did. Was I then rationalising my own behaviour by not admitting I'd make a mistake? Had I developed a new loyalty? I had no idea then – and, to this day, I am still left thinking.

As for my new post, in time my anxieties faded. Fulltime class routines in Cowgate and Tay Street fell into place.

The part-time day release RD student classes filled up, grocery evening classes materialised, and so too did my extra evening class earnings which were so badly required. Class sizes varied – the greatest being around twenty students, and the lowest around six.

John's advice about being 'one step ahead' was helpful, and I gradually built up a pattern of swotting. As a raw recruit, free periods were essential for me. I was putting in as many study hours at home as I may have done working in the shop, but at least I was free of the worries of stock losses and sales.

Your move is a massive act of faith, Robbie. If you work hard, it'll pay off.

Meeting colleagues at both staff rooms gradually helped me connect people and names. There was no competition between colleagues; in a way, it was almost as though we were all self-employed. An additional point was that while a teacher can impart as much as possible, it is up to the student at the end of the day to be motivated enough to succeed and pass exams. To that extent, building motivation was as important as the subject material.

I had no idea how my colleagues dealt with their students, and likewise they had no idea what went on in my classes. Teaching, I found, was a very private matter.

* * *

It must have been about two or three weeks prior to the Christmas of 1963 when John passed me papers about a one-week long residential course I was required to attend in London in June 1964. The course, aimed at teachers across the UK, was tailor-made for lecturers of distributive trades and would be held in University of London accommodation. The outline of the course indicated visits to places of interest, day-time lectures and after-dinner evening speakers. In retrospect, I saw that distributive trades enjoyed a somewhat lower profile. Then, I held the idea that the academic teachers around me – whilst being perfectly respectful – saw distributive trades courses as being rather like "knowing something about shops". Some fifty years later, with the development of giant retail businesses and the interest given by the media regarding growth, performance and organisation of companies such as Sainsbury, Tesco and Asda, distributive trades hold a much greater degree of interest in the country – but of course, this was back in 1963! Retailing was seen then as a 'Cinderella' trade which was characterised by long and unsocial hours, low pay, and the resultant difficulty to recruit staff. The fact that somewhere, influential figures in both the trade and within Further Education circles had put thoughts together to raise the profile of the subject appealed to me. Roll on June next year, and an opportunity to meet other teachers as well as hearing something about the up-to-date situation in retail.

* * *

An unexpected element in my new work was to sense the effect of events in the world had on, especially, my younger full-time students. It would have been unreal to expect such students to engage in serious discussion on world and political affairs, but it was refreshing to hear what 'switched them on' when it came to popular culture. This was highlighted when, after much TV coverage about The Beatles, the quartet of John, George, Paul and Ringo – now the most famous pop group on the planet – arrived in Dundee to perform in the

Caird Hall in early October. The impact that new groups and singers was having in those early 1960s years was electrifying, and I remember thinking the world was never going to be the same again. The students seemed to be distracted by the frenzy. I have to look back now and conclude I was becoming something of a 'fuddy-duddy'. Strangely, because I had so much 'homework' to do, I was not able to spend time watching television, but my students kept me informed on what was going on.

One event during that fateful winter of 1963 was something that caused people the world over to know where they were and how they first heard of the death of John F. Kennedy. In my case, I was walking along Dundee Street, Carnoustie, on my way to a Newton Panbride Church Dramatic Club rehearsal on Friday 22nd November, when I saw fuzzy black and white TV pictures on the screens of television sets in the window of Dobson's radio and TV shop which showed the President's picture with captions. By the time I arrived at the church hall, everyone was shocked and trying to come to terms with the news. This was a good example of how younger students, I found, didn't feel the emotion or the seismic shockwave of Kennedy's assassination amongst all the excitement of The Beatles, Elvis, The Searchers and Gerry and the Pacemakers. The power of 'pop' was upon us.

One day, I overheard Gordon – the art department head – say that he was planning a walking holiday in spring with some other colleagues. This was of immediate interest for me, and I asked if I could join his group. I hadn't walked in the hills since I was a Boy Scout. But this sounded exciting: a walk through the Grampians followed by an arduous trek through the Cairngorms. There were two main reasons to do this: I liked the idea of forging closer links with some of my colleagues and, as a manager in Wm Lows, I would never have been able to consider such a trek. Now I relished this luxury. Shared values with clever people who knew the mountains – I knew I would learn a lot. My demanding life as a message boy and apprentice grocer had denied me the opportunity to spend time hillwalking and mountain-climbing. The last mountain I had climbed was Ben y Vrackie, near Pitlochry, as a fifteen year old Boy Scout. Gordon's plan filled me with great enthusiasm.

* * *

In the week before Christmas, class sizes diminished slightly as businesses required staff in the run-up to the festive season. Before I knew it, I was on a welcome long holiday. The two-week break was something I had never previously enjoyed. In all my years in the grocery trade, right from the time I was a message boy, I had always found the festive period to be the most hectic time of the year. Now, for the first time in my working life, I was about to enjoy a real restful break. Luxury!

It was during that first Christmas holiday I took time to plan the academic courses I must do in order to gain higher qualifications, catch up on salary and have any hope of teaching higher grade subjects. My long-term objective was to obtain a degree, possibly a BSc in economics – but how? First, I would require a set of Scottish Ordinary grade and Higher-grade passes in at least four subjects. Assuming I could reach that level, I would then embark on a degree, possibly by a correspondence course. (Nowadays, of course, it would be more straightforward to achieve via the Open University.) The immediate problem was that while I could study the Scottish courses within Commercial College, there were two obvious difficulties: firstly, would I have free periods to fit in with college classes for mature students in the subjects I needed, and secondly, would I truly wish to put myself in the limelight by failing my exams with a teacher who is also a colleague?

Back to your lack of confidence, Murray! But remember, you didn't want to leave school at fifteen, so now's your chance to get on with it.

After some checking, Gail found I could do English GCE 'O' levels and 'A' Levels by correspondence courses – externally, via the University of London. My plan was to tackle three 'O's in the form of English Literature, British Economic History and Geography, and then attempt Economics and British Constitution at 'A' level. It may take three or four years. Such a tall order was risky for a pupil who left school at fifteen. In hindsight, I'm not sure if I fully comprehended what challenges I was setting myself. I had left a job where I was successful, and was earning good pay – so why now put so much pressure on myself?

The Christmas break also allowed me time to catch up with Peem. We managed to discuss our respective work adventures. "What are your thoughts then, Robbie?" my brother asked me. "Was it a good idea to make your move?"

"I have to admit, there were many times when I was 'within an inch' of picking up a phone and asking Mr Munro if I could be considered for a return!" I confessed.

"What was your problem?"

"The sheer size of the mountain ahead of me. In fact, even now I don't know if I will succeed with all the studies in front of me."

"Do you feel any good has come out of your move?" Peem asked.

"Oh yes. For one, less worry about sales and profits."

"What about the people you work with?"

"Well, this is the strange thing. They're great people, but there's no team feeling to get results. What I do is entirely up to me – and for the first time in my life, I have colleagues to chat with. It's an odd feeling."

"What would happen if, say, all the students failed their exams? Would you be sacked?"

"I don't know," I admitted. "Would I blame the students? Would you blame the transmitter or the receiver? Education is a strange new world for me. Anyway, what about you, Peem? How are you enjoying yourself at DC Thomson?"

"Great!" he replied enthusiastically. "I'm loving it. It was well worth waiting for. I'm doing what I enjoy."

"Back to uncle Alan's advice again, eh?"

We talked for a long time about our contrasting worlds, and it was Peem who best summed it up: "It's what you feel most comfortable doing." The obvious point about our chat was that Peem seemed more concerned about me. He had no worries about his own job. That summed up the situation – do what you enjoy. Later, when I weighed up my current state of affairs, I realised I had merely swapped the nature of my challenges. I still had a challenge, but it was within a more comfortable environment. However, I didn't tell Peem I was still uncomfortable about throwing overboard my Willie Low loyalties.

"So how do you feel about having a quieter Christmas this year, Robbie?" he asked.

"You know, Peem; it's been twelve years since I last had a relaxed Christmas."

"Surely not! You mean when you were eleven?"

"Yes, you were with me. When we had our last Christmas party at Woodside Croft. Do you not remember? I can, as if it was just yesterday."

"I can't remember that, Robbie," he admitted. "Remind me."

"Well, it was at granny and grandad's croft near Montrose," I reminisced, "and the year was 1951. With mum, dad, Isobel and you, we set off from Carnoustie on a utility bus complete with its hard, wooden slatted seats. The bus-stop was exactly positioned at what was Tommy Swan's Café, and is still an important part of the story – I recall mum asking dad to pop in and buy a bottle of Christmas Cordial."

I can still recall me telling him, "Best if you can get black current flavour, dad!" I remember this well, as I thought I was now grown-up enough to sample a real Christmas drink... only to be told, "Oh no, that's for adults only – you'll be getting lemonade as usual!"

"You, Peem, wanted to drink it on the bus!"

"But I thought it *was* lemonade."

The bus journey through the heart of Arbroath and Inverkeiller took us to a bus stop at The White Inn: the landmark, mum had told us, was an inn when she was a young girl. Granny's place was nearly a mile from the bus stop, and it was always an exciting detour for us to run through the beech wood where, in the summer, we picked blueberries and sampled tasty wild gooseberries and raspberries from the small dyke which ran alongside the road.

"You must remember, Peem. It was the week before Christmas Day, and it was a cold, dry day with a blustery wind from the North Sea. When we leaped off the bus, it was around half-past three and almost dark."

"You and I always had a race to see who could get to granny's door first," he recollected.

"Grandad had stoked up the fire in the large black grate, and the kettle sitting on the fireside swivel plate was happily spewing steam that beckoned a warm cup of tea. During all my later life, tea has never tasted as full of flavour as granny's."

"I remember granny's tea too," Peem added. "It had a different taste."

"One of the first things I always wanted to do was to see granny's cow – Maisie – in the byre. It was a ritual for me to pat Maisie on her side and say, 'good girl'. Her ears would twitch, and I always liked to believe she knew me and my voice."

The spacious cottage parlour, complete with a recessed bed and a brass oil lantern hanging from a ceiling bacon hook, was a cosy place to be in winter. The large oak table where my mum and her brothers and sisters had once dined was well known to me from my times when Peem and I had holidayed there. We had picked summer fruits in the garden, gathered grandad's potato harvest and collected eggs from 'cloacking' hens. Now, here it was; the same table, laden with delicious-looking Christmas fayre, holly from the wild wood, bulging homemade Christmas crackers and coloured candles flickering in the breeze caused by us and our cousins running excitedly around as we gazed at the spread we were about to devour.

A choice of hare soup or vegetable broth, chicken or duck with vegetables, and my favourite potatoes done in mint and oatmeal – this was my most anticipated feast of the year. But of course, there was much more to come. The trifle – this was no mere trifle, but a giant dish of layered jelly, custard, fruity sponge and even more layers of strawberries, raspberries and blackcurrants, which I now realise gran must have preserved in her own secret way since summer. This regal sweet was of course topped off with Maisie's delicious cream.

"What were your favourites Peem?"

"Without doubt the hare soup and chicken!" he told me.

"Me too."

We children, in peril of our lives, were not allowed to enter granny's front room. But as soon as we had hurriedly scraped empty our trifle bowls (and at great risk of a telling off if we used our fingers to clean up every morsel of cream), we were queueing up at the door of the party room. The magic Christmas place of wonders.

Grandad entered on his own, daring us to follow. He had important duties and, once we were permitted to enter, we were reminded of his mission. There were paraffin lamps glowing around the room, new logs sparking in the fireplace, and a Christmas tree alive with flickering flames from real candles, each sitting in small cup-shaped holders and all fastened to the branches by thin wire.

"Do you remember the smell of wood smoke and fresh evergreen pine needles filling the air?" Peem asked me.

"I do, and the oil lamps produced dancing shadows of us around the room."

"The mound of parcels under the tree immediately prompted a question: 'which gift was mine'?" he added with a laugh.

We were always told the same thing: "Now remember; we have our little concert before you get your present," the mums and aunties reminded us.

"It feels as clear as yesterday, Peem."

"Who's going to start off this year?" Gran would ask. Deep down I knew it was going to be me, the oldest cousin.

"It always was me. But I held back balancing my timidity with my desperate desire to find out what gift lay in store. 'Come on Robert, it's you to start off,' was always Aunty Jean's way of starting proceedings."

"There was no escape – there never was any hope of that," Peem recalled.

"Granny's question was always the same, too: 'What are you going to sing this year?' I have a poem I once offered, in the mistaken belief that would stave off a song, but that didn't work."

"You *always* had a poem."

"That was just to avoid a song. I think I got away with reciting *The Vagabond* two years in succession."

"I remember your favourite song, Robbie. It was the Robert Wilson version of 'Westering Home' – the one we used to play on granny's wind-up gramophone."

"Don't tell me you remember that!" I smiled. "Younger cousins got away by performing a duet, and Isobel always did a dance like the 'Highland Fling' or the 'Sailor's Hornpipe'. What was your party-piece, Peem?"

"Cousin Sandy and me always did 'Knock, knock, who's there?' jokes," he replied.

"And you did the same jokes every year!" We both laughed. What a great trip Peem and I had down memory lane. It seemed like that last party had been just a few days previously. We both had instant recall of all that had happened.

"There won't have been parties there since then, Peem. We were the last of all the cousins, and now grandad's no longer with us."

"Aye, all good things..." my brother said, though he didn't need to finish the saying.

"You've cheered me up, Peem, and now I'm looking forward to my first good Christmas since all those years ago. But," I added conspiratorially, "I'm not going to sing this year!"

"Thank goodness for that!" he cheekily observed, wiping his forehead for effect.

It was a chat with Peem I would never have been able to enjoy had I still been working in Willie Lows – one of the first joys I remember coming to me in my new world.

* * *

One day sometime in the January of the New Year, John came into my classroom while I had a free period. "You're going to be on telly," he told me out of the blue.

"What?" I asked him, astonished.

"Yes, the College and the Education Department want to publicise how lecturers in Further Education are remaining in touch with the 'real world'."

"Who's going to organise that?"

"You are!"

John suggested that I fix up a place where I could be filmed in a grocery shop. Carnoustie branch was an obvious venue. I remember being filmed by Grampian TV wearing a white shop coat, weighing something on a scale while standing behind the counter. How it was arranged and how I got there I've long forgotten, but I can still recall some of my old boss's running commentary.

"The wee greasy grocer's going to Hollywood!" was one of his chants. Just like the old days – Ian enjoyed his own humour. As it happened, after the trip to Carnoustie and all the effort, Grampian selected about five seconds of a clip on the evening news.

I hadn't in reality done any 'keeping in touch' visits to do something hands-on, and this was a mere gimmick. I never went back to do anything similar again. Probably an Education Department piece of public relations.

Winter passed, classes and studies reached 'anxious point' in students' minds, and revision became the main feature prior to the spring holiday in mid-March. The break was welcome.

Prior to the holiday, I had a humorous yet worrying incident which taught me an important lesson. Students were required to complete a Dundee City Education Department form, indicating personal details and logging which course they had studied and which examination they were to sit at the end of the course. On looking through each completed document I came across an RD1 student's form where he had entered in the space 'Examination to sit?' the words 'Sitting Gulls'. All students except this one had entered the words 'City and Guilds'. Realising immediately what had happened, I had to ask the student to enter the correct words. This was a great shock to me. Did the student have a hearing problem? If so, what other words or phrases had he misheard during the past year? The experience told me I should be conducting more 'checks' on the students' learning processes. It also taught me to think about my own abilities. Was my teaching clear enough? I also realised that I shouldn't be tempted to blame the 'receiver'. It was a valuable lesson for me.

You see, Robbie? You've a lot to learn about this teaching business.

CHAPTER 24

March 1964 to June 1964: "The Cairngorms", or "An Amazing London Experience"

JACK, one of the group to walk with Gordon, happened to meet me on the stairs in Cowgate one morning.

"What boots are you planning to wear then, Bob?" he asked me. "Are you going to buy new hiking boots?"

"All I have are my dress boots, but they're in very good condition," I told him.

"That probably won't be enough. Why don't you bring them in sometime and I'll have a look?"

Jack and I had enjoyed an earlier discussion at Tay Street when we had discussed the matter of boots. I had never owned proper hiking boots, but I'd mentioned to Jack that I had dress boots with fleece lining. In my new married state and with 'setting up' house expenses, I couldn't justify the cost for a 'one-off'.

We met up in Tay Street, and I showed him my boots. "Not ideal," he said. "But I know an excellent shoe repairer in Lochee who could probably stick on climbing boot soles for you. It'd cost a lot less."

"Yes, I'll do that. I'll also wear ex-Army gaiters."

"That should be fine, Bob."

Jack had most likely understood my finances. So that was one problem solved. When I had a free period, I went to report my progress to Gordon, who was busy tidying up his pottery wheel during one of his free times.

"Good," he said when he heard my news. "Now, what about your rucksack and jacket?"

We had chatted earlier, and I was able to report that I had an ex-Army backpack. "Not exactly waterproof, but I can insert a waterproof bag," I told him.

"Fine. And the jacket?"

"Not the best, but I have an ex-Army oiled thick canvas jacket."

"That should be fine."

It was a relief to know I was equipped for the excursion – certainly not the best by today's standards, but probably good enough. What cheered me was the fact that my new colleagues were most willing to help kit me out. Of even greater comfort was the fact that whenever I met any of my new-found walking companions, they or I would ask or report something relevant to the plan. A running commentary developed, and I began to feel a bond even before we had walked. My eagerness to be part of the plan was already helping to build comfortable relationships.

You see, Murray? These are friends now. They don't care whether you have two degrees or none at all. You are one of them.

On another day, I remembered to ask Gordon how much I would need to pay Jack for the cost of his petrol. "Don't worry about that. Jack is loving this. He doesn't walk, and he's only too happy to be the taxi. He's a bachelor – he's got plenty money."

This was the level of informality I now enjoyed.

* * *

With books and my last minute 'one step ahead' notes temporarily put aside, it was now time to set off with my colleagues on the walk which we had regularly chatted about since before Christmas.

The plan was a five day trip. Jack, in his fifties – an English and History teacher – was to drive Gordon and John Buchan (also an English and History teacher), both around their thirties or forties, married men with children; George, a mature man who had been captured on the beaches at St Valery who taught commercial subjects; and myself. We would all travel in his cream-and-red Hillman to the start point at Glen Doll Hostel. We would walk Jock's Road, setting off at 9am, and emerge about fourteen miles away at the Auchallater road-end near Braemar. From there, Jack would drive us to Mar Lodge Hotel in Braemar. We would require only a day rucksack, as Jack would have our overnight gear in his boot.

The next day, Jack would drive us to Mar Lodge and the starting point for day two of our seventeen mile trek through the Lairig Ghru, to be picked up by Jack at the highest point of the track near Glenmore Lodge. Our accommodation for three nights was then to be the Youth Hostel at Glenmore. We would spend two days walking in the Cairngorms.

The adventure began in mid-March on a sunny Thursday with a strong cold wind. We set off from the hostel, having wished Jack a safe drive to Braemar where we would meet up. There was snow on the highest parts of Jock's Road and, to add to the mountain weather conditions, we had to face intermittent 'mini-blizzards'. I had heard a lot about Jock's Road and was pleasantly surprised by the visibility of the track. I recall we came upon a plaque screwed on to a large rock in memory of five climbers – young students, lost in a snowstorm. Unfortunately they had walked in winter some years earlier, and their bodies had not been found until late spring. It was a reminder to us that the mountains can be dangerous places.

The hillwalking experience of George and Gordon was evident, with several stops to chat about glacial features and the flora and fauna. This was a valued expedition for me, and I was learning a lot. Once or twice at the highest points we disturbed ptarmigan, which are Britain's highest living bird. The remoteness and the peace and quiet was something which had to be valued, and I found myself stopping occasionally to take in the solitude of the snow-capped rugged landscape. Despite the short-lived blizzards, we made good time and Jack was waiting for us as planned at around 5pm.

After a luxury bath in the hotel to ease the muscles and an enjoyable meal we adjourned to the bar for a night cap. Here I must confess to a silly prank. George somehow seemed to have been allocated the best room, and we all went to have a look for ourselves. For some reason George had left the room at that point, and we all shared jokes about his posh set up. Somebody suggested giving him an 'apple-pie' bed. Everyone was looking around to see what to insert into his bed when I spotted an under-bed chamber-pot. Yes, a 'potty'.

"That'll do," everyone agreed, and I popped it under his sheets. We all hurriedly left the room.

After a full breakfast the next day, we were driven to our next starting point near Mar Lodge and ready for our bigger challenge – the walk to Glenmore. As we were putting on our walking gear, George – who, with his harsh wartime experiences including imprisonment, didn't take fools gladly – made some offhand comment about not having enjoyed his sleep in a mucky bed. Later on, I had to ask Gordon.

"Is George annoyed about the potty?"

"Yes," Gordon admitted. "He's a bit upset."

This was enough for me. I knew instantly that although the others had come up with the prank, it was me who had done the deed. I had to apologise at an opportune moment. "Sorry about that George," I said sheepishly when the time was right. "It was a silly thing to do."

"Bloody unhygienic!" he blurted. George had obviously ascertained who did the deed, and didn't appreciate the junior stupidity.

Gordon later told me George was not annoyed only at me. "He knows we all had a joke at his expense," he reassured me. "He'll get over it."

Watch out, Murray. Don't get over-familiar.

The Lairig Ghru path followed the River Dee which rises at a spot termed 'The Pools o' Dee' in the mountains, and in the early stages was quite an easy walk. The features ahead of us were more obviously glacial, and we had to cross a boulder field followed by a walk across the frozen Loch Etchachan. Names of places of interest I'd heard about were in my thoughts, and the first of these we reached was the Shelter Stone – a massive boulder the size of a large villa resting on a smaller rock, thus creating safe shelter for climbers, hence the name. We all explored the cave-like space amid imagined tales of how many lives may have been saved by the geographical feature. Not so far away, we approached the Curran Refuge – a small, stone-built cottage-type building. We were looking forward to a rest and some food from our rucksacks, but were shocked to find the place wrecked. Gordon reckoned that cold and tired walkers in need of help had burned every scrap of wood in the building.

From memory it was Easter weekend, and accommodation in Glenmore Hostel was cramped. The communal sleeping arrangements for males were totally spoiled further by noisy, physically sick students. Nevertheless, we managed two days of walking in the Cairngorms, and I can remember the joys – after some strenuous effort – to reach the summits of Braeriach and Cairn Toul. It was a glorious adventure, and one I marvel at today not only for the walking but for the shared experience with my new colleagues.

Back at the college, and for many days after that spring holiday, my colleagues and I would stop and briefly chat about one or two of the many interesting and humorous tales relating to our unique adventure. The 'potty' prank, although an early topic, was soon put to bed (or at least permanently under it).

Murray, that walk planned by Gordon was a piece of real fortune. You couldn't have asked for anything better to get to know your colleagues.

Thereafter, in later years, I joined them on many college walks around Glen Clova and Glen Doll. This was a major uplift to me, as I would never have had that kind of comradeship had I remained in Wm Lows. Hearing of Gordon's plan of a mountain walk was truly a serendipidous moment.

In April 1964, a can (or cans) of corned beef packed in Argentina caused a major scare in Aberdeen. Nearly 150 cases of typhoid fever were reported, and sadly the grocery store involved was Wm Low & Co Ltd.

As the news became clearer, it was found – fortunately – that Wm Low was not responsible for the outbreak. What had happened was that when cans are sealed in the cannery, a vacuum is created, and if there is a pin hole in the seal then the water in which the cans are cooled is 'sucked' into the can. Unfortunately the water in Argentina had been found to contain the harmful bacteria, thus spreading the disease when the cans were opened in Scotland. I had to read all about the damaging incident in newspapers, and could only imagine the frantic efforts that Mr Rettie and Mr Munro – amongst others – must have been through to limit the damage of their good name.

I was able to conjure up a picture of the agonised directors in the boardroom where I had my excruciating interview, and I felt for my old company. My concerns told me I still held a strong feeling of identity and loyalty with my former employers.

Distributive trades classes ended in May with City and Guilds ('Sitting Gulls'!) examinations held in June. Whatever results would come were now in the hands of students themselves. It was a scary feeling. Session 1963/64 – my nervous first college year – was over, and there were no guarantees about the results.

Within a few days of the courses ending, I was on a train from Carnoustie bound for King's Cross Station, London, and on to my accommodation in University of London residences. Technically I was not yet on holiday, so I would not lose any part of my summer break. The course was attended by around thirty or forty teachers, such as myself, from all over the UK. We were accommodated and had our meals in the University. Lecture rooms were used for various talks and discussion groups during day-time.

The group made two outside visits which, to this day, I am still able to recall with accuracy. The first was to Harrods, where we had a tour of the entire 'back shop' – which is not entirely an accurate word to describe the vast network of underground storerooms. Two features of the cavernous storage area remain with me: one is the electric railway circuit, complete with tracks, which is used to carry stock in and out of storage. The other is the system for packages to arrive in the huge underground distribution centre. A chute system from every retail department in the entire store delivered packages of various sizes (except furniture) to a massive bank the size of two or three terraced two-storey houses. Each parcel was addressed, and the purpose of being centralised was for weighing and posting to the customer. Our guide picked up a parcel at random from the mountain of boxes – the label simply read "Baroness Thyssen, Switzerland". This aptly demonstrated that packages were probably bound for every part of the world and to a high-class clientele. Following our below ground level tour, we visited every floor of the store to be given a briefing of the work of each department.

The other interesting outside visit was to the Marks and Spencer headquarters at Marble Arch. Here we were given an insight into the high degree of testing carried out by this high street multiple. In those days, and still today, M&S was well-known for its reliable clothing, and we were given a glimpse of how – by impressive product testing – that success had been achieved. I remember seeing a machine which was designed to constantly stretch a piece of elastic. Our guide told us the test could run into thousands of 'stretches' until the elasticity was exhausted. This was the degree of testing a manufacturer's product underwent before being given the M&S stamp of approval. In another test, a sample of cloth was attached inside a drum not unlike a centrifugal device and was exposed to a flashing light to simulate daylight. Like the elastic test, thousands of exposures of the light were measured to see if and when the colour was damaged by light. Our guide told us every product was tested to this extent before accepting a manufactured batch from a supplier. This was quality control at its best, and the images of the M&S system remain with me.

Our evening lectures were, in their own way, equally impressive. Two stand out, and to this day I marvel at the interest taken to assist teachers like myself by arranging the course and the care taken with the content. One evening after dinner we were given a talk by none other than Lord Sainsbury himself. In 1964 he appeared to be in his seventies or eighties, and he was able to tell us about the origin of the Sainsbury business in 1868 – incidentally, the same year when Wm Low & Co Ltd commenced trading. He painted a picture of the start of the enterprise being one ordinary grocer's shop which was run by his grandfather, and how he as a child was permitted to swing on a rope suspended from the door into the back shop. Lord Sainsbury came across as a normal person who valued his modest, hard-working roots, and he emphasised how hard work and attention to detail had been the essence of building the business. I could sense the responsibility he felt in maintaining and developing the family business.

On a later evening, we heard a talk from Mr Lloyd Jones – the then-Trade Union Congress leader. He gave us 'the other side of the coin': talk about care of employees and training, development of staff, and the responsibility of employers for the welfare of their employees. Lloyd Jones' ability not to sound his "ings" appealed to me. Vaguely, I recall one of his classic statements was something like: "Teachin' and trainin' are very important in modern day retailin'." I had the utmost respect for the high-ranking figure in the trade union movement, but it seemed novel to me that someone in that position would not sound his 'ings'.

Having heard Lord Sainsbury talk, I felt his organisation had an enlightened approach to employees and the sense of a paternalistic ideal came across to me – and equally, the part played by responsible unions was made in such a way that we were given a well-balanced view of running an enterprise.

This is top level, valuable stuff, Robbie. Not run-of-the-mill. Soak it up!

Several factors made the course such an eye-opening success for me: the time to speak and discuss with other teachers, the outside visits, the speakers, and the very fact that the 'system' had produced such an uplifting and thoughtful course at a time when the distributive trades were then described as the underdog in the employment market.

I returned to Carnoustie and the college with a stronger purpose, and feeling more comfortable in my shoes. The course, I remember clearly, created a positive uplift and improved the feeling of wellbeing within me. It improved my self-esteem, and gave me an enhanced view of the important impact Further Education should have on the commercial world. In fact, the very substance of what Mr Rettie wished it to have, but had been sadly disenchanted with the Dundee Commercial College experience. I now had an inkling of what standards Mr Rettie was seeking.

If ever there was a course designed to achieve intended results, I think this was it. My spirits soared.

* * *

With students – apart from the full-time class – now gone, there was time to tidy up notes and paperwork and chat with John about plans for 1964/65 session. Budgets featured at about this time. This required John to provide his Head of Department with a cash figure for equipment for the coming year. Being more involved with fabrics and clothing, John asked for appropriate supplies. He had also started to design and erect shop window frames made from something he called 'Speedframe', which was a system whereby a length of square metal tube with a hollow section of approximately 1.5 inches square could be cut to length and formed into a frame by ready-made joints. John's plan was to create window displays with dressed dummies.

My idea was to obtain product cans and packets from grocery suppliers, in order for me to start to create a shop environment complete with a checkout. Additionally, I wanted appropriate posters to display around my classrooms. Apart from letters and postage, my needs would not cost anything but would help towards creating a retail grocery atmosphere.

Coincidentally, a Dundee Trades Exhibition was being held in Caird Hall in June. John asked me if I would prepare an appropriate 'stand' displaying the retail courses offered by the college. Somehow – I can't quite remember how – I managed to find some display panels and enough information to put on a show. Jim Lindsay of the art department offered to add some clever promotional features to enhance the stand. I recall all of this for mainly three reasons. Firstly, that I felt for the first time a fellow teacher had offered to help. This gave me a feeling of being part of a team – something I had hither-to felt did not exist between departments. Secondly, I noticed that during the three-day event no-one from the college came around to see what efforts I had made. Thirdly, not a single person stopped to ask any questions about the courses which were advertised. Mr Rettie was nowhere to be seen either!

This is a poor response, Robbie. But keep in mind that London experience. That's the big picture.

However, the feeling of getting to know colleagues had a further boost when, about a week later – one day after lunch – Ron, John and I walked to the harbour wall area to have a closer look at the building progress being made on the Tay Road Bridge. That day I recall for an unfortunate reason. My full-time class was being held in one of the two classrooms in 'The Tinny'. Ron, John and I lunched together, and Ron happened to say he hadn't realised the classrooms in 'The Tinny' were currently being used. I offered to show him the room I had used immediately before lunch.

I had been talking about advertising and marketing, and had put a word in chalk on the board. The word was 'motif', but I had wrongly spelled it 'motiff'. "Ah," said Ron, "motif should only have one 'f'." For a number of reasons I was an-noyed at myself. First, I had made a mistake and transferred it to my students; second, I did have a doubt when I wrote it on the board and didn't deal with the doubt; third, it exposed my junior level of education . Of course, there was another point – I really ought to have cleaned the board when I had fin-ished. I hated myself for showing my ignorance. Ron would probably go off thinking the level of education of teachers had definitely slipped.

On the last day of the session, around fifty teachers from all over the college gathered in the Cowgate library, which was in its embryonic state in a space created by opening the divider between two rooms on the middle floor in Cowgate. Evidently, teachers in the English department had been asked to develop the reference library. With the efforts of John and myself and the creation of a library, there was a real feeling of the college itself in its infancy. Although we played our own part, what was missing was the commercial or business atmosphere and the drive from a 'managing director', as I cannot recall seeing the principal visiting the Tay Street 'branch'. I began to sense that growth came about by education policies rather than by team selling.

Mr Newlands updated us on new courses to commence in the next year, and changes that were to take place. One was that yet another primary school, Wallacetown, was to be prepared for use by the college. Amongst other news items were recent staff arrivals. It was a gentle, unassuming approach by the principal, who I'm certain read the pulse of everything going on. He was the study of a very clever man who did not seek a high personal profile in what he said or did.

To this day, I still quote something he said that day to his staff. He was referring to the stresses and strains caused by growth in student numbers, and to the extra efforts required by all. (Nobody, I'm sure, in that gathering had ever experienced retail grocery.) Mr Newlands asked the question in a friendly way: "Are you made of oak or bamboo?"

One or two voices said 'oak'. I kept quiet.

"But no!" he exclaimed. "Bamboo can bend in the gale, take the strain and bounce back again. The oak may break."

We were all wished a happy summer break of six weeks after a very busy year. On my way home (we were all let out early!), I did wonder what pressures the principal felt. Was there an annual assessment of student successes, pass rates or achievements which Mr D.G. Robertson, sitting in City Square, was waiting to see? What would be the outcome if he or any head of department was not meeting the required criteria – whatever they were? As had been the case with Mr Munro, was there a league table somewhere?

Hang in there, Murray. It's getting better all the time.

It was, for me, an important gathering as I had gradually built up a knowledge of people and names and now felt part of an organisation which – as I saw it – was so different from any profit business. I was very much a junior figure in a staff of seniors, both by age and by level of work. This was the place, for better or for worse, where I now belonged.

CHAPTER 25

June 1964 to August 1966: "Swotting During Summer Holidays", or "Teacher Training Dominates"

O N a warm, sunny morning I walked along Carnoustie High Street and – quite by chance – met Alan Craigie.

"How are you Robbie?" he asked me. "I'd lost track of you. I've looked into Logie Street shop a few times, but was told you'd moved to another shop." I gave Alan a run-down on my recent moves, and explained how I had spent the last winter keeping one step ahead of my students. "Heavens above, Robbie!" he exclaimed. "That's quite a move. How are you enjoying it?"

"I'm missing the hustle and bustle of the grocery world, but I've taken a huge gamble on the future. But what are you doing in Carnoustie wearing a long white coat? The last time we spoke, you were all set to start work in NCR." (That is, National Cash Register – a US company.)

"I've got a huge problem," Alan confided. "My father and mother want me to join them in the bakery shop and eventually run it, but that's not my scene. They have been desperate to have me in the business since my apprenticeship ended. So I never joined NCR in the end, and I agreed to do a probationary spell in the shop. I'm hating it, though – it's just not where I want to be."

"But Alan, you could be running a successful business and be your own boss. You may even create a bakery empire someday! Why hate that?"

"Look, Robbie, I'm an engineer. I don't want to be an expert on jam tarts, or any other kind of tart!"

"But what's so bad about it?"

"I want to know the profit margin of every item we sell, and how much we lose if we have waste left over – or don't bake enough in the first place."

"Have you not asked your dad to give you the costs of each product, or how he decides how many pies to bake each day?" I asked him.

"That's my problem. I can't stand his ways of working! When I asked him how many meat pies he decides to bake, he tells me when he leaves the house at midnight to go to the bakehouse, he looks at the sky and decides."

"I suppose he has to decide on the basis of temperature and rain." Which I could understand, as I knew from my own experience it had a bearing on selling 'hot' meals or 'cold foods'.

"Robbie, I need to know exactly how many of each product are we likely to sell each day – it's key to profit and loss. The bakery needs to be run based on facts and calculations."

"Is that practical, Alan?"

"It has to be. We are in a very short shelf-life world, but every time father sees me with my slide-rule doing calculations he goes mad. But that's the only way I can deal with this."

You see, Murray? You're not the only one with worries.

I could sense Alan's frustration, and that of his parents too. He was the only child, and they probably wanted to see him settled and on the road to success in the family business. "I've put pressure on myself, and I may have made a huge error – less anxiety, but still little time to relax," I explained to him.

"My aim is to get into micro-electronics, Robbie. I noticed recently NCR have a base in South Africa. That's what I would like – away from this climate, too."

"Well there's a lot of tension there, Alan," I mentioned. "I read this week that Nelson Mandela's been sentenced to twenty-seven years' labour on Robben Island. Will that not stir up even more trouble?"

"Don't know, but it sounds better than working in a city with over a dozen cases of typhoid!" he laughed. Alan was referring to an outbreak which had no bearing on his own life, but it indicated to me his frustrations. He was downhearted, and I didn't think the recent outbreak of typhoid in Dundee was all that relevant. "Maybe we're just both a bit too ambitious to do well," he added.

Wishing him well, I offered to keep in touch – knowing full well how difficult that was.

* * *

Continuing along the High Street that day, I had time to pop in to see my ex-colleagues in Carnoustie branch. I wasn't certain if I wanted to coincidentally encounter Mr Munro while I was there.

"Oh, look who it is! He hasn't forgotten about us after all," said Ian. "He's decided to come and see real workers."

"So how's the real world these days?" I asked while my old boss went dashing past in his usual style.

"Don't worry – we're the ones making the money for your pay," he joked. (I think?)

"What's the news?" The words were just out of my mouth when Cathie appeared. "Oh, Isobel's gone to England now, and we're as busy as ever."

The shop *was* busy. No time to distract my friends.

"Bring your students here to see how it's really done. Go, go, greasy grocer, go!" My old boss was still as hearty as ever.

The buzz was still there, and I picked up all the well-known scents of cheese, bacon and cooked meats. Deep down, I knew I could have stepped in behind the counter in an instant and started serving customers. My grocery instincts were still there.

Did I miss them? Yes, I did.

* * *

It was 1964, and I was on a six-week summer holiday! Such a thing had not been enjoyed by me since 1955 when I had my last summer holiday before I left school at the October 'tattie holidays'. So now I had time on my hands. Well, not exactly, as I had signed up with Correspondence School of London for my 'O' Levels and received the prescribed books. The two subjects I chose to study were English Literature and British Economic History. Aware that once the next session – which was 1964/65 – got underway, I may not have time to study, I opened my books and started to read during my summer break. Plenty of time, but no money to go anywhere!

My intention was to sit GCE (General Certificate of Education) exams as an external student of London University sometime during 1965, and I set a studying regime for myself to meet that deadline. However, it was not until the new session commenced in August 1964 that I was told by John that I had been booked by the college to attend Jordanhill Teacher Training College, Glasgow. This was the standard course for all teachers in Scotland who, like me, had been recruited from commerce and industry to teach in colleges. Looking back, this was a significant stage in the development of Further Education in Scotland, and must have laid the foundations of future commercial and technical education. The course was structured so that six weeks were to be spent attending classes at Jordanhill during June and July 1965, and the subjects would be Education, Teaching Methods, Speech Training and English. During the winter session of 1965/66, six 'in-class crits' would be carried out by an assessor from Jordanhill. The 'crits' would relate to real 'live' lessons appropriate to any one from my normal curriculum. In 1966 there would again be six weeks' attendance at Jordanhill, when the subjects would be Psychology and Sociology. The course was a legal obligation to teach in Scotland, and would have no bearing on pay grades.

Cheer up, Robbie. Get through this and you'll be a real teacher.

With such blocks of time at Jordanhill along with the preoccupation of 'crits' throughout the winter all on the horizon, I could foresee studying 'O' levels would be interrupted, but I kept reading and studying both subjects with a revised view of sitting exams – probably in 1967.

During that unreal summer period, I managed to keep more in touch with Peem. He gave me positive reports on his artwork at DC Thomson. It was also a time to occasionally visit mum, who always enjoyed me running through the pages of the *Courier* newspaper. "I miss our half-day Wednesday afternoon chats and you reading the news," she would tell me. It seemed like another world when, less than a year earlier, I had those valuable minutes with her.

One day I picked up the *Courier* by chance and, amongst all the reports about the new Overgate, the airport and the typhoid scare, I read out that on the 9th of July in the recent force nine gale on the River Tay, the Abercraig Tay ferry had crashed into the new road bridge – not yet opened.

"That must be a worry, Robert," mum said. "Do you think it's a good idea to build the bridge so close to the city centre?" Mum always had a very practical view about things.

"Yes, but the ferries will stop so there shouldn't be a problem," I suggested. But she was right, as there had been discussion about where exactly the bridge landfall should be. Some had argued that it should have been near Stannergate, and well clear of the city centre.

I missed my chats with mum.

"You'll have more time on your hands now," she said one day. But I had to remind her that it was not all spare time, as I had to study now.

"Are you sure you have made the right decision, Robert? You enjoyed your work in Low's." Of course, I had to reassure her that I was comfortable with my decision, but I detected her nervousness about *my* nervousness.

Looking back, I lived for a long time wondering if I had stepped too far too soon. This was not helped when one evening, one of my Round Table friends made the jocular remark that, "Maybe Professor Murray will be able to tell us?" It was meant to be humorous, but I was very sensitive about teaching at my young age. I thought he was taking the mickey, and it struck a delicate chord.

* * *

That first real summer holiday allowed me a welcome trip down 'memory lane'. Mum and Dad invited Gail and me to join them on a picnic. When I was younger, family outings like that had always been adventures. On this occasion we were driven to Glen Clova and, with great relish, mum laid out the tablecloth and food while dad set about his procedures to get his beloved primus stove into action. As soon as I saw the well-used biscuit tin (the twelve inch cube) wrapped in its cloth parcel and tied up by hairy string, I watched with fascination his meticulous ritual. First assembling the legs, then carefully placing the top grill on which the kettle would sit, then topping up the paraffin in the base followed by carefully pouring about a tablespoonful of methylated spirit into the circular trough. Dad then lit the spirit, which would ignite the paraffin when pumped up through the hairbreadth jet. All very easy, except that I knew risks were always there. Was the stove on a firm flat base? While pumping, would the spirit spill out of the trough? Was the jet clear, or did he face the unwelcome chore of pricking it clean with the supplied gadget?

Once everything was working and the primus stove was burning forcefully, dad placed the kettle – already filled with water from Mum's lemonade bottle – onto the miraculous travelling hob. We all then relaxed and looked around at the mountain tops until the whistling kettle signalled it was time, at long last, for mum to make the tea. It was one of those time-honoured pursuits that dad loved, albeit with a high degree of tension. Mum's joke was that it was 'dad's pressure cooker'.

In September 1964, almost exactly a year after joining the college, I had a pleasant surprise: my long-awaited CRMP certificate arrived in the post. This was not hugely important, but it reminded me that when Mr Robertson interviewed me, he had not asked to see the certificate – he had merely taken my word for it!

A second surprise was that uncle Tom arrived from Edinburgh for a few days' holiday with mum and dad. It was always a pleasure to hear about his life as a gardener in Edinburgh. He never married, and always turned up carrying a tiny suitcase – only about twelve inches square and about six inches deep. He called it his 'tiddly' case, and said he had managed to pack everything he needed for a week-long stay. I have subsequently found he kept immaculate records of his work and the weather over many years. He had served in the Royal Navy during World War II, and had a story or two to tell.

Around August 1942, his ship happened to be based at Sierra Leone, and he somehow learned that the Black Watch were aboard the *Empress of Australia* which had stopped off for supplies. Knowing that his younger brother Jim was likely on board, he made a request to meet him ashore. I have often admired the fact that the respective senior personnel in a time of war allowed this meeting of two brothers to take place. I'll never know how they spent that valuable time, which was perhaps only minutes. But it was the last they saw of each other for – although neither would know where they were headed – Jim was in fact on his way to El Alamein where he was killed, aged 22, on the first night of the fighting. It's a human story which I have often thought about – especially my granny in Montrose, who must have yearned for news of her sons. She would have been thrilled, back home, to think their meeting took place.

"What's the latest about Donald Ford, uncle Tom?" I asked him.

"Great news!" he enthused. "He's signed for Hearts. He's still an amateur, but he'll do well."

"I have a bet with a pal that he'll play for Scotland someday. What do you think?"

"Bit early yet to say. But likely."

"Must tell Jim next time I see him!"

* * *

A new full-time class of young students arrived, and after a year of learning I felt better prepared. It was a testing time. I well remember trying to widen their scope of thinking by 'chipping in' some topical news events – for example, the opening of the Forth Road Bridge. I used examples to find a way of encouraging them to think of events, as this would help them in their retailing studies. The opening of the Forth Bridge on the 4th of September and, a few months later, the death of Sir Winston Churchill on the 24th of January 1965 had little impact compared to the arrival of The Beatles in October to perform in Dundee, when 6,000 teenagers packed the Caird Hall. I had to learn it was best to understand their motivations than to fight against them.

Two weeks into the new session of 1964/65, results came through from City and Guilds in London giving examination results. "Nothing to worry about," was John's comment. "It's never likely to be a 100% success."

Running through the names of students at each level, he nodded approvingly at each pass. Individual pass rates were not provided. When it came to the 'fail' category, John observed, "You see, Bob? We could probably have predicted the 'fails'. We both knew those students had such a poor attendance record it was inevitable."

"Are you satisfied with the results?" I enquired.

"Yes, I am. I'd like to see a few commendations and placings, but it's early days for us."

"What does that mean, John?"

"Perhaps a first, second or third placing. But we're okay with that." This, to me, seemed to imply we had achieved a satisfactory result and there was no more discussion about it beyond that point.

The Jordanhill course commenced in June 1965, and I had to make arrangements to travel to and from Glasgow. This was a major obstacle, but Jim Lindsay – the artist in Gordon's department – took his car and offered to give me lifts. When that was not available, I managed to get a lift in a car driven by a student colleague from Arbroath. One way or another, the travel plan worked.

Arranging accommodation near Jordanhill seemed at first glance to be a difficulty, but a long-lost aunt of my wife who lived in Paisley, near Glasgow, was contacted by letter and agreed to accommodate me on a bed-and-breakfast basis. Initially I intended to travel daily by bus to Jordanhill, but again luck came to the rescue when I met, out of the three hundred students attending the course, a namesake by the name of Sandy Murray who – like John, my boss – had studied through the Co-op courses. It was through Sandy that I learned the Co-op College at Loughborough offered courses up to graduate level. This, I thought, may be of interest for me in future.

Sandy wore extremely thick spectacles and had no car driving licence. He drove a pale blue Robin Reliant, since his motorbike licence allowed him to drive the three-wheeler. Most generously, Sandy came off his route to pick me up each morning and delivered me home each evening.

In the early stages of the course it was normal for all three hundred students to file into one large hall for main lectures. This was quite a daunting experience, and I was relieved when we were split up for all other subjects. This was my first taste of Higher Education, and everyone I spoke with was aware this was something we could not fail as our jobs were reliant on the qualification. No pressure then!

We were given examination questions in advance; all we had to do was to acquire the appropriate textbooks and write, in the examination room, approximately 1,500 words on each topic. Knowing how nerves may affect me, I decided for each exam to use my amateur drama experience to learn by heart the entire 1,500 words of my essays. This worked for the Education topic in year one, and I repeated the technique for the Psychology and Sociology topics in the second year.

Although sociology was a major subject in year two, we occasionally had lectures on the subject in year one. One lecture stands out very clearly, even to this day. The message was two-fold: one was that Glasgow was viewed as "the blackest place in Europe". I'm sure Fergie would not have liked to hear that comment, yet this was stated seriously and related to poor housing, poverty and inadequate roads. Secondly, we were informed that – at the present rate of population growth – city schools, housing and hospitals would become totally inadequate. It was an alarming and desperate picture of the future. We were taken on a tour of a new town (East Kilbride) built to alleviate the housing problem, but which was already feeling the strain. Glasgow's future looked grim.

We now know that two unexpected events began to resolve the problem. For one, 'the pill' and its impact almost immediately allowed the projections of population growth to be favourably revised. The other was a storm in January 1968 which tragically killed twenty people and brought ancient tenements crashing to the ground, thus kick-starting a process of demolishing buildings and creating new housing estates. It was the start of Glasgow's road to recovery, and removing the 'blackest place' picture we were told about in 1965.

To give ourselves a break from the pressure, I well remember Sandy and two of his friends joined us on a very hot July day when we 'skipped' a lacklustre class and drove – not in the Reliant – to Balmaha on the shores of Loch Lomond for a cooling dip. On another occasion, Sandy had to meet some engineers who had done a 'homer' job for him using materials and tools inside a Greenock shipyard. The arrangement was to meet in a pub, which we did. His friends had dipped some screws and bolts for a chrome finish (probably an illegal free dip within the shipyard?), and Sandy had to collect and pay for dipping. These were lively lads, and before long Sandy and I were urged to try 'Black and Tans'. This, I found, was a half-pint of stout topped up to a pint with draught beer. From memory I had only two pints, as did Sandy, but I had to re-

Sandy took a turn too early.

mind him he was driving home in darkness. It was one of the most hair-raising drives I have ever experienced. On one sharp left-hand bend somewhere between Greenock and Paisley, Sandy took the turn too early and – wearing his thick glasses and with two pints in him – he drove his three-wheeler at a forty-five degree angle with his left-hand wheel on a high grass verge. How we survived driving along at 45 degrees I will never know.

* * *

As time went on, I found less time to meet up with my family, but with the first year over I had a welcome weekend break from my Jordanhill studies when my sister Isobel turned twenty-one years old on 26th July and a party was held for her in Carnoustie. This was an opportunity to meet the family after what seemed a long absence.

The mystery of Mr Leitch continued. He simply didn't appear for the commencement of the 1965/66 session. No announcement. No retiral farewell. There was guilt on my part. Had my appointment effectively ended his career? Or had Mr Leitch declined to take up the Jordanhill requirement? Maybe he had tried and failed? It is still a great sadness not knowing the true facts.

Come on, Murray. Get real. You can't dwell on Mr Leitch's situation. There must be some good reason behind it all.

My time that summer was also taken up by moving house to Broughty Ferry, where we had purchased a two bedroomed semi-detached bungalow. The prospect of the pitter-patter of little feet was in the air! It was a reminder to me that had I still been managing a shop I probably would not have found it easy to deal with all those time-consuming matters.

On the last day of the first year of the course, my wife came to Paisley and we took her aunt to Glasgow to see *The Sound of Music* which had recently been released. It was a most apt finish for me at Jordanhill, and the music for me had never sounded sweeter. After numerous lectures, a good deal of reading, an examination on 'Education' satisfactorily completed and a few adventures with Sandy and his Robin Reliant, the course was over. Only six crits during the ensuing winter, and another six weeks at Jordanhill to go!

Robbie, if you can do the first half you can do the rest!

My closer connection with Paisley meant that Cassius Clay's exhibition fight in the city at that time had slightly more meaning. The chat in the staffroom, I remember, was whether he could become a world class boxer. Somehow the winter went speeding past, all crits were signed off satisfactorily, and I again blessed my early dramatic club experiences.

* * *

It seemed too early for the patter of tiny feet, but a baby girl, Carys, arrived on the 24th of April 1966. My nervous wait for Carys's arrival was over when, in the early hours of the morning, I telephoned Maryfield Hospital from a friend's house. A nurse announced. "Yes, Mr Murray; a girl at 12.07."

I was cock-a-hoop, and drove with a friend to Carnoustie to tell my parents. It was a sunny Sunday morning in April, and – until I visited Gail in the afternoon – I had been telling friends and relatives the good news, to which they all replied, "My goodness! What a big baby!" I was highly pleased with myself until I visited the hospital and saw Carys lying in one of a long line of cots and noticed she was the same size as all the other babies. Upon enquiring, it was then clarified that Carys had been born at seven minutes after twelve midnight. Silly me!

A few weeks later I was again off to Jordanhill – this time for the second leg. The tension and nerves were less noticeable, and everything went well. After a total of twelve weeks concentrated study, six classroom crits and more than a few adventures with Sandy and his 'Robin', the course was over and I received my Teachers (Scotland) Further Education Certificate on 18th July 1966. This was followed much later by a surprise letter of commendation on 10th April 1967. The mystery of the commendation letter was solved when Mr Newlands, in a seeming chance meeting in the main corridor, told me, "You did well, Mr Murray! You were in the top percentile of the group of three hundred students". He must have received a letter. Would he ever have told me if we hadn't met? I didn't query his terminology, and later found it meant I was within the top 30 of the group. This was a monumental piece of encouraging news which left me flabbergasted – I can't recall my response to Mr Newlands' casual 'legalistic' style of praise. Neither John Ferguson nor Mr Marr, the Head of Department, ever mentioned it. This was an example of the uncertain, uninspiring and impersonal element in the education universe.

* * *

Carys's arrival made me more aware of how serious my earnings gap was. We were living frugally. One evening I had insufficient bus fare money in the house to enable me to make a return trip to Dundee. To this day, I vividly recall searching throughout the house to find enough for a return fare. Miraculously I found a florin down the back of the settee. Deep within me, I realised how true it was that I lived in 'spam valley', which was the nickname that my neighbours cheerfully used for their similar plight.

Robbie, your granny had a good phrase: "They dinna hae twa pennies tae rub the gither!" Well, that's you!

Granny's oft-quoted remark about 'other people' now also applied to me. She would not have been impressed to know I'd put myself in this situation.

I recall in those days it was quite common for all teachers, quite openly, to study *The Times Educational Supplement* which seemed to appear regularly in the staff room. Some of my graduate qualified colleagues were interested in promoted posts. This related to Section Head or Department Head posts, which were advertised as available in schools and colleges throughout the UK. In my own case, whilst I could chat openly with John about better prospects, the reality was that in the Distributive Trades sector – while posts were advertised – they were no better than my own situation. There was no point in moving home and suffering heavy costs just for the same job. All this did heighten my anxiety. I was still earning a low salary, and improving my qualifications was still an urgent requirement.

On the 18th of August, John, Ron and I made our daily lunchtime trek to The Tinny and found the city centre crowded. The excitement was caused by the arrival of the Queen Mother, who was visiting the city to formally declare the opening of the Tay Road Bridge. The Tay ferries had now stopped, and I remember thinking of happy days with my school pals in Carnoustie doing our annual bike run to St Andrews. The trip on the ferry was always a welcome 'breather', especially on the way home.

There seemed at this time to be a growth and excitement about Dundee. One other example of this was John Cairney's portrayal of Robert Burns in Tom Wright's play *There Was a Man*. The play ran for a week in the Rep, and was a sell-out. I learned only recently that Cairney found those performances highly emotional, and was in tears at the end of each evening. I had studied a good deal of Burns' works at school, and the play had me glued to my seat. It implanted in me the thought to try and write my own Burns play someday.

An additional centre was made available for the growing number of students when the former Wallacetown primary school was re-opened. The policy by then seemed to be that Cowgate was given over to secretarial, typing and office studies, Tay Street was primarily used for mature students studying SCE 'O' and 'H' grade subjects and some distributive trades classes, and Planet Wallacetown now offered some distributive trades classes along with banking, hospital administrators and other professional and business classes.

It was around this time that some attention was being paid to develop 'programmed learning'. Looking back, this appears to have been an attempt to introduce a basic form of learning by flow charts on a screen with yes/no options for students. It was probably a very early attempt to build learning by computer programmes. I think then the theory was that students could work at their own pace and arrive at conclusions by their own discovery.

CHAPTER 26

March 1967 to May 1968: "Fergie's in Trouble", or "Escaping to Sit an Exam"

ENGLAND'S football team, by winning the World Cup in July 1966, created a massive amount of interest – but John 'Fergie' Ferguson was on his own mission for his beloved Rangers. Even the news that Pickles, the wee dog, had found the missing World Cup trophy had done nothing to amuse Fergie.

An incident which was both amusing and serious took place in March 1967. The scene was the Tay Street staffroom on Wednesday 3rd May, when Fergie's heroic 'Gers were due to play the second leg of the European Cup Winner's Cup semi-final. On the 19th of April, Rangers had won the away tie against Slavia Sofia by one goal to nil and now faced the prospect of getting into the final if they could draw or win the second leg at Ibrox Park, Glasgow. This was to be a magnificent crowning glory for his team.

Fergie had been talking up "the 'Gers" for many days. He didn't say it, but his very pro attitude was, I think, emphasised to 'windup' his colleagues of a different religion who supported the 'other' famous, rival Glasgow team. So proud was he of Rangers' achievement to date, he – by some unknown means – had borrowed a small portable TV and set it up on top of a tall metal cupboard. Fergie's enthusiasm had spread through the staffroom during tea break and, with the match due to begin immediately afterwards, several teachers were enticed to watch the dramatic game. The fuzzy black-and-white TV picture made it difficult to follow, and John was standing on a chair trying to adjust his set when Mr Marr, John's head of department, walked into the room.

Mr Marr's timing was no accident. He must have

"Should you not be teaching a class, Mr Ferguson?"

heard rumblings from other teachers about Fergie's infatua-
tion with his team and the irritating boasting that accompanied it. There was an immediate deathly silence. Some teachers, including John, had delayed going back to their classroom
and students – and that was a serious issue. I, like a few others, had a free period... but free periods were not meant to be
used to watch football matches. I slinked back to my classroom and got on with my swotting. No more was heard about
my schoolboy prank and being caught 'amongst the crows'.

*This is all good fun, Robbie. Enjoy it! You would never
have had this in Perth Road.*

Rangers won that match by one goal to nil, and – much
to John's delight – they reached the final when they were
defeated by Bayern Munich by a goal in the 109th minute of
extra time. Great excitement, and a story which shows the
boyish enthusiasm of some teachers who were meant to instil
discipline and common sense.

Fergie was nowhere to be seen or heard when Celtic
FC won the European Cup on 25th May 1967.

* * *

Achieving my teacher's diploma had come at a cost: my 'O'
level studies were delayed. In my mind they were important,
for they would take me on a route to get a meaningful qualification. With the Jordanhill experience behind me, I set out
with renewed purpose to sit my first two 'O' levels. Free periods were essential for me, and I found two quiet places to
read and swot. One was a small, low-ceilinged classroom on a
half landing (the room where the garage storekeepers classes
were held). My vivid recollections are that as I wrote my
notes in the added light of the setting sun, I could gaze dis-

tractedly at the silhouettes of Dundee University towers and domes. The soporific feeling seemed to add to the learning environment.

On occasion, if my papers and study textbooks were in my usual large classroom then I would remain there. My experiences in that room were totally different for, with no noises to be heard around the building, I would occasionally look up and see a group (a nest, horde, herd, mischief or cluster?) of mice running around the classroom floor. Not mice again! I'd had mice problems when delivering to the farm bothy at Westhaven when I was a message boy and, then again, as an apprentice when one of my duties was to empty mouse traps. What was it with me and mice?

What appeared to be the problem was that some of the 'dummy' product packets which I had sent for had been filled with sawdust, and the mice seemed to enjoy nibbling the packets and eating the contents. When I told Dave the janitor, he told me, "The whole building's full of mice – they run up and down inside the walls."

"That can't be very hygienic," I said.

"You're telling me! They drive my wife mad with their scratching around in the ceilings and walls."

I sat my 'O' level exams in February 1967 at the GCE examination centre, which happened to be Cowgate. I then learned around April that I had passed both English Literature and British Economic History. My spare time had also been spent reading and studying for my two 'A' level subjects – Economics and British Constitution. Although I had no dates to sit the advanced subjects, I wanted to be ready to sit exams as soon as my 'O' levels were completed.

"The whole building's full of mice," said Dave the janitor.

I didn't need any reminding that to survive in teaching I must raise my qualifications. What would I have been doing and earning in Wm Low & Co by now? Had I made a huge mistake? The answer was still not clear.

Look, Murray, you can't go back now. You've finally got on the road towards your degree.

* * *

Somehow, around the August of 1967 I learned about a three-year postgraduate management course being run at Dundee College of Technology – known locally then as "Bell Street Tech", and today called Abertay University. The title of the part-time, one day a week course was the Diploma in Management Studies (DMS). I spoke with John, and found that this may well provide me with a step up the pay scale. He

305

agreed to my one day a week release. After an interview, I was accepted for the course and started year one in August 1967.

After that interview, I recalled that during a similar meeting in 1961 – when I had applied to commence the CRMP course – that the Head of Department had used the word 'paradoxically', which had me scampering home to see what the word meant. This time I'd got through without the need to refer to a dictionary. Since the DMS included Marketing, Management and Training, I decided to speak sometime with John about membership of three Institutes. This would allow me to display membership of Marketing, Management and Training Institutes.

Around this time, John – due to an increase in student numbers – engaged two additional members of staff. George recruited from Burton's the tailors, and Ron recruited from Justice's furniture store. This was to give balance to his section, reflecting the need to cover additional areas of the retail trade. Growth within the college continued. The number of mature students seeking to obtain university entrance qualifications seemed to double. This reflected my own situation, and it was to the credit of the Government's policy for Further Education that people like myself had the benefit of 'a second chance' in life. Development seemed to race at such a pace, I began to imagine the quiet-natured Mr Newlands being overwhelmed by the burgeoning growth. It was no wonder, I guessed, that he had no time to carry out any human relations activities by visiting Tay Street.

With the launch of the *QE2* in September that year, Fergie was again in full flight with his Clydeside stories. One of his tales – which no-one could challenge – was that half the population of Greenock and the surrounding area now had new carpets. "Everybody knew about this," he said, "because every second house had a piece of the same tartan design that was laid on the ship."

I remember asking him, "Was it deliberate over ordering, or was it simply theft?"

"Easy," John replied. "The management wanted new carpets too!"

My association with the SSA Scottish Schoolmasters Association, through the enthusiastic Ron, had an unfortunate outcome. Something foreign to me – a strike – had been called for. Luckily it was a token strike of one day, but for me it was as if I had become a bad person – the worst kind of employee. None of my classes were affected, so I didn't let any students down. Strangely, it was something which in my Wm Low days would have been unthinkable for me to participate in. It served to remind me that Mr Newlands had no involvement. There was no apparent 'them and us', or employee/employer situation. The action by the union was simply aimed at the ultimate employer, the Scottish Education Department. Had Mr Newlands been an SSA member, he could have been on strike too!

Robbie, you can't make any waves. Just grin and bear it.

As an insight into the way I was trying to develop, John and I did eventually discuss our qualifications. We were aware of a culture in education whereby it was 'smart' to gain as many qualifications as possible and have the initials behind your name. This would look good on the college prospectus, and we felt the principal would not disagree. Apart from the fact he was my boss, I began to feel that I was on equal terms with John because I too had completed a teacher's course. I wrote to the Institutes and, for a fee, was made a member of each. I was becoming indoctrinated into the false world of presenting a favourable standing for myself and the college.

Looking back, it was rather pathetic to dream up such ideas. It was simply a need to present an impressive, superficial image for the college. Sad, in a way. I was now listed as 'Robert T. Murray, M Inst of Mark., AMBIM, MITO' on the prospectus. Talk about vanity! (Of course, I had to be sure I didn't appear to have more qualifications than my boss.)

When in Rome, Murray!

* * *

Two pieces of news were reported in March 1968, and both – strangely – had a potential impact on retailing and customers. As time went on, I found I was always able to introduce news items to stimulate discussion in the class. An example of this was that The Royal Bank of Scotland introduced cash dispensing machines capable of giving out up to £10 a day. This raised some interesting viewpoints, one of which that young students did not think too kindly about being put out on to the pavement in the rain with no cover. One other example with less immediate impact was the introduction by Autair to commence flights from Leuchars to Luton.

In April 1968, and as part of my attempts to recruit next year's grocery students (numbers had been dropping alarmingly), I prepared a booklet complete with sketches drawn by Peem to take to employers. I obtained finance to produce it by contacting employers in the area to subscribe, and then had it professionally printed. When the supply of booklets was published, I spent several days visiting grocery organisations and leaving copies in the hope that some interest could be generated. As a means of showing the Grocers' Institute the efforts I was making to 'sell' Institute courses, I sent a few copies to the headquarters in London. A week later I received a request from the Institute to send on 50 copies of the booklet.

It was announced on the 23rd of April (St George's Day) that 5p and 10p decimal coins would be introduced. More information to expand on with the students. But there were other developments to attend to. My DMS studies had been continuing during the past winter, and assessments were being carried out on each subject. In early June there was to be a one-week residential course at 'The Burn' near Edzell, a stately old property adorned with Adam fireplaces amongst other period features. Study was quite intense, and I was determined to finish the year successfully. Unfortunately my Geography 'O' level exam was timed for Wednesday 2nd June of that week. Here I was attending a postgraduate course on management and I had to sit an 'O' level in Commercial College, Dundee. It seemed far too ridiculous and, in order to escape, I had to invent an interview in Dundee in order to drive to the exam venue. Luckily, I had recently been given a loan to buy a Morris Minor 1000cc car, otherwise I may never have made the journey. I recall driving like a madman to the location, again at Cowgate. Only the recent tragic death of Formula One racing driver Jim Clark, who had been killed in a crash in West Germany earlier in the month, slowed me down.

For that exam, I didn't study through the correspondence school. In a chance discussion about my qualifications in the Cowgate staffroom one day, it was suggested that Anne – a geography teacher – could perhaps help me study for my Geography 'O' level. She was a full-time teacher and had a full programme of teaching, but she very generously provided me with textbooks and gave me homework exercises. After six weeks of intense study and guidance by Anne, I sat and passed my examination during that fretful week at The Burn.

Success, Murray! Three 'O' levels now 'in the bag' – time to concentrate on your two 'A' levels now.

The exceptional piece of luck which had taken me into teaching was now matched by an even greater inexplicable event that may take me out of the education sector altogether. With only two or three weeks to go before the end of the teaching year, I decided to spend as much time as possible studying in my classroom. My focus was now on sitting both 'A' levels sometime in 1969. So what was the luck?

One day John, Mr Marr – the head of department (football frolic forgotten) – and me, were discussing the usual 'game' of budgets. For the last four years, John – when pressed to set a budget and spend money – had been inventing purchases he didn't actually require. A variety of materials, dummy models and clothing which he had purchased over the years was lying around in heaps on desks, tables and on floors. The head of department's rule was that each year something must be purchased because, if not, the budget would be cut the following year. Somewhere in Westminster, I imagined, the government was trying to cut spiralling costs – and here was an annual ritual in one small part of the education world inventing unnecessary spending. It was an unreal, bizarre situation. John was scratching his head about the pounds, shillings and pence he had to spend.

"Come on, Bob!" he urged me. "Surely you need something in the grocery area?"

"There's nothing I need," I replied, "but why don't you indent for some cupboards to put all that superfluous stuff you've been buying all those years?"

"Brilliant, Bob. That's what we need!" John had finally found a need to spend some money which, in reality, he didn't require. For all the years since that day I have had a jaundiced view about Government spending within education – and where else besides?

With that budget decision made and my feeling of 'achievement 'in finding a solution, I went upstairs to the staff-froom as it was approaching teatime. The room was quiet, and Dave hadn't yet brought in the teapots and cups. In pre-paring a place on the table for his cups, I moved some papers and happened to glance at a page in *The Grocer* magazine. This was my slice of luck, for dominating the page was a job advertisement for a Training Development Officer, required to work for The Grocers' Institute in East England. Grocers' Institute qualification and grocery management experience required, along with a training or education background de-sirable. 'Salary £1,950 plus car and expenses,' the advert read.

Wow! That package, with expenses, would overtake a graduate teacher's salary. It seemed just too good to be true.

Time to check your space suit again, Robbie!

This was almost as much of a shock as I had felt when reading about the teaching post five years previously. Like the advert all those years ago, this reflected my exact situation. Quite extraordinary! There was only one snag. The magazine was dated – in fact, it was nearly a month old.

With the magazine in my briefcase, I headed home to prepare a letter of application and posted it early the next morning. My salary then had risen slowly to around £1,200 per annum – plus some precarious overtime earnings. This was roughly what I was earning in Wm Low when I started teaching five years previously. What would the Perth Road manager be earning now?

With such a lucrative prospect, I also telephoned the Institute and explained my situation. "Thank you for your call," I was told. "We will wait until your letter arrives and be in touch." I was a little relieved not to have been met with something like: "Sorry, but the position has now been filled."

Well, well, Murray. All you can do now is pray. Yes, you may have to get your spaceship ready!

The next day I received a letter from the director of studies informing that I had successfully passed year 1 of the DMS course, and that they looked forward to me commencing year 2 in August.

CHAPTER 27

March 1967 to June 1968: "Interview at the Grocers' Institute", or "Another New World?"

WITH loud banging on my sleeping berth door, the attendant wakened me as arranged. "Cup of tea, Mr Murray, sir?" came an efficient-sounding tone of voice. It was 6am, and the overnight Aberdeen/London train was approaching King's Cross station. Somehow I'd managed to sleep, in contrast to my trip to London only nine years previously when, along with my Grocers' Institute classmates, I had set off to sit Institute exams. Then, we sat up nearly all night playing cards and having a restless time lying flat out on unoccupied seats. Now I was in comparative luxury, and the Institute was paying! My letter of application had obviously been considered, and within a few days I'd received, at home, a call from the Director of Training asking me to attend an interview at the headquarters in Doughty Street, London.

It's all looking good, Robbie. But don't take it all for granted.

Not for the first time, I emerged from that famous railway station. It was around 7.30am, and I wondered how to spend time until the rest of the world 'clicked into gear'. My interview was arranged for 9.30am, and with no appetite for a breakfast I took a taxi to 50 Doughty Street in the hope there may be a café nearby where I could read a newspaper and enjoy a coffee. *Don't make assumptions*, I told myself as I pulled the gleaming brass doorbell. As expected, there was no response and no cafés to be seen.

The Institute offices, marked by a highly-polished brass plate, were located in a residential street complete with an unbroken terrace of three or four storey elegant Georgian dwellings which ran the length of the road, and with a uniformity of black painted railings which curved elegantly up to each front door, access to which was up a flight of three stone steps. This was obviously a classic 'listed' street of residences which reflected an historic period in London high-class city dwelling. With time on my hands, I enjoyed the warm sun of a June morning as I strolled around the block. Alas, no cafés could be found in spite of my best efforts to track one down, so I walked further afield and took in the scene. Quiet electric milk vans moved about on their routine pattern, and I could see cleaners emerging from offices and the occasional black-cab taxi picking up or depositing 'fares'.

At the doorway of a large hotel, a gathering of tourists with suitcases strewn around a coach were milling around in readiness for their next adventure. The coach operator was Evan Evans, which appealed to my sense of humour – so they are off to Wales, I imagined. Walking back to number 50, I noticed – almost next door – a wall-plaque which declared that none other than Charles Dickens had, at some time, resided there. The setting was high-quality Dickensian, and I stood there trying to dream up a scene of the man himself emerging from one of the glossy black enamelled doors. Having recently learned something of the famous writer's colourful background, the scenes I conjured up could have been quite interesting – but perhaps not yet revealed then.

As time ticked on beyond 8am, and having soaked up the local scene, I decided to remain at the front door with my briefcase at my feet. It occurred to me that it would not be such a bad thing to be discovered on the doorstep at opening time. It wasn't long before a taxi stopped at the kerb nearby, and out stepped a middle-aged, distinguished and tidy-looking suited gent.

"Hello!" he said in greeting. "You must be Mr Murray?"

"That's right," I replied, offering a handshake.

"Kilburn. Sam Kilburn."

"Pleased to meet you, Mr Kilburn."

The name registered with me. Yes, of course! He's the Chief Executive. I'd seen his name on various documents. In fact, his signature was on the Institute certificates I'd received years previously. So, this was the top man!

"It's Robert, isn't it?" he said as he used his Yale key to open the pristine black lacquered door.

"Bob, Mr Kilburn," I replied.

"It's Sam, by the way. Right, Bob – let's get the kettle on for a cuppa."

Jings, Robbie! You've hit the big time. Mr Kilburn – no, Sam – unlocking the Institute front door for you and

about to make you a cup of tea! Yes, unthinkable... and amaz-
ing!

Sam asked me about my journey and, in the course of our chat, he told me he commuted from Brighton every morning. "You must get to know your travelling companions well," I said as I recollected hearing tales of such commuters who were set in their ways.

"Oh yes – same coach, same seats and the same six in the compartment."

Making small-talk with Sam now! "What happens if a stranger sits in your compartment?" I asked.

"We'd tell them to bloody well move out!" said Sam in what was not a Southern English accent.

His accentuated accent intrigued me. "So this is not your native heath?" I asked, rather boldly.

"Nay, lad; I'm Yorkshire!" he replied, accentuating some genuine Yorkshire accent. Somehow, I'd picked up that this fresh-faced, rosy-cheeked, friendly man with a curious crinkly smile, and who exuded confidence, was on my wavelength. I felt comfortable in his company. We were chatting when there was a definite Southern English voice from the passageway.

"Good morning," hailed the voice.

"Come in, John!" Sam said in response. "John, meet Bob – on our doorstep and eager to start when I arrived. Bob, may I introduce John Simpson?"

"How do you do?" John responded in a cultured, friendly but unemotional tone, and with a definite 'plum'. No sound had come from John's entry at the front door and I wondered why but the mystery was soon solved. "Yes, I heard the doorbell," he said.

My curious glances between the two men prompted Sam to say, "John lives in Suffolk, but he dosses down in the coombe space on the top floor."

"Good way to avoid commuting," I pointed out.

"He was used to bunking down in small spaces in the Navy," the jovial Yorkshire man told me. After a few minutes of general chat, Sam then announced, "Right then. Let's get on with the good work."

Sam's down-to-earth, no-nonsense, straight-talking Yorkshire approach appealed to me. John Simpson had a more studious, authoritative and precise demeanour. "Let's get to my office," he said in a friendly but commanding voice.

John's interview was more like a chat. There was no rigid formality. He started by giving me the background. "The Institute courses have been declining over recent years," he told me. I nodded in response. "Things are changing. Super-markets are on their way. The government is dedicated to raising the profile of training in businesses. Training boards are being set up for each industry, and companies will be charged a levy which will be repaid if a business reaches certain criteria. The Distributive Industry Training Board is now in the process of being set up, and the levy will be 0.7% of a company's wage bill."

I listened intently. "Where does the Institute fit into this?" I asked him.

"We are dedicated to assisting grocery businesses large and small throughout the UK by encouraging the use of Institute courses in colleges, and also by training people inside companies to set up their own training systems – thus helping them to claim back their levy. That's why we have appointed Training Development Officers. Or TDOs, as we call them. I was recruited to set up and run the training initiative only nine months ago."

"Yes, I have heard of an appointment in Scotland. It sounds like a good move for the future."

"We make no bones about it. The role of the Training Development Officer is not viewed as a long-term one. It's pump-priming and a stepping stone."

"What is the expected lifespan of a Training Development Officer?" I enquired.

"Good question," John remarked in his clipped Naval officer fashion. "We see the role as one where individuals can move on to work within a Training Board, move into Further Education or become a training officer within a company. So the answer is probably no more than two or three years."

"Does this mean the Institute is working itself out of its function within the trade?"

"Not exactly. We'll still be here to provide guidance, and of course to continue offering our redefined college syllabuses."

To bring the discussion more closely to bear on my own situation, I asked the question: "What exactly would the TDO job entail?"

"We have TDOs covering areas across the UK, except for East England. We have Mike covering south of the Thames, John covering west and south-west England, and another Mike working in the north-west of England. You've probably heard of Norma, who is responsible for all Scotland and south to the Humber."

"Yes, Norma looked into the College one day about a month ago to say 'hello'," I remembered. "What is the area to be covered by the East England TDO?"

"That's easy: north of the Thames, south of the Humber, and east of the M1 Motorway."

"Quite a patch," I responded, trying to play down in my mind the enormity of the geographical spread that was being talked about.

"It's an excellent territory. You'd have the headquarters of Fine Fare at Welwyn Garden City, London Co-op, Key Markets in Essex, International Stores, and a number of smaller multiples spread throughout the region."

The picture was immediately clear. To fulfil this post, I'd have no choice but to move home. The extent of the area was daunting and travelling would take up a lot of my time. It would not be conducive to family life... BUT, training and education within the grocery trade was changing and I would be in the forefront of that fast-changing world. There was no question that having the Institute on my CV would look good.

I wanted a little more clarity. "What would my typical week look like?"

"You'd probably visit a couple of colleges and one or two companies. In due course you would be involved in running our Instructional Techniques course which we are planning, and being part of our Training Administration course to be run by Mike in the south."

"Where would the courses take place?"

"Mainly London. Possibly one or two in Scotland. And some, of course, inside a company where we – I mean you – have identified suitable personnel to be trained."

"I see. Some time away from home, then?"

"Yes, occasionally," he acknowledged.

"Where would I need to be based?"

"Anywhere you like within your territory, but I'd suggest a strategic spot depending where your expected greatest volume of work will develop."

"And what would my remuneration package be?" I enquired, half expecting to have the salary cut back because of my hitherto lack of training as opposed to education.

"Exactly as quoted," John said. "All TDOs are on the same conditions. Plus all car and telephone costs, but no pension scheme as we don't view this as long-term. Come, let's have a coffee and I'll show you around." His clarity and brisk approach was impressive.

My prospective boss's office was on the third level, and I took it that his unofficial sleeping quarters were in what may have previously been a maid's room upstairs. As we walked about the impressive design and layout of the property with its tight, winding classical staircase, I picked up the grandeur of the building and how prestigious it was as a headquarters for a national institute. The real gem in the accommodation was a majestic board room which John referred to as the place where key figures in the UK grocery world regularly met. "The Institute plays a prominent role in acting as a meeting place for discussions on the big decisions of the day, and is a figurehead not only for education but also for trade development and legal matters."

Time had passed and the office staff had arrived. John opened a glass panelled door and introduced me to John Simpkins. "May I introduce you to Bob Murray, John?"

"Ah yes, Bob Murray. I've seen your name 'Robert' over the years. Pleased to meet'cha!" he said with smiling enthusiasm in what I guessed was an East London accent.

"A pleasure to meet you, too. I've seen your name as well. You have a big job keeping the education syllabuses up to date."'

"Never-ending!" he told me gleefully. John Simpkins, I knew, had the responsibility to send out all syllabuses to colleges and Institute students. Even from a distance, over the years I could tell it was a demanding job.

In the basement I was introduced to George Reid, the accountant/treasurer. "This is the man who checks all expense claims," said John in an undisguised way of making a point.

"Important job," I remarked as I shook hands with a man who looked every inch the precise accountant.

We moved on. "It's a lean, busy machine and a tight ship," John pointed out as he ushered me into another office. "Pauline is Sam's secretary," he said, introducing me to another new face. "Pauline, Bob Murray."

"Pleased to meet you, Bob," said an attractive lady surrounded by what appeared to be many dozens of filled but unsealed letters. "Got to get this lot out by tonight's post."

John guided me to a small waiting room where he explained in some more detail the general role of the Institute and its central role within the trade. It had a far more extensive influence within the trade than I'd previously appreciated.

"When are you setting off back north?" asked John as he glanced at his wristwatch.

"Two o'clock from King's Cross," I replied.

"Right, then. Let's have a wander round to the Red Lion for an early spot of lunch."

* * *

"What do you think then, Bob?" John asked as he picked up his half-pint of Best Bitter.

"I'm extremely interested," I replied. "It's obviously a stepping stone, as you said, which I understand. But for me, the involvement in running courses and learning more about training in-company is attractive."

I recall chatting about a plan for my future within the education world, and John's clear (if biased) comment that training within companies was the way ahead. This confirmed my worries about the decline in Institute students at Dundee Commercial College. "What are your thoughts, Bob? Does the job have any appeal to you?"

"It certainly sounds interesting. If I was a young, unattached man, I would give you a 'yes' right away. All I need to do is speak with my family about the move."

Since it was declared as a short-term employment prospect, I wondered at that point if I could move south myself and leave the family back home – perhaps with myself in lodgings. A permanent move may arise in England, on the other hand, so a move would probably be best.

"That's perfectly understood. I don't want to rush things, but ideally I'd like you in situ for around the start of the academic year." Deja vu! "When does your college year end?

"End of June," I told him.

"Would I be wasting my time by sending you an offer letter?"

"No, not at all."

"Good."

John organised a taxi for me, and soon I was on my way back home. Once settled into a quiet compartment, I started to jot down the pros and cons.

Robbie, this could solve a lot of problems for you. But there are downsides...

I listed the readily-identified plusses first. Moving on to a higher salary is not only good for now, but a better base for future jobs. It could remove the need for 'A' levels and a degree, and alleviate my slow salary progress worries. Training within companies is undoubtedly a likely future direction for me, or perhaps within a Training Board anywhere in the UK. There was also the prospect of a stimulating experience. After five years, I now felt out-of-date with the fast-changing modern grocery world. Visiting top companies such as Fine Fare would provide me with state-of-the-art training policies and practices. I would be at the cutting edge. It felt like a breath of fresh air, and a new world beckoned. The English business culture was attractive. It seemed like a brand new world beckoned, with which I had an immediate rapport.

On the minuses, however, there were a number of things to consider. Moving away from Carnoustie and Dundee to a new, unknown part of the world, for one. There would be lots of driving around and time away from home. Also, there would be upheaval for Carys – now two years old. Would England be good for her schooling? The stepping stone, although a plus, still means another move somewhere at some point in the future. There were no guarantees! I'd have no time for studying if I wanted or needed to, and I'd be deviating off the route I had planned for the next few years.

Picking up my *Daily Telegraph*, I happened to focus on two items which, had I read them the day before, would have had less impact. "Government on target with Industry Training Boards," was one of them. The piece went on to say: "To meet growing competition in the world, the Government was determined to improve the nation's standards of training within commerce and industry, and to have all Training Boards in situ by end of the decade." A smaller piece on the front page reported "M1 complete by year end." Front page news, and suddenly all very relevant in my possible future employment.

Sitting back in my seat, I started to feel the tingle of a big opportunity coming my way. Not for the first time, luck had intervened in my life. Was it too good to be true?

Looks like you'll better prepare your jet engines, Robbie boy!

CHAPTER 28

June to August 1968:
"A Job Offer from the Institute",
or "Farewell University Education"

"**W**ELL? How did you get on, Bob?" John 'Fergie' knew why I was absent and, as I stepped into the staff room next morning, he was ready with that obvious question.

"I've not made up my mind yet, but it sounds attractive," I told him. "I'll need to speak more with the family about it. It's a similar job as that done by Norma, who looked in to see us a few weeks ago."

The fact I could speak openly about the situation with John indicated what I had always felt – that Further Education teachers didn't work in teams, but are each contracted by the Council and get on with the job they are designated to do. To chat with your boss about leaving your company would be unreal in the commercial world.

John would obviously be anxious about his staffing level, and potentially faced the same problem he had when I arrived in 1963. If I were to leave at the end of the session, would he have insufficient staff to start off the new session? He now had George and Ron, and I felt quite certain he would find ways of coping.

My concerns were two-fold – would my family situation suffer if I moved to England, and would I still manage to go on two weeks' holiday in July to south-west Scotland, which was booked and already paid for? The priority was my family, and I discussed the pros and cons with my wife. "It's up to you," she told me, "but it sounds better than studying for the next five years."

Robbie, this opportunity demonstrates how 'high risk' it was to leave Willie Lows. Another five years of low pay makes the decision to leave Lows a bad move. This pay package on offer means that you will possibly overtake where you would have been as a manager.

I spoke with Peem. The telling sign was that I didn't feel the need to sit at my favourite place at Westhaven, where I had always mulled over problems. This indicated to me my situation was not a problem, but one where I felt attracted to this bold new opportunity. What I found odd was that although I had met the Scottish TDO, I had never given thought about such a move myself. Fergie and I had never discussed the training boards. Looking back, it indicates just how inwardly-focused we must have been within our college world. From a personal viewpoint, I must have been so absorbed by my DMS and Geography 'O' level studies. What was more amazing is that *The Grocer* magazine appeared as it did. Luck kept following me.

John Simpson's offer letter soon arrived, signed "John Simpson, Commander RN (Ret'd)". That figured. By now I'd spoken with my wife, mum, dad and Peem, and all independently saw the move as positive – albeit with regret about a move so far away. The letter gave a starting date in July. This was a pity, as my holiday booking was for the last two weeks in that month.

I wrote accepting the offer and pointed out the holiday problem. John replied and graciously accepted the holiday delay, asking if I would instead commence a week after the end of the holiday. That date, I remember, was the 5thof August.

Robbie Murray! You've just pressed another big button. Space suit definitely required!

The next step was to officially inform Fergie and write my letter of resignation to the Dundee City Education Department. On this occasion I had none of the high emotion I experienced when leaving Wm Low. There was an announcement around then that the college was now to occupy the old St Joseph's Primary school in Blackness Road, and that the end-of-session staff meeting would be held in the spacious drill hall there.

Robbie, your landing on Planet St Joseph's was merely as a visitor – your spaceship is already programmed for London. So it's farewell to education.

The memory of that last staff meeting is still vivid today. The total college staff now numbered approximately a hundred and fifty – a far cry from the fifty who attended at the end of the 1963/64 session. Sitting listening to the principal's report and the plans for the ensuing year sounded only vaguely interesting, and I sat there with a massively different adventure ahead. Fergie, I was sure, could not have been as excited about his year ahead as I was about mine. John wished me well, and I said I'd keep in touch. Sadly, I have no recollection of finding the time to do so. I said cheerio to my hill-walking colleagues but, for some reason, I have no memory of meeting the principal. Looking back, it somehow crystallised my view that I and all my colleagues were self-sufficient individuals. We worked together, but we didn't work as a team. To this day, I don't know if that would have had any impact on student pass rates. Probably not. It was a unique situation. During the period of my five years of employment, the principal spoke to me only once – when he congratulated me on my commendation from Jordanhill. It was, I'm sure, not a personal issue – it served only to demonstrate how the education system worked. Come to think of it, John never once sat down with me to ask how I was getting on, nor to ask if I had any questions or ideas. Whether by design or otherwise, the 'swarthy one' played his cards close to his chest.

* * *

Prior to my holiday and after chatting with John Simpson, I decided to drive to Cambridge and have a hasty look around the housing market there. It seemed the perfect place to be based. My brother-in-law offered to join me and to use his car. We planned to stop off at a hotel at Richmond, just a few miles off the A1 main road. Our journey, however, was slower than anticipated, and after loud knocking on the hotel's main door at midnight – to no avail – we were facing a sleepless night in a lay-by. Driving on, we spotted – somewhere around Catterick – road signs for the army base. On enquiring about possible accommodation, we were most kindly offered Army bunks. A good free night's sleep followed. Bravo for the British Army!

The reconnoitre was successful in as much that it told me Cambridge properties were too expensive to consider. But on driving around the region, I felt it would be more practical to base myself near the A1 for driving access to London combined with a rail link to the city. No websites in those days to do some research!

During my holiday, I took a few opportunities to think over my college experience. It seemed I had never stopped reading, studying or planning. What were my main thoughts? There was no doubt that the graduate teachers I rubbed shoulders with were paid a handsome salary, but there were occasions when – quite openly – some would take a day off to attend interviews for a 'promoted post' such as head of department. Again, this was something done quite openly. From a principal's point of view, I could see he was the leader of a moving group of people – which in commercial or industrial life would not happen. From my first day, my driving force was to occupy myself with plans to recapture my salary level in Wm Low. Looking back, I had taken a huge risk by going to teach. It's possible that I may never have achieved my 'A' levels, far less a degree.

In retrospect, I had made a teaching contribution to John's section, but to what extent I'll never know. Retail students' achievements were satisfactory, which reflected something had gone right. I had also gained considerably by my employment: I had used college time to study for my 'O' levels and 'A' levels; the opportunity to gain my teacher's qualification was gifted to me by the system, and the college allowed me time off to study for the Diploma in Management. All in all, while I was living like a 'kirk moose' my time and experience had been profitable. Looking back, my college years had been a route rather than a destination.

With the holiday over, I was off to London on another overnight journey and – learning from experience, and with the comfort of 'traveling expenses' – I enjoyed a breakfast before being back at the Institute door shortly before Sam arrived.

John had sent me a timetable for the next six months, on which were plotted key events including meetings of TDOs, two days labelled 'Debach', some overnight stays in London to attend some trade dinners, and dates of two training courses – one in Peebles, Scotland, and one in London. A box of index cards containing names, addresses and contacts for all colleges and companies in my area was also handed over to me.

John had arranged for introductions and a meeting of TDOs to be held on my first day. We sat in the grand boardroom and had a briefing, then went to the Red Lion for "half a pint of bitter and raw beef sandwiches".

Welcome to Planet Institute, Robbie.

I was briefed on the weekly report to be sent in by voice tape, my expenses and telephone claims. I was also given instructions on how to calculate my petrol claim, and the need to send or phone in my planned travels for the ensuing week. Anxious to continue my DMS course I asked John for his advice. Without hesitation, he said, "Ipswich Civic College – that's what you want. We have an excellent relationship with Colin Dewsbury, the Head of Department there."

"How many miles to Ipswich, John?"

"Probably about seventy miles from Cambridge," he told me.

"Hmm, I'll need to think about that."

"The college has an excellent reputation."

"Thanks, John. It's year two I want to do."

"Why don't you give him a visit and fit in other calls? In fact, you may be able to do that each week."

This was typical of the Institute's generous help to de-velop the TDOs every bit as much as companies and colleges.

* * *

Jack, another TDO, drove me to the car dealer where I picked up my car en-route for Cambridge. John had, through a con-tact, found lodgings for me which would be available until university term time commenced in October. The white Cortina MK2 with red interior looked a powerful machine compared to my Ford Prefect and Morris Minor.

It was a hot August day in London. I had never driven in the city, and I had a scribble on a scrap of paper describing the route to take out to Cambridge. To cap it all, I started driving without realising the car heater was switched on – but being so pre-occupied with traffic and a new car, with nowhere to pull over, I had to sweat it out until I could park in a layby.

My first expense item was to buy a wall-map covering my area. Using the cards showing businesses and colleges in my 'patch', I would see patterns emerge where I could maxim-ise visits with minimum time and travel. This would also as-sist me to select priorities which were the 'big boys' – Fine Fare, Keymarkets and London Co-op. Superimposed on these journeys, I would be able to make a final decision where to base my home – and it would be beneficial if I could combine house-hunting, or at least 'base' hunting, whenever I was travelling around my area.

CHAPTER 29

August to September 1968: "Ipswich College", or "A London Training Course"

"GOOD evening. Sorry to trouble you. Are you Mrs Pittam?" Somehow, with no GPS or Cambridge city map, I had managed to follow John's verbal directions to St John's Road, Cambridge. It had been quite a nerve-wracking drive, and I probably looked like a sweaty scared rabbit when I reached the address.

"Yes," said the tall, smartly-dressed lady. "You must be Mr Murray."

I was invited to park my car in the correct place within a narrow lane and bring in my suitcase. "You must be needing a cup of tea, Mr Murray," she suggested, obviously noticing that I did.

"Certainly. Very kind of you."

With great relief, I sat and relaxed in Mrs Pittam's front room while we chatted about arrangements. She explained to me, "The students have gone, and I have only one short-term boarder at present. You will be only other one for the summer.

Mrs Pittam was a gentle person and kept a low profile, and before long I was able to sit down and plan my visits. Cambridge was a busy university town and, on summer evenings, it was a joy to walk around the town and along by the river Cam at the 'Backs'. My arrangement with Mrs Pittam was for bed and breakfast, and sometimes I could arrange in advance to be home in time to dine with her. Her husband had recently been killed in a road crash in Stoke, and she was happy to eat with me. It was holiday time, and she was alone in a large B&B house. When I knew I would be late home, I had to eat out. This was not a problem, as I had found the ideal answer – Berni Inns. As soon as I saw the rows of chickens roasting on a spit inside the restaurant window, I was a captured customer. I seem to recall roast chicken and side salad, and an ice cream was seven shillings and sixpence (37.5p), with steak and salad available at 10 shillings (50p).

This is it, Robbie. Planet Cambridge!

John had said I should choose a base to suit, but suggested for my own sake to settle myself in the best strategic place. The predominance of work appeared – not surprisingly – to be nearer London, and trips to Doughty Street and planned courses in the city indicated somewhere in the northern daily commuting belt. To help plan, I drew concentric semi-circles at ten-mile intervals emanating northwards from the city.

Two priorities, then – my DMS course and house-hunting. Both personal, but John's attitude was brilliant. The Grocers' Institute was prepared to pay my fuel to continue my studies, which was in keeping with their declared policy of encouraging training and education within the trade. I couldn't have asked for anything more.

* * *

Ipswich was, as John had advised, about seventy miles from Cambridge. However, it was a worthwhile journey, for I secured a place – amazingly – on the second year of the course. Ipswich just happened to be offering the second year subjects at the same time as Dundee College of Technology! The course was due to commence the next week, and would run on an all-day and evening class every Wednesday. Colin Dewsbury asked me to produce a letter confirming my successful conclusion of year one. He also outlined to me how things were going generally as regards retail courses, and specifically Grocers' Institute courses. The picture mirrored the declining situation at Commercial College, Dundee. Knowing I was a qualified FE teacher, he asked if I could help take classes if he was ever short-staffed.

My first report therefore related to Ipswich Civic College with a dual element – an enquiry about how things were generally, and my personal arrangements for Wednesdays. To my great relief, Sam and John agreed without question my attendance, and at the Institute's acceptance of my day-release and travel costs.

My plans to visit contacts soon got underway, and Wednesday trips became routine. The semi-circles on my map began to make a good deal of sense. What I learned was not only mileages, but the direct relationship between miles from London and house prices. I had to carefully consider my house value (and therefore mortgage commitment). My three bedroom property in Broughty Ferry, purchased for £3,500, was worth then around £4,750. This meant I had to consider something similar. What I also began to realise was that with fuel costs and heavy parking bills, it was advantageous to travel by train. This directed my attention to towns near a main-line railway station. With house prices and commuting in mind, I settled on St Ives, Huntingdon.

The course which I was to run at Peebles Hydro would take place some six weeks after I had left Scotland, and it seemed an excellent idea to think about making a quick dash home for a weekend. TDO Mike (South of the Thames) joined me on the course to run the administration aspects. All went well, and it served as a useful curtain-raiser for me. For the first time ever, I felt completely at home – not just being in Scotland, but because I was now making use of my teacher training in a direct and practical way, knowing that the results were going to be picked up and used inside companies. Teaching students had seemed useful enough, but now I felt I had direct input into corporate management.

* * *

A weekend in Broughty Ferry, including a trip to Carnoustie, was a welcome rest from many miles of driving. I took my daughter Carys to see Westhaven, where we had a walk along the shore and some time playing on the 'swings'. As we walked along to the fishermen's huts, who should I meet but Jim. "Where did you disappear to?" was his friendly greeting. "I gave up looking!"

"I know it all happened quickly when I was moved to Perth Road." As I told the story, I could hardly believe that five years had passed and how much my world had changed.

"How are you doing – or who are you doing, these days?" was his joke. I briefly told him the story, and his comment came as expected: "Oh, a nice cushy number, then?"

"Aye," I replied. "No break-ins, robberies or shop lifters." I didn't try to respond to the cushy comment; all I said was, "I expect the crime rate in Lochee will be well and truly curbed by you now, Jim."

"An on-going job," was his dour reply.

While staring out at the receding tide, we reminisced about our freedom to run around Westhaven and our treasure trove of tales. "What are you doing here anyway, Jim?" I asked him.

"I come here as often as I can, just to sit and think about all those great days."

"I don't get here often enough, and I'm miles away from here now," I said wistfully. "Anyway, you owe me a pound, Jim."

He looked surprised. "What for?"

"The Donald Ford bet!"

"Wait a minute, Robbie! He hasn't played for Scotland, has he?"

"Yes, he has – nine times!"

"Naw, he's played nine times for the Scottish Amateurs."

"Ah, but I said *Scotland*. So, hand over your pound, Jim."

As Jim handed over the pound note, he added, "He's done well in the Hearts squad. Runner-up in the League Cup in 1965, and the Scottish Cup this year."

"Aye, Jim," I agreed, "he's done well."

"And it a' started here at the Ballaster, when we showed him the best fitba' and cricket tricks."

"Did you notice then how he ran on his tip toes, Robbie – he was a nippy wee player." It was great to catch up with Jim. Incidentally, Donald Ford went on play professional football for Scotland three times in the 1970s. He also played cricket for West Lothian County, and was selected to play for Scotland.

We said our cheerios and, as I walked away, I was thrilled to think that Jim had exactly the same feelings as myself. The emotions of Westhaven had never left us. Those boyhood days were a magical piece of history.

Later that day, I remember driving along to Jock's house. As expected, he was not at home, and his mother told me he was now running a fruit and vegetable shop in East Anglia. I made a mental note. It was too much of an opportunity to miss.

Next, I popped along to Alan Craigie's parents' bakery shop. Mr Craigie was about to go home after his night's work. "He's gone to work in NCR," was all he said. I knew of the disappointment within the family about Alan not following his father in the business, so I didn't say much. "He's away to a wedding today, so you won't see him here."

"Please let him know I was asking for him," I asked.

To be based in Cambridge and find myself back in Carnoustie was a real tonic. I was never homesick, but hearing Jim's stories of coming to Westhaven gave me a great comfort that after all those years – although spread around the country – we each had those fond memories. When I chatted with Peem later that evening, he too mentioned his many moments of sitting at Westhaven thinking of those wonderful days.

"Coffie and Ollie tell me the same thing," he said. "We were greatly blessed."

As I drove alone back to Cambridge on the Sunday evening, I had many warm memories of Westhaven – but even more so the knowledge that all my pals also prized that golden heritage we shared.

* * *

A one-week Training Administration course with Mike and John was held in The Great Northern Hotel, King's Cross, later in September. On that occasion, John had arranged – as a means of publicity for the institute – to invite the trade press to 'look in' on the event. Two weeks later, the *Super-marketing* trade magazine ran the story with a front cover picture and the caption: "Grocers' Institute courses: Simpson, Pope and Murray show the way." The picture almost certainly would end up beside Dave the Janny's tea pots and cups, and Fergie and my other old colleagues would see it. Great feeling to imagine they would see I'd made a flying start.

By the end of September, my property in Dundee was sold and I was awaiting an agreed entry date from the buyers. I had made an offer of £4,750 to Ekins, Witherow & Handley for a similarly-priced new property in Acacia Avenue, St Ives, which was accepted and signed for. My improved salary would pay for the bigger mortgage. Arrangements for my furniture removal were made, and I was set to move on a due date. By chance I met the site manager in charge of builder's property keys, and mentioned all was organised and my furniture would arrive two days later. So it was time for me, if I may please, to have the keys for my house.

To put it mildly, the poor man almost exploded as he fell off his stool. "What?! You can't do that! I've not been notified!"

"Well, I'm notifying you now," I told him. "I've signed for the property, and the furniture van is on its way as we speak!"

"But you ain't got completion yet!" he spluttered in his increasingly high-pitched voice.

"But I've signed!" I informed him.

"Don't care what you've signed! You can't get keys yet!"

Hold on, Murray. You're in England now. There are different rules.

After hasty phone calls by the shell-shocked custodian of keys to the property owners' lawyer in London, it was established that my furniture, when it arrived, may be deposited in the house – but strictly no occupation of the building could take place, as there was no 'Habitation Order'.

The next day, I spoke with the lawyer and apologised for the confusion. I tried to establish why the problem had occurred. "Well, Mr Murray," they explained, "what you signed was an 'exchange of contracts'. We haven't got 'completion' yet."

"Oh? How do we get that, then?"

"I need to be sure that monies have passed hands, that the property is surveyed to say it can be occupied, and that the selling agents are satisfied the sellers have received the sum due."

"I'm sorry. In Scotland we simply have an offer and acceptance – even verbally, that's binding, and the money is paid over. My apologies."

"We need to get our skates on if we want you living in the property!" they told me.

I recall the lawyer mentioned, a Mr Deas, as being the sales agent, and I asked for his telephone number. The name sounded Scottish, so I thought I could explain my ignorance.

The sales agent listened to my tale and suggested he would speak with the seller's lawyer and that, if it could be agreed, I should make an urgent trip to London and sign the completion papers. All was well, and next day I made a hurried visit to the legal offices in London.

"This is highly unusual, Mr Murray. We don't normally manage to deal with things as promptly as this."

"Very sorry about that," I said, pocketing the signed contract. I silently mused that I had somehow budged a London lawyer to move quicker than normal.

My furniture, having arrived at Number 8, Acacia Avenue, was now safely stored. Until my family arrived, I would continue to live at St John's Road.

CHAPTER 30

September to October 1968: "Knocked Out by a Boxer", or "Nearly Killed by My Plants"

"**W**HAT'S the charge for a deck chair please?" I asked the attendant with typical frugal instinct.

"Two and six, sir!" came the prompt reply.

"Thank you," I said as I passed over a half-crown. That was my initial enquiry some weeks previously. Now I knew the kindly park employee as 'Harold'. It was now September, and the autumn sun glinted on the silver instruments of the band joyfully playing in the bandstand situated in Jesus Green, Cambridge. My family were living with my in-laws in Scotland, and soon we would all be together under one roof in St Ives. My regular visits to Jesus Green – where I sat on a deck chair and read *The Sunday Times* while the band entertained – were nearly at an end.

There were many aspects of life and work in England which I began to enjoy, and sitting in a park in one of England's most historic cities was one that I treasure to this day. The ambience was so uplifting, and there was a timelessness about it which had me thinking about the heritage of the place. I can't explain it but, as I have remarked many times to friends and family, I have a deep feeling of rapport and 'belonging' with England.

Robbie, you're a true Scot, but there's something about England you enjoy.

One evening as I drove from the A1 to Cambridge, I did a detour to St Ives to check on the property at Acacia Avenue and stopped off at The Seven Wives hotel for a bite to eat. As I was making my exit towards the front door, I turned a corner in the hallway and collided with the tallest and biggest man I had ever seen.

"Oh, sorry!" I said, looking up at a blond Adonis of a man with sharp features, piercing eyes and wavy hair.

"My fault!" he immediately replied.

Immediately recognising the giant figure, I blurted out: "It's Mr Bugner, isn't it?"

"Sure, it's me," he confirmed in an unfamiliar accent.

I'd seen a picture of this promising Hungarian-born, heavyweight boxer in Mrs Pittam's local newspaper, along with an article about Joe digging ditches in the area to help keep himself fit for an upcoming fight.

"I'm from Scotland," I told him. "I just want to wish you all the best."

"Kind of you," he replied.

Over the years I have kept up a little knowledge about his progress: he was three times European Champion, and twice held the British and British Commonwealth titles. I

344

"My fault," said Joe Bugner.

read that he suffered a Technical Knockout (TKO) delivered by Frank Bruno and, after a comeback at the age of forty-eight years, defeated James 'Bonecrusher' Smith.

Weighing in at nearly sixteen stones, he was massive – and when I look back, he must have been only eighteen or nineteen years of age when we collided. Unfortunately, I have no bruises to show off or to boast about and say were caused by that most polite, pugilistic gentleman.

In preparation for the family arriving at the new home in the pleasant market town of St Ives with its wide main street, I decided to travel by train on a Friday afternoon to Broughty Ferry and then make the return journey to St Ives in my Morris Minor. I'd had no time to arrange a sale, so this was a useful way to get the car to St Ives while at the same time transporting some excess shrubs and plants from my own garden, and that of my father, to start up a ready-made garden at the new property. Unfortunately, a science lesson I had at Carnoustie school was completely forgotten, for – when I set off one Sunday afternoon – I experienced, by the early evening, somewhere near Scotch Corner, a feeling of great drowsiness. Finding it increasingly difficult to stay awake, I realised the problem – the vegetation was emitting carbon dioxide! Being a typical Scot, rather than abandoning my toxic cargo I decided to continue my journey with all windows down. Luckily, with some 300 miles still to go, it was a dry evening for the remainder of my drive.

* * *

My programme of visits was working well, and I became quite accustomed to mapping out my routes in advance. No GPS systems in those days and, with no navigator, I simply had to carefully jot down the route. The Cortina MK2 had no radio as standard, but I solved that problem by wedging a battery radio (a wedding gift from Peem) about the size of a brick between the rear window and the back seat. This was useful, especially on long drives – and even more so in traffic jams. I had to set the radio station, which of course I couldn't reach to alter or to adjust for atmospherics or signal. It was the only way of getting road reports and news. I remember listening endlessly to the radio disc jockey of the day, Jimmy Young, and his jaunty and humorous chit-chat. An oft-repeated message on radios in those days was the plea for "relatives of Mr or Mrs X to please get in touch with X police force or X hospital, where their son/daughter is critically ill". Those must have been the preferred quick and effective ways of getting in touch with relatives about serious illnesses in those days, but as the years wore on telephone communications have improved.

On a warm, sunny evening sometime in early September, my wife and Carys arrived at Luton Airport having flown on a commercial Autair flight – a recently-inaugurated service from RAF Leuchars, Fife. I was now based in St Ives, and began to enjoy the small-town environment and exploring the countryside at weekends. Cambridge was a favourite place, and a walk along 'the backs' was a special place of historical interest where Carys could safely pull along her little set of quacking wooden ducks.

A week or two later, the mystery word on John Simpson's six-month programme was revealed. "Bob, you'll see 'Debach' comes up a couple of times in next week's plan."

"Oh yes, I see that, John. Is that a debrief session?" I said – thinking, in my ignorance, that Debach was possibly a naval term.

"No, nothing like that," he replied. "It's a place name."

"Oh, Debach" I replied pronouncing the 'ch' as in a Scottish 'loch'.

"No, no, Bob – *Debach*." He pronounced the end of the word as 'atch', as in 'batch'.

"Oh, 'Debatch'! I see! Where is that, John?"

"It's where I live. It's in Woodbridge, Suffolk, near Ipswich. All TDOs are invited to my place for a policy review."

Aye, Murray, but remember – you're a Scotsman in a foreign land.

John gave me route instructions, and told me his property was named 'The Old Rectory'. He finished up, Navy style, with an ETA for dinner the evening prior to the first day. We were to spend two nights under his roof, for two days of discussions.

When I duly arrived at The Old Rectory, I found it was a substantial cream-coloured 'London-type' brick-built building within a large wooded acreage, and learned later it was a seven-bedroom property. John's wife had prepared an excellent supper for us, followed by a pleasant chat in his spacious lounge completely furnished with woodworm-riddled antiques. This was a shock to see but I soon accepted it as part of the quaint English charm. Chatting late into the evening, we then each enjoyed a separate bedroom furnished with even more 'wormed' furniture.

It was then I got the sense of John's world. A retired Naval Commander, now living in a majestic old rectory with the quiet orchard surroundings. For me it was again part of the English charm that I had come to appreciate. John lived in two worlds – his 'coombe ceiling' room in Doughty Street, and his delightful country retreat. All very English.

Looking back to that rectory meeting, I don't think there were any serious issues to address: it was a moment to assess how our courses were going, and what if any changes were required. Perhaps John simply enjoyed giving a Commander's briefing to his 'ship's crew'. Nowadays, this would be described as a 'bonding' session.

It was at this meeting when Jack took me quietly aside and asked me about my petrol claims. "Our treasurer George has questioned why you're claiming less petrol costs than the other TDOs. If he follows your calculations then we are all going to lose money. The others have asked me to have a word with you."

"Oh dear. What's the problem, Jack?"

"Well, how do you calculate your claim?" he enquired.

"I submit a note of all my miles travelled and fuel bills paid by me," I told him.

"Yes, but George says that means you are claiming fuel at the rate of around forty miles to the gallon."

"That's right. That's what I claim."

"But Bob, all TDOs have historically claimed *thirty* miles to the gallon. George isn't sure what to do."

"Sorry, Jack. My mistake. Okay, so I'll claim thirty miles to the gallon from now on."

It was a good example of George not wishing to cause a problem, and the team keeping me right. It helped to make me feel part of the team, though I felt bad about over-claiming in future. I remember it so well, because it was my first ever brush with a 'business fiddle'.

Murray, that's something you could never have told your students. But 'when in Rome'...

* * *

Meeting staff in the colleges I visited was of great interest, as I was able to relate to my Dundee experiences. What was sadly evident was that there seemed to be little support for Institute courses. These findings had to be included in my weekly taped messages to HQ. Changes in the retail grocery trade were now having an impact. As I drove away from each college, I could not remove the growing realisation that grocery product knowledge over the many earlier decades had been of immense importance to students but had now drained away. The changes such as I had seen in a mild form at Logie Street were having a marked impact. It was clear that there was now no need for retail staff to detect the different characteristics in tea, coffee, or indeed any product stocked. Fred Leitch had told me that a few years ago. Only an expert at head office would need to know the variations of quality. The Institute had already read the signs, and was reflecting the changes by introducing in-store training concepts. As I drove around, my thoughts often returned to Dundee Commercial College. What were the numbers in retail classes now, was Mr Leitch's coffee roasting machine still sitting in that former classroom of mine, and were the mischievous mice still enjoying the sawdust? Sadly, those images now conjured up the sense of the decadence of Institute courses.

A week after we moved into the house in St. Ives, I received a piece of news which temporarily stunned me. John telephoned me to say, "Bob, I just want to let you know before you read about it in the trade press. Norma has resigned her post in Scotland. She is about to join the Distributive Industry Training Board (DITB). Do you want to be considered for the Scottish territory?"

This piece of news shook me initially, as I quickly recollected all my efforts to leave Dundee and find a home in St Ives could have been avoided, and I could have continued with DMS in Dundee. I wasn't upset or annoyed. My reaction was that, had I not been so wrapped up in my 'A' levels and Geography I would have – or, perhaps, should have – been more alert to what was going on in the outside world, in which case I may have been in closer touch with Norma. The most telling reaction however was my reply to John.

"That's kind of you, John, but I'm finding the DMS course in Ipswich helpful – and my exposure to the world 'down here' is exciting and expanding my knowledge hugely. I wouldn't want to have missed it." It was true; I was getting involved in training in the trade at the highest level, and my 'love affair' with England was growing.

Norma phoned me a few days later to apologise. "Not a problem, Norma," I told her. "In fact, I'm quite enjoying myself down here."

CHAPTER 31

October to December 1968: "Peebles: Running My First Course", or "A Rabbit or a Hare?"

IN October I travelled to Peebles in the Scottish Borders to run the Institute's one-week Instructional Techniques course. Course attendees came from large and small grocery companies; it was obvious the Training Board's levy had owners of businesses thinking about training. The prerequisite for companies was to appoint someone in the business to identify the needs and set up appropriate training. Being self-sufficient in developing staff was the new approach: in-house training would be key. More courses were planned, and there was a feeling within the Institute that we were providing a useful training start-up point for companies.

Coincidentally, my sister Isobel was to be married in Carnoustie while I was in Peebles. It was a three hour drive away, and would be a glorious opportunity to stop over for two or three evenings. Sitting in Newton Panbride Church, our family church when we lived at Westhaven, my thoughts went back to the day 'Baby Jean' was christened in that same place. It had come as a massive shock to me when, aged thirteen, I fully realised mum was pregnant with Jean back in 1953. Looking at her now as a bridesmaid to Isobel, I marvelled at how well she looked as a teenager of fifteen years of age. Isobel, too – the young prize-winning dancer, who could only practice when our downstairs neighbours were out – was now aged twenty-four and looked radiant as a young lady. Where had all those years gone? My grocery world had demanded long hours followed by my teaching experiences, which forced studying upon me. Now I was based in England, and my sadness was that I had missed so much of sharing family time in Carnoustie.

With such a busy schedule, I had decided to get a haircut in the town before the afternoon service. "Why don't you go to Ian McDougall's salon?" mum suggested.

"What, young Ian?" I was surprised to hear this. "Has he got his own business now?"

"Yes, he does. He runs a newspaper shop as well."

I dashed along Carnoustie High Street. Looking through his window, I could see three men sitting in a queue and decided to have some fun with Ian, who I had last seen as an apprentice in Dundee in 1963. I put my head around his door and pretended I was a stranger in town... which really was almost the case. With an accentuated Scottish accent, I popped my head around the door of his salon. "Excuse me, barber. I don't know if I have come to the right place, but can you help me? I seem to have developed a bald patch on my crown," I said as I turned my head to demonstrate. "Do you think you could cover that up?"

To his great credit, Ian looked up, recognised me, and immediately played my game with the bemused audience of three men reading newspapers.

"Oh yes, I certainly can. I'll draw a rabbit on the bald area."

"Gee, what will that do?"

"From a distance, it might look like a hare."

Everybody had a laugh and, when it was my turn in the chair, we chatted about his old days as an apprentice in Dundee. "So, you did what you planned, Ian. Are you enjoying it?"

"Best thing I ever did. Now hold your head still!"

"You said that the first time you cut my hair," I observed.

"Yes, that was the first thing I learned – and I notice I still have to tell you!"

That haircut was an added bonus during my trip home to Carnoustie, and he impressively charged me two shillings. He would probably need it to help make up for the three customers he had now lost! I was loving life in England, but it was wonderful to be back in Carnoustie.

Ah yes, Robbie – happy days. You were always too nervous to enjoy yourself, but you're improving.

After the wedding reception, Peem drove me along to Westhaven. We sat and reminisced about our gloriously happy days of fishing off the rocks, catching crabs and lobsters, and playing games on the grassy area we called the 'ballaster'. How often had we done that over the years?

"The fishing boats are out of the water for the winter now," Peem noted.

"Remember how we used to smoke Woodbine cigarettes underneath the upturned boats? Oh, yes – five Woodbine for eight-pence, and we took matches out of the box so mum wouldn't hear them rattle!" I reminisced.

"Remember one day, Jim – our leader – rowed us, and Coffie and Ollie, out in a boat, and we all screamed when porpoises or dolphins dived all around us?"

"Ollie thought they were sharks!" I said with a laugh.

Taking this unusual time, I wanted to chat with Peem and asked him how he was getting on in his art world. "Seems a long time ago since we last spoke, but how are things for you in DC Thomson now?"

"Well, it's a lot different from when I started."

"Oh, in what way?"

"The artwork done in Dundee has gradually been cut down and passed to places with less expensive labour costs, in countries like Spain and the Far East, and is now almost totally gone."

"So what are you doing now?"

"I've been moved to a new building on the Kingsway, where I'm a page planner for weekly newspapers like the *Weekly News* and magazines."

"Do you enjoy that?" I asked with genuine curiosity.

"It's a responsible job with no two days the same, so yes. But I miss the real artwork."

We chatted for some time, and remembered the times when we both helped each other out when we had worries and had to make big decisions.

Driving back to England, I felt so pleased that we had that valuable time together to think back on our earlier days. Peem's final parting shot was so appropriate: "Well, Robbie, it was uncle Alan who gave us our first valuable advice – look for progress, he said."

* * *

A beautifully handwritten letter arrived in my Acacia Avenue letter box sometime in October. It was addressed to me and, when I opened it, the contents took my breath away.

Robbie Murray, you have a message from a previous Planet.

It was from May Cameron, a teacher of English at Dundee Commercial College. She wrote on behalf of all my former colleagues to say how much they missed having me around, and wished me well in my new job. In all my years in the college I was never asked to subscribe to a collection for a departing colleague, and I found this staggering. Enclosed was a cheque which, I think from memory, was for twenty pounds – inviting me to buy something to remind myself of my days in Commercial College. It was a genuinely warm letter, and I was hugely touched by the gesture. Looking back at the day when the end of session meeting was held in St Joseph's school at the end of June, I sat there knowing I would not return after the summer break. There was no farewell and no announcement by Mr Newlands – and, in truth, I think I was probably grateful to go quietly without any fuss. Technically I hadn't received my formal appointment, and so had not written my resignation. But this letter gave me a huge boost – and to think that I had constantly made a point of there being no team feeling amongst the staff! I had been wrong all those years. I purchased a desirable looking table-lamp and shade, and still have the base to this day to remind me of my intense learning curve at Dundee Commercial College.

Now, Murray – take that as a lesson. Don't make these assumptions in future.

Only recently, during the Covid-19 coronavirus pandemic lockdown, I took the opportunity to tidy up my attic and came across a long-forgotten letter from Mr Newlands. I had, it seemed, replied to Mrs Cameron thanking her for the gift and bringing her up-to-date with my work. In his letter, he thanked me for my contribution to the work of the college and wished me every success in my new career. Another moment of regret; Mr Newlands, a busy man in days of college growth, may not have been greatly visible at Tay Street, but now I realise he was a caring manager after all. Able to reflect, I look back and see how that gentle, undemonstrative man conducted himself so professionally in a milestone period in Dundee's educational history.

The feeling of belonging to the long-standing Grocers' Institute with its proud history was amplified when it hosted an awards dinner and ceremony in November at the prestigious London Hilton Hotel. Every owner and chief executive of a 'big name' in grocery retailing in the UK was represented. We TDOs were involved in trying to recognise top names arriving and greeting each one. In fact, every Institute staff member was present that evening, and Pauline was able to see the fruits of her typing and posting dozens of invitational letters. The evening was a measure of the organisation's influence within the trade as a meeting place in Doughty Street for chief executives, managing directors, buyers, marketing people, and now trainers. Approximately two hundred people attended, and each TDO was assigned to a separate table. To say I was out of my depth seemed an understatement, but it was an event where I learned a great deal simply by hearing the chat. Sitting next to Tony D'Angelo, the well-known editor of *The Grocer* magazine, was a highlight for me.

Visits around my patch continued, and once I had built up some experience in the 'know-how' and jargon I visited the high-profile Fine Fare multiple organisation at Welwyn Garden City to ascertain their training progress. I spoke with the Director of Training, and was given an opportunity to speak with members of the training department. What emerged was that an entire team of 'writers' were busily engaged producing job descriptions, personnel specifications and training plans for every job title and function in the business. Each element of training administration meant that levy was not charged. For an organisation of their size, the cost saving would be substantial, and the policy was to create the paperwork. When I reported this observation to HQ, John Simpson replied with the obvious comment: "Writing plans on pieces of paper is fine, but what is happening on the ground?" This, I learned later, was an example of one of the pitfalls of the Training Board's approach.

This was an important point, as writing theory was seen – by some, at least – as simply a means of doing a clerical job. Nevertheless, I had the feeling that with such a progressive retailer, once the paperwork was complete action would follow. When an offer was made for me to join their training department, I was justifiably impressed – but with a lengthy drive each day from St Ives and a salary less than I enjoyed, I found myself put off.

Robbie, don't rush – other opportunities will come. False alarm, space suit not required.

With so many absences from home and considerable driving around my 'patch', we decided to return to Scotland for a Christmas and New Year and joined the exodus of exiled Scots heading back home for the holidays. With Carys's presents from Santa surreptitiously placed in the St Ives lounge, to be discovered on return to prove that Santa had answered her letter, we set off.

No festive season was going to be complete without a stay with both families. With Carys now approaching her third birthday, it was an important visit to find out what Santa Claus had also delivered in Scotland. Despite the amount of driving, it was a restful break. In addition to visiting families, I thought I could catch up with my friends, but it was no surprise to discover that – for various reasons – I was unable to meet up with Bill, Alan, Jock or Jim. Yet again, another example of how in those days communications were seriously limited. One easier aspect was that I was now quite well accustomed to the drives north and south, mainly using the A1 and A68. My routine was to leave St Ives at around 4pm. This allowed Carys, while we travelled, to change into pyjamas at her normal bedtime around 7 o'clock and sleep for the entire journey and then be carried, still fast asleep, into her gran's house at usually 1am. Not only did the driving time become quite habitual, but I became well-acquainted with the route. Both Tay and Forth Bridges had been recently built, but there remained the frustratingly slow movement of negotiating through the city centre streets of Edinburgh – development of the city bypass was still a long way off.

While visiting my family in Carnoustie, I had a stroll along the High Street and met Norrie – an old school pal I hadn't seen since I'd moved to work in Dundee in 1959. "Goodness me, Norrie!" I exclaimed. "How are you?"

"All well; keeping busy," he replied.

He didn't seem to want to say much about his work, and I didn't pursue it. I also played down my own recent job changes.

"Are you doing anything special for New Year, Norrie?" I asked him.

"Naw," was the response.

"Will you be going along to the Cross?"

"Naw, it's no' the same now. There's no big crowds going to the Cross these days." Norrie was referring to our schoolboy days, when we were silly enough to go first footing.

"What, no dressed herrings and lumps of coal?"

"Naw," he confirmed. As we chatted, I began to be aware of how foreign these Scottish customs were to me. It saddened me to think they were diminishing.

* * *

When I sat down that evening, I found my chat with Norrie had sparked off many reminiscences of days long gone when I had my first New Year outing with my pals. I was an apprentice at the time. Suddenly everything came back to me in great detail...

Rita McBeth's bagpipes skirled into action to signal the magic moment and, amid her rendering of 'The Rowan Tree', a loud cheer erupted. Immediately, everybody who'd gathered at Carnoustie's Cross was animatedly handshaking and wishing each other a Happy New Year. The well-wishing crowd then dispersed in all directions, diminishing like the proverbial 'snaw aff a dyke'. They, like my friends and I, had probably set off on pre-determined routes to 'first foot' their friends and relatives.

With a walk across the golf course ahead of me I was able to think back to the moments immediately prior to this: my introductory, daring 'first footing' experience. It must have been almost fifteen minutes to midnight, and a large crowd of around a hundred hardy, well-clad merrymakers had congregated at the more elevated and sheltered viewpoint on Queen Street. Meeting my friends at Willie Clark's cycle shop doorway (our agreed meeting spot), I immediately felt it was the ideal place out of the cold wind. Before long, as the crowd swelled, I recall we had busied ourselves as we compared our respective collections of herring.

After minor disagreements about how many pieces of coal we each needed to carry, I remember the banter. "Oh, Robbie, your wee fish is dressed in pretty red crepe paper!" Willie scoffed. "My wee herring's dressed in tartan!" he added by way of a boast.

"Listen, you two," Richard chimed in, "my wee fishy's got nae claes on, 'cos the wind blew them aff on the way here!"

"Why herring, anyway?" piped up Timothy, Richard's cousin from Coventry. He'd been sent north from England to Carnoustie while his mum was ill.

"So, you'll aye hae guid fishing harvests!" replied Willie.

"What?" queried Timothy, genuinely bemused.

"This is a fishing part o' the world, Tim," he explained. "It's an old tradition tae wish your fishing friends good catches. If you didn't have good harvests, you'd starve."

"I dinna ken any fishers. We should hae brocht tobacco plants so we'll aye hae plenty fags!" chirped up the shivering, scarfless Norrie as he lit up another ciggy from his posh Christmas box of du Maurier cigarettes.

Timothy's face looked blank. "And the coal? Why the coal?" he wondered, warming to the mysteries of Carnoustie.

"So, you can say 'lang may yer lum reek wi ither fowk's coal'," answered Willie.

"Say that again?" Tim's English voice raised.

"If you run out of coal, you may always get some from your friends to keep you warm in your house," his cousin explained.

"My mum said we need a' the coal we hae," stated Norrie, emitting the words as he exhaled into the cold night air.

"Gee, you guys have got some weird customs," Timothy said with a degree of admiration.

"You must hae something like that in Coventry, dae ye no'?" questioned Norrie.

"No, just Christmas," replied Timothy with some dejection. "We do have coal, but we don't see much fish."

"Never mind, Timmy. You'll get used to our customs the nicht," Willie assured him.

As I trudged along the uneven ground with my head turned against the wind, I reflected on this comparison with an earlier time when dad, after begging him for weeks, had taken me and my brother Peem to see what went on at The Cross at midnight. Now I was free and beginning to sense the thrill.

As we approached a desolate cottage with its welcoming lights, Norrie called out an instruction. "Mind now, Willie; you have black hair, so you go in the doors first," he advised with surprising knowledge.

"And wi' your red hair, Robbie, you're aye last!" was the chorus which followed.

"Gee, what next? Don't tell me; what's that custom all about?" voiced Timothy.

"I'll tell ye why," Norrie called out, full of his previously-unknown New Year protocol.

"Aye, we a' ken – it was aboot the Vikings!" groaned Willie.

"Well, you'll have to tell Tim."

"You see, Timmy, the Vikings sailed around Scotland and raided towns and villages on the coast. They had red hair, and they killed the men and bairns and took away the women."

"What were Vikings?" asked Timothy

"They came from Norway."

"When did all this happen?" he asked, puzzled.

"Oh, two or three centuries ago."

"Dinna be daft, Norrie! It was in the 10th or 11th Centuries!" Willie corrected him. "So it's bad luck tae allow anybody wi' red hair tae enter a hoose and be your first foot."

"And that's why Robbie's got to be last?"

"Aye, you see, fowk wi' red hair must have come from a Viking – and that's bad luck."

This first port of call was to a pal of Willie's, and I remember the huge fire in the over-burdened grate, the warmth of the cottage, and a table groaning with the spread of festive fayre fit to feed the entire crowd we'd just left at the Cross. Then the custom of drinking a wee dram out of each other's bottle commenced. Timothy, of course, wanted to know what a dram was, and his cousin had to explain.

And so it went on. We were off to friends of Richard at Barry, then another two houses, more carved ham and black bun at every stopping point – from freezing winds into unknown, over-heated homes, meeting of course more unknown faces but nevertheless wishing each of the unknowns all the best and exchanging an unknown number of wee drams.

At one point we all had to wait for Norrie to dry off his left foot, which he had soaked when he misjudged a jump over the Barry Burn. Amid mocking cheers of everybody telling him the year was not yet two hours old and he had already not put his best 'first foot' forward, we finally were on our way.

A walk back to Carnoustie with more visits and meeting robust revellers was still to come. That's when the singing started, as we all walked in a line across the road with arms linked and Timothy – now thoroughly enjoying himself – locked in the centre and trying to join in on the words of 'We're No Awa' Tae Bide Awa''. Then on to Muirdrum where, at long last, I met people I knew and proudly passed over my well-travelled herring – which, after successive freezings and warmings, must have been as relieved as I was to finally reach the home of its new owner. *A poor-looking symbol of hope for good fishing harvests*, I remember thinking as I passed it over to the host – a man I thought had probably never even paddled in the harbour at Westhaven, far less being a fisherman. Frying, I'm certain, would have come as some relief later in the morning to the unlucky symbolic creature.

It was the early hours now, and no sign of dawn creeping. As I sat on a floor with my back to a marble-top cupboard, I looked at the seemingly pointless Christmas decorations and baubles of the festive scene and dozed off while quietly beginning to feel repulsed by the entire adventure. I looked across the room and saw Timothy, fast asleep and wearing a tartan scarf which had appeared from somewhere.

As we walked to Carnoustie, the first streaks of dim light appeared over the North Sea – but, of course, there were more merry-makers heading in the opposite direction: another moment to provide liquid hospitality from my now-meagre supply. By now, Norrie was almost unable to walk and was supported by Willie, while Timothy – who kept repeating "Have a wee dram!" – was aided by Richard and myself.

The moment came when I arrived home, then tried to tip-toe my way to my bedroom. I imagined no-one in the house heard me stumble to my room and flop on to my bed. In a haze, I vaguely saw my brother fast asleep. But why was he wearing my football rosette? I was trying to make sense of that question when next I heard mum saying, "Come on, Robert! It's nearly one o'clock – time to get up. The game starts at two."

I recall mum's plea as if it was yesterday. I had my rosette and a new home-made red and white mascot ready. (Well, it was maroon and white actually, but only because I couldn't find red wool in mum's sewing bag.) So with my new display of support, I was ready for the big New Year's Day football match... but I felt ill. Perhaps I had eaten something disagreeable. Or could it be the onset of flu?

I pulled the covers over my head and lamented on how robbed I was to miss out on Carnoustie Panmure's top table tussle against fellow Juniors – Dundee's Lochee Harp – which I had looked forward to with great excitement. How had my intentions all gone so badly wrong? Did my brother know I wouldn't need my rosette? What was he trying to tell me?

My senses feebly flickered into action as I struggled to piece together the story of the previous evening's events. I remember the shop remained open until the last shopper had left the street. My boss told me he had discretion to remain open for as long as he liked to maximise sales. Eventually, somewhere around 8pm, he thankfully decided it was time for me as an apprentice to tidy up and get home – "Go, go, greasy grocer, go!" he had chanted with a broad grin. He probably had his own plans for the evening. It had been an exhausting and hectic day, and I couldn't wait to get home. Mum's meticulous preparations would be well underway.

As I cycled along the High Street, I remember I kept my head down against the blustery wind whipping up dustings of snow around me. Nevertheless, I could see some shop blinds being lowered and displays being removed from doorways. My boss's timing was right.

As soon as I opened the front door I knew mum had been busy, for I was enveloped in the sweet, mouth-watering aroma of family favourites being baked – mince pies, shortbread, and my beloved melting moments. Of course, the beef cubes were cooking too, and she was vigorously rolling out the pastry for next day's steak pie. As always on such an evening, the stoked-up fire was glowing and the living room was looking spick-and-span. I'd also noticed the front doorstep had been scrubbed clean. "Watch you don't sit on my knitting needles!" she said, pointing to her ball of wool and needles left temporarily on dad's rocking chair.

"Why are they there, mum?" I asked.

"Because I had to take my knitting off the pins so that I can start knitting Isobel's scarf again in the new year." Mum was looking different too. What was it? Ah, yes – she'd had her hair done up in curls. It was all part of her special routine.

The clock had raced away its remaining hours of 1956, and I thought back to the moment when I enjoyed a bowl of mum's next day's Scotch broth. I recall after, a wash and spruce up, I was armed with my dressed herring, a brown paper bag of small pieces of coal, and a bottle of Odds On cocktail. Wrapped up in a thick coat and scarf against a cold east wind, I set off to the town centre.

Now, in the darkness under my bed clothes, I struggled to conjure up a reason why anyone would have wanted to go out on such a cold, windy night – and especially why I had chosen that bottle of refreshment. Why that one? Oh yes, it was my pal Jock's boss who had said it was a good bargain, and that it would meet my mum's strict rule not to be silly and buy anything strong. The description I gave to mum was that it was a half-bottle of Odds On *cordial* – somehow the word 'cocktail' must have become confused.

As I massaged my numbed skull, I had already conceded I'd been duped by my pal's boss. I had to blame someone! But now, lying in my bed and feeling ill, I began to have repulsive feelings about the whole first footing experience.

"Are you going to the football match or not, Robert?" Mum urged. "James wants to know if he can wear your rosette."

This was the final realisation that I would not be cheering on my team against Lochee Harp. "Alright, he can," I groaned in total despair.

"What's wrong with you?" Mum asked, starting to get angry.

"I don't know. I think I'm getting the flu!" I said, feeling close to playing my own harp as I pulled a blanket over my head and muttered, "Never again!"

That was an emotional, if not harsh, memory of a long-ago Hogmanay. My new life in St Ives now seemed to be on a different planet – Planet England.

CHAPTER 32

January to August 1969: "Jock Found in Deepest Norfolk", or "The Bardolph Mystery"

IN January I was again engaged in running the one-week Instructional Techniques course. This time it was in South London. My DMS course was proving valuable, and I requested permission during the week to attend Ipswich College for the usual Wednesday afternoon and evening class. Looking back, it was an extremely ambitious plan, but once more – with eternal gratitude to the Institute – I was given time off and expenses. Wednesday was scheduled to be Mike's teaching day, so I was free.

Leaving the Richmond Hill Hotel, Richmond-on-Thames, at around 6am, I drove to the nearest tube station. I then took two trains to the British Rail terminal – at Liverpool Street, I think – where I boarded a train for Ipswich. To this day, I recall the main lesson for me that day was an important one on Work Study: a crucial one I would not have wanted to miss.

Having checked the return train from Ipswich, I retraced my steps to the tube station for my journey back to my starting point. I remember running on to the platform and – around midnight, with seconds to spare – jumping onto the carriage. On the journey I was told by the guard that I was on the last tube train to my destination. Looking back, I was a fraction away from sleeping all night on an underground railway station platform!

My coverage of my territory developed, and I planned to visit Norwich College. While in that area, I remembered that my old rival message boy – Jock – had moved to work in the East Anglia area. On my way home through some flat countryside, I stopped and looked up Jock's name in the directory inside the red telephone box. Amazingly, there it was! I decided to call, and pressed button 'A' when I heard an 'English' voice. "James Street Greengrocers," came the greeting.

"Hello, this is Scotland Yard," I said jokingly. "We are trying to trace stolen cabbages, and believe you may be able to help us with enquiries."

"What?" came the puzzled response. "Who's that?"

"Detective Inspector Murray here."

"I thought I recognised that voice! How are you? *Where* are you?"

"I'm fine, Jock. How are you?" I asked. "I'm in a call box in the wilds of Norfolk."

"Yes, Robbie; I've made a few changes."

"Are you running a greengrocery now?"

"That's right. Last time we spoke, I was Production Supervisor with Armour Star Group. But I joined Derby

Brothers in Norfolk in 1963 as Production Manager. Then, in 1966, I started up my own mobile greengrocers van."

"But you're in a shop now?" I asked him.

"Yes, Robbie. You know me – always looking to make my fortune."

"I remember in the old days listening to you charming the ladies in your Bradburn's grocery shop van," I recalled wistfully.

"You were only jealous!" he laughed. "How are you, Robbie?"

"Since we last spoke, I've been teaching in Dundee – retail distribution subjects alongside Fred Leitch!"

"Never!"

"Yes, but grocery classes hardly exist now."

"So, what brings you to this part of the world?"

I gave Jock a run-down on my last few months work in the Grocers' Institute. "If you can't beat them, join 'em," was Jock's cheery reply.

We were too far away from each other to meet up, but we exchanged news and decided to meet up sometime. "It's after 6pm now. We must get together when you are in the area again."

"Sure thing," I agreed.

* * *

My Scottish working background caused both a ripple of amusement and disbelief in the Institute offices when, one week, I sent in – by tape – my planned programme of visits for the ensuing week. I received an anxious phone call to ask me to alter my plan and inform the client. I can't recall who the contact was, but I had – without realising my mistake –

made an appointment to meet up the next Friday. "You can't visit them next Friday!" was the urgent message.

"Why not?"

"That's Good Friday!"

Good Friday had, in my grocery experience, been a normal busy day. But it was still held rigidly as an important religious holiday in England. Nobody at the Institute joked "heathens", but they could have.

During my Institute days I'd had a few nervous adventures, but in the early spring of 1969 I had one which even today I still talk about. John Simpson had received a request from a successful small, family-run multiple grocery retailer based in Grimsby (which may have been called Hall's or Hill's). John, I think, had the scent of possibly running an in-company course – and, more probably, having one or two senior managers attend one (or both) of our one-week all-comers courses. He asked me to join him in Grimsby on a Thursday morning in the company's headquarters at 9am. With the DMS revision sessions coming up, I knew I must not miss a Wednesday by travelling to Grimsby. Rather optimistically, I decided to attend my usual Wednesday afternoon and evening session which finished at 9pm.

Checking and mapping out a route from Ipswich to Grimsby, I gauged a journey of around four hours which would get me into the hotel by about 1am. It transpired to be an unusually wild night, with strong wind and lashing rain, but I set out full of certainty. My route was to take me on the main roads through Fenland towns – Needham Market, on to Thetford and beyond Downham Market. It was around four miles beyond Downham when, with the wind howling and the rain pelting my windscreen, I found it almost impossible to keep the car under control. Then I saw a road sign in my headlights. The shock of seeing the name of the village had my mind reeling, and – on instinct – I braked hard to avoid going off the road. Why this reaction? What was the name?

It was "BARDOLPH".

Instantly, the next word which came to mind was "SWARTHY". Yes, the very word I'd used to describe Fergie's looks. Why? What was the connection?

My mind was in turmoil, and I sat there motionless in shock with the car engine racing. Everything seemed out of control. Eventually, I parked the car sensibly and tried to make sense of the situation. I could recall using the word 'swarthy' when, on my first day at Commercial College, I described John Ferguson's looks to Gail. She reminded me, then, that we had played the Ouija Board game one evening with friends in 1959, and that the board told me 'beware swarthy'. That evening I told her I didn't believe in such nonsense I put it out of my mind. But now, here was another link with that evening – Bardolph!

My secret question to the 'spirit of the glass' had been, "What will I be doing in five years and ten years' time?" Doing a quick calculation, the 'Swarthy' connection had first materialised in 1963 – only four years later. But this was 1969, exactly ten years later as predicted by the glass. As clear as day, I could recall the way the 'spirit of the glass' had swirled around the table and spelled out B-E-W-A-R-E S-W-A-R-T-H-Y and then, after a pause, burst into action spelling out B-A-R-D-O-L-P-H. The exact village name now facing me at the roadside. Swarthy, although I had earlier dismissed it, had proved accurate... and now Bardolph. What dangers lay ahead for me with such difficult driving conditions? Long grasses waving across the roadside in front of me, canals alongside many parts of the road, and fen ditches around every bend.

Seeing the village name had literally paralysed me with fear, and I was convinced something dreadful lay ahead of me.

Eventually driving many miles at a snail's pace, I found myself out of the Fenlands and onto better roads. Now I could think clearer. John 'Fergie', with his dark-complexioned skin and Latin looks, had clumsily thrown books at me on my first day at college and had left me with a strange uncertainty about him. But why 'beware'? Well, I'll never know. But what were the forces that predicted John after five years and Bardolph ten years later? What mysterious power predicted both events? What were the odds of me ever being in the middle of the Fenlands on such a journey, conjured up almost at the last minute to accommodate a college class?

Reaching my hotel at 3am and breathing a sigh of relief that the hotel porter was awake, I managed to join John's meeting at 9am. I may have looked white and shaken, but I never told him the story. Phew!

* * *

With visits to Macfisheries and London Co-op, I had visited nearly all major grocery organisations within my area. Regular trips to Doughty Street had been logged and, after several training courses were conducted, I felt I had achieved something. The problem was that there was no way of measuring the success or otherwise of my efforts.

The DMS exams were held in May and, much to my relief, I had passed all parts. My admiration went out to the college team under the leadership of Colin Dewsbury. From the first day I travelled to Civic College in Ipswich back in September, I had an immediate connection with the "Scottishness" of the people, the attitudes and the countryside of that part of England. As I have said earlier, I had an inexplicable affinity with England, but in Suffolk and Norfolk I felt the connection to be stronger. Was it simply the coastline and the agricultural hinterland which gave it that feel?

Third year DMS would start in September, and I couldn't wait to get back to Ipswich. If truth be told, and all things going well, I began to seriously consider a teaching job in Civic College if a suitable post and salary came along. It really had a dynamism about it.

Months passed and it was summer, with a chance to further explore England. John had obtained approval from Sam to send all TDOs on a Training Officer course. The thinking, I imagined, was to give all of us the opportunity of running our own complete training courses which would include both instruction and administration.

The course was to be run as a residential one near Ipswich, and the instructor was to be a qualified trainer employed by Civic College. Another TDO, David – who had attended one of our courses – had been engaged by John to fill the vacant West region, and also attended along with others from around the country. The course was to be run in September.

Robbie, how lucky can you get? The Institute is preparing TDOs for jobs in the industry.

* * *

Yet again, luck – my constant companion – was with me. From the day my pal Jim found me a job as a message boy, which led me to my grocery apprenticeship; the luck of my boss Mr Munro, who looked after my early 'manager' life; the relative who spotted the college job; and then the magazine on the desk in the staffroom where I accidentally found myself a 50% salary increase. Even more, the chance to experience life at the top of the grocery training world. But now, an even bigger piece of luck...

The TDOs had a routine meeting in the Doughty Street offices. It was nothing particularly special, but at lunch time we routinely went to the Red Lion for a 'half a pint o' bitta' and a rare beef sandwich. Someone suggested going to The Globe, as the Red Lion would be too busy, but one or two said "Let's stick with the Lion". While standing at the bar with my half pint jug of 'bitta' (despite my 'mouse dirt' shock many years before, I had a half pint occasionally – 'when in Rome'), I heard, above the general hubbub, a voice behind me saying, "I hear Watson and Philip in Dundee are looking for a training officer." I didn't look behind me, but I guessed the voice was from someone – perhaps a sales or marketing director – who had been at the Institute offices that day. It was not the time for me to relate my interest to colleagues, but that evening – from home – I phoned my friend Alastair McDonald, a former student of mine and now a Watson and Philip sales manager who had helped me with my Institute recruitment booklet. Wasn't it so amazing that I happened to be in the Red Lion and not The Globe, as had been suggested?

Robbie Murray, how on earth do you do it? Time to check your space suit again.

"Hello, Alastair," I said by way of greeting. "How are you?"

"I am well thanks, Bob," he replied. "How is life down south?"

"It's great, Alastair. But a little tinge of homesickness for the family."

"It's funny you phoned," Alastair said, "because the boss is looking for a training officer."

This was the confirmation I needed. "Really?" I enquired. "I had heard a whisper, but wasn't sure if it was true." I wasn't telling a lie.

"Yes, would you like me to mention you to him?"

"Well yes, but I am not in a position to move at present."

A few days later, an application form arrived in my mail. It was from Harry Gardner, Director of the Delivered Grocery Division, Watson & Philip Ltd., Dundee. The covering letter briefly stated, "Dear Robert, If you are interested in coming back to Dundee please give me a call to discuss a date when you can come up to the city for a chat." After all my work in England promoting training inside companies, here was a sizeable wholesale grocery company on my home doorstep seeking a training officer.

Was it too good to be true?

CHAPTER 33

September to November 1969: "A 'Feel Good' Fit", or "Back to Reality"

FIRST thing I did the next morning was phone my boss. "Hello John," I said, "I just wanted to let you know that I've been invited to meet with a Mr Gardner at Watson and Philip's offices in Dundee."

"Well, you must go, Bob," he replied. This was typical of John's encouragement.

Once more on a train bound for Carnoustie! It was a daytime journey in September, and my plan – thanks to mum and dad – was to stay overnight in Carnoustie and travel to Dundee to meet Mr Gardner the next day.

It was a warm Autumn day in Dundee, and at 2pm I walked into the head office in Blackness Road and reported my arrival to a cheery receptionist located in a cramped space that she shared with an old-fashioned reception telephone exchange. An ancient-looking system, seemingly strangled by its own numerous wires and plugs.

"I'll let Mr Gardner know you are here," she told me.

"Thank you."

As advised, I sat on a chair on the first floor landing. On previous interviews I had always been nervous and uncertain, but for some reason I had no nerves that day. Perhaps it was because I felt confident about my qualifications, or maybe something to do with my recent work where I had been visiting so many senior figures in the trade. But my dramatic club days always reminded me never to be too confident.

You may not feel nervous, Murray, but don't get too cocky either. This may feel easy, but it could be your most important interview so far – so watch how you go!

After only a few minutes I was met by a secretary who, in an English accent, invited me to follow her to Mr Gardner's office; a spacious room with traditional wood panelling walls up to dado height and what looked like original leaded glass windows. "Hi, how do you do?" said the tall, slim gentleman in a smart, dark green, silky-looking suit. His face was sharp-featured with a golden tan, and his big eyes glowed. I took him to be around forty years old.

"Hello, pleased to meet you," I replied. It immediately felt quite informal – nothing stuffy.

"How was your journey tae Bonny Dundee?" he grinned as he spoke with a pretend, accentuated Scottish voice above his slight Cockney sounding accent. He hung his jacket on a coat-stand near the door

"Very smooth," I grinned, acknowledging both his enquiry and his attempt at a humorous accent. "I travelled yesterday by rail, and stayed with my parents in Carnoustie last night."

"Nice place, Carrrrnooostie." (Again, his friendly take-off of Scots). "I've been here for less than a year, but we've had walks around Barry Buddon. Aye, the gulls were pretty fierce down there," he said as he took a tipped cigarette from a black box on his desk and inserted it into a holder, at the same time offering me a cigarette. I smiled and shook my head.

"Oh yes, that would probably be the terns – they can be very protective. You must have been near their nests."

"Aye," he agreed amiably. "So, Robert, what brings you here?"

This man had a charm and an eagerness. He was extremely courteous, and his lean, hungry look gave me a sense of his dynamic nature. Not a man to be meddled with – but I felt an immediate rapport.

Without too many interruptions, I gave him my background: grocery apprentice with Wm Low, branch manager, teacher, and latterly my Training Development work with the Grocers' Institute. I found myself telling him of the job options which John Simpson had outlined for TDOs, and how I felt it was time for me to get back into the real world of grocery.

Mr Gardner explained he was Director of the Delivered Grocery Division, and that there were other divisions – Cash and Carry, Import and Catering Supplies. The company had originated as a partnership in 1873, and had now been a public company for twelve months. The divisions were now managed as separate units, each overseen by a Director.

"What do you know about us, then?"

A favourite question in interviews, but – with no Internet in those days, and no time to find a copy of accounts – I was merely able to say that I had visited a grocery wholesaler in West London called Harvey, Bradfield and Toyer (HBT), which, like Watson and Philip (W&P), operated the VG franchise (in their case, around London) and also had a catering section. I was able to describe the general style of operation and to relate my meeting with John Paul, the HBT training and personnel manager, as well as to say that I had met Len Jackson, the Sales Director.

"Ah yes, I know them both well. We've got young Peter Philip doing his introduction into the trade down there right now." I'd visited HBT and found it also to be a vigorous business, and had been told someone from W&P was under training there.

"How many employees are employed in the division?" I asked him.

"About two hundred now, and – in the group at present – nearly four hundred. But we have plans to grow." Mr Gardner went on to explain that there was no formal training going on within the company, but he was convinced he needed help within his division. "What are your plans, Robert? I mean, what is your availability?"

"I have a programme of visits to make in my patch," I responded, "but I'm sure someone can take that over. There is one recently-arranged course which I have been asked to attend later this month."

"Oh? What's that?"

"It's a residential training officer's course run by Ipswich Civic College."

"Do you think it's important to attend that?"

"Very important. It would give me a necessary basis for working in training."

"You wouldn't want to miss it, eh?" he observed. "What does it entail?"

"The A to Z of training administration, instruction, and a 'training needs analysis' project within a company," I told him.

"Hmm. Have you got a company where you can do your project?"

"Not yet."

"How long would a project take?"

"About a month at least," I said thoughtfully. "Maybe more, I should think."

"How would you like to do your project here?" he suggested.

At first, I thought that the eager Mr Gardner was jumping on the bandwagon for a free analysis, but he then went on to ask how much notice I would have to give the Institute. When I told him one month, the quick-thinking Director came up with a suggestion. "How would it be if you do your course, give the Institute a month's notice during October, then do your project here during November? You could come on the payroll on the 1st of December."

So yes, he *does* get a free analysis, but he is committing to offer me a job as well. "That sounds like a good arrangement," I confirmed. "I would need to ask John Simpson if he would pay me up to the end of November, though. There's one other thing, Mr Gardner. I've completed the first two years of a three-year postgraduate Management Diploma course. I did the first year in Dundee, and the second in Ipswich. The Dundee classes are held on Wednesday afternoons and evenings. Would I be able to have a time off to attend year three here in Dundee?"

"You can have the evening off," he teased with a wide grin. Then, added after a timed pause, "Of course, the afternoon too, if you think it will be beneficial."

"I can assure you it will be helpful to me in my job," I declared.

"Good, Robert. Now I need to think about salary, but I can come back to you on that later."

"That's fine."

Time to check out that space suit again, Murray!

"Now, before you go, I'd like to bring in our Finance Director for a few minutes," Mr Gardner said as he pressed a switch on a telephone console. Speaking into the machine, he said, "Can you come down now Jim, please?"

I recalled the day six years previously when Mr Newlands had similarly pressed a switch to summon 'Fergie'. I felt far more relaxed than I had on that previous, nerve-wracking occasion.

Watch it, Robbie! Don't get too carried away. The finance man may hold sway.

The chat moved along at a fast pace, and it seemed like there was a pre-arranged plan for 'Jim' to meet me. Now Mr Gardner wanted him to cast his eye over me. Perhaps more questions?

"Jim, meet Robert; Robert, Mr Jim Hadden." The finance director looked as if he may be in his fifties, of small build and dressed in a grey striped suit. His serious face was tired looking, and he had very bushy black eyebrows. "How do you do, Mr Hadden?" I said by way of introduction.

We all remained standing, and Mr Gardner gave a two-minute report on our chat. "What salary are you on now, Robert?" Mr Hadden asked me.

"£1,950 p.a."

"Any bonuses?"

"No, but I have a car and telephone expenses."

"When do you travel back?"

"I'm going to jump on a train as soon as I leave here."

"Good, Robert. By the way, are you always called Robert? John Simpson refers to you as Bob."

"Yes, I'm a Bob," I nodded.

"Right, Bob. I'll drop you a note – and please let me know your travel expenses sometime." Shaking hands with both gentlemen, I thanked them for their time and said I'd look forward to hearing from Mr Gardner.

As I walked briskly down the sloping Blackness Road in the warm sunshine, I had a comfortable, confident feeling. I was quite sure there was a future for me in W&P, and already I had a project arranged even if I didn't join the company. But I was pretty sure I would, if the offer came.

I wondered, as I made my way to the station, why it all seemed to flow so smoothly. There was no word of any advertisement or shortlist of candidates. Then I realised Harry Gardner had said John Simpson referred to me as 'Bob'. Had he been doing some behind-the-scenes intelligence gathering? Had John and Harry Gardner already worked out a plan including the project work? Probably. Harry Gardner seemed like an energetic leader, and I felt comfortable with his brand of humour.

Time to check your space suit again, Bobby Boy!

* * *

My planned visits kept me busy, but exactly a week after my interview Mr Gardner's letter arrived offering me the position of Training Officer, Delivered Grocery Division on a salary of £2,200 p.a. plus participation in the division's profit bonus scheme. A Vauxhall Viva car would be available from the start of November, and telephone and business expenses would be paid on what he called grade two of his structure. A relocation package would apply. He asked me to confirm that I would work October within the Institute, spend November on a training needs analysis for his division, and would join his payroll on the 1st of December – provided that I passed my Training Officer examination. No pressure! He said he hoped I would enjoy my employment within his division, as I was joining it at an exciting stage in his plans for development. He understood that the training analysis was technically the property of the Institute since Sam Kilburn would finance it, but he hoped it would be kept confidential after I made my presentation of it as a case study to the TDO team.

Robbie, time now to confirm your space suit is ready!

My remaining programme of visits for October continued, and my final reports to John were submitted. I passed all my contact cards over to David, who I learned had been assigned the territory. During the week of the course, I had received a telephone call from Colin Dewsbury asking if I could take an evening class of National Retail Distribution Certificate (NRDC) students. Of course, I agreed immediately. It was such an unexpected and enjoyable way of helping, and one where I realised my Dundee experience would be useful. Colin had been a most supportive person during my entire employment with the Institute.

Now, Murray, you are teaching the NRDC syllabus; something you were told in Commercial College you may do only if you had higher qualifications.

A date in early December was agreed with John, when I would present my training analysis as a case study to the team. A requirement of the Training Officer's course was that I also had to present my analysis to the course instructor.

Farewell Planet Institute.

Yet again I took a train to Carnoustie, and would stay over with mum and dad during November. On the 1st of November I reported to Mr Gardner, and was directed by his secretary to an office near to his own. The office was bare but for a desk, a chair, one filing cabinet and an uncompleted Distributive Industry Training Board claim form with a note attached which read: "Trust we won't need to pay the levy." It was signed by a director of the Philip family. So that was the second objective! Then I thought: *no... perhaps the first?*

Welcome to Planet W&P. Be ready for a change of atmosphere!

"You've got the use of a spare car while you work here," I was told.

"Excellent. Thank you."

I had time to chat with Peem – something I had not enjoyed since Isobel's wedding. I didn't go to my thinking place at Westhaven; those days were long past, though they had helped me considerably all those years ago. "Gee, Peem; long time since we chatted," I joked. "How have things been going with you?"

"Great!" he replied. "I'm still getting a lot of interesting lino film and planning work to do. Do you think Watson and Philip will be a good move?"

"Absolutely. It's a public limited company, and the director of the delivered grocery division is a go-getter with progressive ideas."

"Do you think a Training Officer job will be difficult?" he asked me.

"I think initially it will be challenging. But my last boss, John, has always said that the obvious progression for a Training Officer is into personnel management. So we'll see."

"Was there a training person in the job before you?"

"No, I'm the first. I have to come up with a training plan, and I have to prevent the company from paying a training levy. If I do that, my remuneration package will cost the company nil and a credit bit left over."

"Will your new job be easier than the one in England?" Peem enquired interestedly.

"No, it will be a bigger job and I'll need to show results. But I won't have to drive the 45,000 miles I drove during the last fifteen months!"

"You didn't want to leave school. Do you think you feel any better now?"

"Yes, I do. The amazing thing is that Further Education has been a saviour. Without all my courses I would never have got to this job."

"Looking back, was teaching a good move?"

"Yes and no. I managed to gain some valuable education but, in hindsight, I don't think I did a good job there. While I was there we had excellent student results; in fact, some of our City and Guilds students won national prizes. But if I went back today, I would do a far better job."

"So, what's the best thing about this move?"

"I think it's simply the fact that everything I have ever done has, one way or another, been part of a long apprenticeship of fourteen years. Now I'm back in the real world."

Peem and I chatted for an hour or so. It was like old times, but I now felt a more confident person. "Thanks for listening over the years to all my problems Peem," I told him. "It's always been a great help."

"We both learned a lot from Uncle Alan that day when you were a nervous manager and I was worrying about not finding a job," he remembered. "I remember you told me about walking across that imaginary line when you left school."

"I think it was then that I made up my mind to work hard to try and achieve something. By the way, Peem, remind me: what is it that mum tells us she has – you know, those premonitions? She was the seventh child of a seventh child, wasn't she?"

"Oh, you mean the second sight?" he said.

"Yes. Well, I think either she has been influencing my life or I have some strange powers too."

My brother seemed curious. "What do you mean?"

I reminded Peem about each piece of amazing luck I had experienced along the way, and about the inexplicable 'Swarthy John' and 'Bardolph' predictions. "Some people say you make your own luck in this world," he told me.

"I don't think so, Peem. I think I had pure luck and some spooky luck too! But somebody up there seemed to look after me."

CHAPTER 34

November to Christmas 1969:
"Last Time in Ipswich", or
"Full Circle Back to Dundee"

"**H**I, Bob. Pop into my office, please," Harry Gardner asked me over the internal telephone.

When I got there, he greeted me with the words: "Just been looking over the structure charts, and there appears to be a problem."

"Oh dear. What is it?" I asked him.

"No, no; no problem. It's just that you are out of line."

What did he mean? "How's that?"

"Well, you need to display the same authority as the two senior department heads, so you've got the wrong car. You're going to get a Vauxhall Victor, the next level up." It sounded to me like the principles John Simpson would advance to companies trying to launch a successful training and personnel presence within an organisation.

"That's very good of you, thanks. But do I need that?" Not being a salesperson, I didn't feel I required such a car, but I understood his thinking.

"Yes, you must – it's fitted with all the latest conveniences: radio, heated front and rear windows, heated driver's seat," He grinned broadly as he reeled off the benefits as if they were a list of 'must-haves'. I'd noticed the discrepancy and had kept quiet, because it impacted only on me. But it was a pleasing sign to see the way he was applying principles.

You're in another world now, Murray – a long way from the grocery back shop with no chairs or teacups! Just think; you left Commercial College annexe across the road just last year. Did you ever imagine, eighteen months later, that you would be told you must have a car with all the latest features?

I was now installed in my office at Planet Watson & Philip plc., wholesale food distributors to the retail and catering trades throughout Scotland. The Training Officer course near Ipswich had been successfully completed, and my Training Needs Analysis was presented to the course tutor at Ipswich and accepted. I'd been presented with my Training Officer's Certificate, which allowed me to apply for membership of the Training Institute. At long last, there were some initials after my name which I had earned and would mean something. But in the down-to-earth grocery world, it would not go down well to 'push' letters after my name – those fanciful days were over. My TDO colleagues said they would find my training analysis helpful in their own work with companies, so that was complimentary feedback.

The Watson & Philip analysis was completed slightly later than planned, as I had started work on some aspects to avoid the Training Board levy. Harry Gardner was delighted with the content which I had compiled for the training analy-sis. It was the first ever professional piece of work in the com-pany to establish training, and personnel action required for it included structure charts of the total Division and depart-ments, identified training required, and offered management succession recommendations.

Aware I had a long way to go before understanding the entire workings of W&P, I knew that at the root of the oper-ation would be service to customers. I had learned that previ-ously in my Willie Low days. Customers are customers wher-ever they might be. My thoughts went back to 'the Colonel', Mrs Rice, Mrs McCleary, and all the others I'd experienced along the way. Be sure to look after the customers.

* * *

Mum and Dad had always taken a great interest in my pro-gress and, when I told them about the change of car, mum said, "That's fine. You'll be a 'ticky' better off now, will you?"

I smiled. "After all I've put myself through, mum, the size of car is not all that important. But it means a lot inside the company."

Time was short, but one evening Peem and I managed to have an hour at the Station Hotel for a celebratory drink. "It's great you're soon going to be living back here," he told me over the rim of his glass.

"Yes, it is. The last years in England have been hectic. I've learned a lot, but it can be very tiring on the roads."

"What a decade it's been for you, Robbie! Look at all the changes you've gone through."

"The sixties will end in a few days, and I don't know what the seventies will bring you, Peem. But you have gone through many stages too. When the sixties started, you were picking and packing potatoes in all weathers at Tattie Thompson's. Then at DC Thomson you've been drawing and sketching, and now you're doing high-tech computer work."

Peem grinned, knowing that we had both seen major progress in our lives. "But your changes are far more obvious to the world," he said.

"I suppose you're right. Counter service, apart from corner shops, has nearly disappeared. My old jobs, like weighing up bags of sugar and scooping up butter, are ancient practices. The equipment I used will soon be in museums!"

"Look at the massive changes inside your old grocery world," my brother reflected. "Shopping centres being built, and now out-of-town supermarkets being talked about."

"You're right, Peem. And just think of all the changes outside my trade. Road bridges across the Tay and Forth. Motorways, not to mention the old Fordie Prefect that I had to crank up on those cold mornings. And my grocery order arrived on a flat-bed lorry with just a tarpaulin over the load."

My brother seemed contemplative. "There's been good and bad in the last ten years, Robbie. Steam trains gone, New Towns to replace slums... but then Kennedy's assassination, and now decimalisation on the horizon. Why do we need that? Do you think it will catch on?"

"And not forgetting pop culture. Since the Beatles came along, I'm lost in the music world now. It all seems foreign to me. But then, I suppose I've been studying all that time and not taking notice."

"Your attitudes to all that will have changed," he thought aloud.

"Talking of attitudes, Peem, I'll tell you a strange thing I noticed just the other day."

"Oh? What was that?"

"I saw a Willie Low truck, and yet I felt no close feeling towards it. I may never live without feeling some guilt, but the question of *have I done the right thing?* has gone at long last."

"Glad to hear it. I remember the tortured time you had back then. You know, when you think about it, you've done a complete circuit: Dundee retail grocery, college, Institute, and now wholesale grocery back in Dundee."

I nodded sagely. "You're right, Peem. I've been on a tour of space, stopping off at a few planets on the way. What's more, did you know that Willie Low's headquarters, St Joseph's College annexe and the Watson & Philip offices are all within two hundred yards of each other? When you think about it, I've been on a circular trip! So cheers: you helped me a lot. Here's to the next decade – what will that bring us?"

We clinked glasses.

* * *

The training needs analysis had, in effect, created the agenda for a long programme of planning and training. That had been exactly what it was intended to do, but I could sense other matters were on the horizon. Decimalisation was only a year away and it seemed to herald a training programme of its own, as Harry had pointed out that I'd be involved in training 'our' VG retail customers across Scotland. That evening, I read out to mum – just like old times – an item in *The Courier*. "Our half-crown coin will go," I perused from the page, then went on to say that in January 1970 the coin would disappear forever.

"Oh dear. Is all that necessary?" she asked me.

This was another special time with my family – mum was fifty-five years old on the 3rd of December, and dad was the same age three days later. On the 9th, they would celebrate their thirtieth Wedding anniversary. After all my travels, I happened to be there with them at 'celebration' time.

It was approaching Christmas, and my family were 'marooned' in St Ives. But before heading south, I was invited to attend the office party to be held in the employees' canteen. I'd never witnessed such a party, and I was in for shocks. Two young lads – sons of a Director – played guitars and sang songs, which went down well. A group of 'office girls' sang a cheeky song about their boss, and then a manager who was more than tipsy was sick and was last seen searching for his false teeth amongst the sawdust. I'd made a few risky job decisions in the past. Had I just made another one?

It took me some time to become accustomed to this office culture. My boss, a relative newcomer like me, had sought my objective impressions and views as he witnessed the same behaviour. In the end we realised this was indeed a laudable characteristic, for it was the 'work hard, play hard' attitude within Dundee which shone through in the workforce. My 'personnel' role was already beginning to take shape. There was never another party held in the offices, and thus these scenes were never repeated.

My family were in St Ives, and I went to spend Christmas with them there.

* * *

Postscript

During that December of 1969 I met Alan Craigie. He told me he was now working with NCR as he had planned, and was now hopeful of a senior NCR job coming up some day in South Africa. As usual, our favourite topic was discussed, but I sensed we were – at long last – getting over our big psychological barrier of not getting to Arbroath High School.

I learned that my friend Bill McGregor was still in India and, although I didn't know it then, it was going to be twenty years before we would meet up again. I didn't see Jock until 2005 when he, Alan and Bill all turned up – along with thirty others, and two teachers – at our school class reunion in Carnoustie. Many reminiscences!

Year three of the DMS course was successfully completed in 1971. It had felt like three hundred years to get there. The Delivered Grocery Division grew by acquiring other depots across Scotland and, in time, employed around 400 people. After two years, I was appointed Personnel and Training Officer. Following three years of studying the Institute of Personnel Management's part-time course at Dundee Commercial College (now situated, after years of debate, on Constitution Road – otherwise known as "The Conshie"), I became a qualified personnel manager at the age of thirty-five. More initials, but – like my training ones – they were 'real'. At long last, I felt that my twenty years' apprenticeship was at an end... but the learning certainly wouldn't stop.

Following another three years, I was appointed Group Personnel Manager for the company, which then employed around 1,000 employees. After further national acquisitions in the UK, the Group employed approximately 3,000 people. I continued as Group Personnel Manager and was made redundant at sixty-two years of age, after thirty-three years of employment with the company. Not bad for a job opportunity overheard in a London pub!

On many occasions I sat looking out over the River Tay from my home in Wormit, Fife, and looked back at my luck. Being pointed towards a 'message boy' job in the grocery shop of Wm Low & Co Ltd in 1953. How my spell as a radio and television apprentice told me that retail grocery was where I was happiest. Obtaining an apprenticeship with Wm Low in 1956. Mr Munro providing time off for me to attend night classes. Finding, by accident, a job opportunity for the post as lecturer at Dundee Commercial College aged twenty-two. Again, by pure chance, seeing a job advertised by The Grocers' Institute at age twenty-seven. Hearing in a London pub about the opportunity for the Training Officer job in Dundee, aged twenty-eight.

But my real luck? Being born into my family, and the guidance and upbringing in a church-going household. Barry, Westhaven, Woodside, Carnoustie JS school, Newton Panbride church... all key milestones, or 'nursery' Planets. Support from my family when I thought of myself then as being poor when, in fact, I was rich. Everything seemed to fall into place. I'd taken high-risk decisions, but luck saw me through.

These days, whenever someone asks me, "And what job did you do, Robbie?" I say to them: "Well, I was a personnel manager." Then I correct myself, and say, "I was a grocer!"

You're a very lucky boy, Murray... but you'll never know if you made the right decision to leave Wm Low in 1963.

The End? Not yet...!

YOU MAY LIKE TO KNOW...

MY brother James (Peem), after completing four years at Art College followed by one year working as a farm labourer, worked for DC Thomson newspapers for thirty-one years as an artist and later a computer page planner, eventually becoming redundant due to computerisation at the age of fifty-two. He then found huge pleasure working as a highly-respected caddy well into his seventies on Carnoustie's Championship Golf Course. He also worked as a trained barman and now, in his retirement, expertly paints friends' cats and dogs in oils to order.

My school pal and fellow message laddie Jock, after a successful career in food processing, ran his own fruit and veg businesses. He eventually ran his own hotel in Cromer, Norfolk. We meet in Carnoustie occasionally, when I try to beat him at golf – a game which we enjoyed together as boys in the 1950s. He joins me and other classmates who left school in 1955 when I organise reunions.

Ian McDougall, the young apprentice hairdresser, ran his own newspaper and hairdressing business for 55 years in Carnoustie, finally hanging up his scissors and jacket in 2019. We meet regularly in the town.

Alan Craigie, who resisted going in to his parents bakery business in Carnoustie, managed to leave the short-lived radio and TV technician world to follow a micro-electronics career in Dundee and then South Africa, where he spent all his adult life. Sadly he passed away there, shortly after reaching his 'three score and ten'.

Bill McGregor came back to Carnoustie after more than 25 years in a banking business in India, returning to pick up a second banking career in Scotland. We meet now again for a coffee and a 'blether' about old times.

Jim, my leader and hero when Peem, Coffie, Ollie and I fished off the rocks at Westhaven and mucked about on boats, is now approaching his mid-eighties and can still reel off the names of all the fishing boats and their owners who fished at Westhaven in the 1950s

My wee sister, 'Baby Jean', who surprised and embarrassed me when she arrived when I was thirteen years old, is now 67 years of age. She lives in Ayrshire with her husband and family.

The "'wee' fleet and gifted cricketer and football player", Donald Ford, who we played against at the ballaster when he was eight or nine years old, had a highly successful career as a capped international cricketer and footballer for Scotland. As well as gaining amateur caps, he became a professional and won three senior Scottish football caps during 1973 and 1974. (Come to think of it, Jim hasn't paid me that pound yet!) Donald, who spent many boyhood holidays at Westhaven, has now retired to Carnoustie, and I meet him occasionally in the town.

Two great joys emerged from the success of my first *Grocer's Boy* book. John Allardice, my young apprentice in Logie Street, went on to become a successful branch manager and then area manager with Wm Low & Co., doing what I could have (or maybe should have?) done. He worked closely with Mr Munro, and was made redundant when Tesco acquired Willie Lows. My other joy is that John Thomson, my former boss for a short time – and whose wife was my fruit and veg assistant in Logie Street – has also been 'found'. The three of us spend time going back through many chapters of our Lows experiences.

My managers Mr Munro, John Ferguson, John Simpson, Harry Gardner and Jim Hadden have all passed away, and so – sad to say – has Wm Low & Co.; Commercial College, Dundee; the Grocers' Institute; and Watson & Philip plc. So it's just me left, telling the story of my luck.

You may also like to know that my dad died at the age of 86, and mum passed away in 2015 in her 101st year.

APPENDIX 1
SOME OF THE DECADE'S NEWS

THE 1960s was a decade of decisions and discovery for me, and set the foundations for my working life. On reflecting on how many changes happened to me, I can now look back and see how much of an action-packed, change-giving period it was. Ten years dominated by news of the Vietnam War, race riots in USA, protests and revolutions in Europe, wars and famine in Africa, and many technical advances. Some of the items mentioned in my story are included below:

1960

World News
- Prince Andrew born
- Princess Margaret weds Anthony Armstrong Jones
- John Fitzgerald Kennedy elected American President
- Cassius Clay wins Gold Medal at Rome Olympics
- Harold McMillan's "Winds of Change" speech is delivered
- *Lady Chatterley's Lover* by D.H. Lawrence is published
- Traffic wardens first appear in London
- First Motorway Café opens at Newport Pagnell
- St Paddy wins the Derby
- Last British Steam Locomotive is made
- Queen's Bridge, Perth is opened

Films

- *Ben Hur*
- *Psycho*

TV

- *Coronation Street*
- *Sykes*
- *Maigret*
- *Bootsie and Snudge*
- *Wagon Train*
- *Take Your Pick*

Pop Music

- 'Tell Laura I Love Her' (Ricky Valence)
- 'It's Now or Never' (Elvis Presley)
- 'Only the Lonely' (Roy Orbison)
- 'My Old Man's a Dustman' (Lonnie Donegan)

1961

World News

- Russian Satellite with dog 'Laika' orbits earth and returns
- Yuri Gagarin goes into space and returns
- Adolf Eichmann sentenced to death for war crimes
- The contraceptive pill goes on Sale
- Boy Scouts permitted to wear long trousers
- Smallpox outbreak in Britain

Dundee News

- Only 750 pickers needed for potato harvest, consequently boys only required
- Dundonian Noel Gordon is the first person to be filmed in colour on TV during experiments at Crystal Palace
- Dundee's new Commercial College to be built near Park Place, Nethergate
- Charles Gray (builders) obtain contract for phase one of the new Overgate re-development
- Admission charges to climb the 160-foot Old Steeple introduced; sixpence for adults and threepence for children
- Caledon shipyard secures orders for three diesel ferries and five ships, including one for New Zealand
- Parking crises in Dundee

Films

- *The Hustler*
- *West Side Story*

TV

- *Coronation Street*
- *Sunday Night at the London Palladium*
- *Emergency Ward 10*
- *Probation Officer*
- *Double Your Money*
- *Rawhide Wagon Train*

Pop Music

- 'Are You Lonesome Tonight?' (Elvis)
- 'I Remember You' (Frank Ifield)

- 'Let's Twist Again' (Chubby Checker)
- 'The Young Ones' (Cliff Richard)
- 'Walkin' Back to Happiness' (Helen Shapiro)

1962

World News
- Smallpox outbreak in Britain
- John Glenn orbits the earth in *Friendship 7*
- Panda crossings introduced
- 'Telstar' Live TV link starts
- Nelson Mandela is arrested in South Africa
- Death of Marilyn Monroe
- *Z-Cars* TV series first shown
- Safeway opens its first supermarket in Bedford
- Smallpox outbreak in Britain
- Scottish airline Loganair starts flights
- 'Night of the long knives,' when half of the UK Cabinet is sacked
- *Dr Finlay's Casebook* is first televised
- John, Paul, George and Ringo of The Beatles give their first public appearance
- Racing cyclist Bob McIntyre is killed in a motorbike accident
- Last tram operates in Glasgow
- Scottish rugby team beat Wales 8-3 at Cardiff and Ireland 20-6 in Dublin
- Ford Cortina Mk1 first on the market at £573
- No frost free nights from December 1962 until March 1963

- 'Pay Pause' announced, preparing for Britain's entry into the Common market

Dundee News

- British Transport Commission worries about tunnel under the harbour and Tay Bridge building works
- Messrs Caird & Sons, Reform Street, advertises 'give away' price bargains
- La Scala cinema presented *Night of the Eagle* (the emotional shock of a lifetime)
- Dundee's Lord Provost plans to visit USA to seek business set-ups in the city as the city needs 3000 jobs
- Scott's Travel Agency advertised an eight day holiday to France, Belgium and Holland, for £27, 5 shillings and 9 pence including travel, accommodation, tip and four excursions
- Top Ten Club presents Tommy Dene, Frank Kelly and the Hunters; 4 shillings entry fee
- Last tram runs in Dundee
- Royal Arch, originally built in wood for arrival of Queen Victoria in 1844, is to be demolished
- Andy Stewart visits Baxter Bros. and Dens Works
- Dundee's £40m re-development scheme is announced, including £2m for Overgate scheme

Films

- *Dr No*
- *West Side Story*
- *Breakfast at Tiffany's*

TV

- *That Was the Week That Was (TW3)*

- *Laramie*
- *Eric Sykes*
- *Dr Finlay's Casebook*
- *Z Cars*
- *Steptoe & Son*

Pop Music
- 'Stranger on the Shore' (Acker Bilk)
- 'I Remember You' (Frank Ifield)
- 'Let's Twist Again' (Chubby Checker)
- 'The Young Ones' (Cliff Richard)

1963

World News
- President Kennedy assassinated
- Sir Alec Douglas-Home elected Prime Minister
- Cliff Richard in *Summer Holiday* opens in London
- John Profumo MP resigns after major political scandal
- Great Train Robbery takes place
- British Rail chairman Baron Dr Beeching announces cuts of 2,000 railway stations, 8,000 coaches and 68,000 jobs
- Duke of Edinburgh opens the Hillman Imp Linwood plant at Paisley
- Last National Servicemen released from service.
- The Beatles occupy top three spots in pop charts
- Henry John Burnett is last person hanged in Scotland
- Robin Hall and Jimmy McGregor concerts take place throughout Scotland

Dundee News

- Rep Theatre in Nicoll Street burns down and is temporarily housed in a tent
- Car parking crisis continues. Constitution Burial ground used for parking
- The practice of GPs issuing Death Certificate without seeing deceased is stopped
- Drama group *63* starts, actor Brian Cox (aged 19) joins
- The Beatles perform at Caird Hall, Dundee

Films

- *From Russia with Love*
- *Billy Liar*

TV

- *Coronation Street*
- *Sunday Night at the Palladium*
- *Emergency Ward 10*

Pop Music

- 'From Me to You' (The Beatles)
- 'She Loves You' (The Beatles)
- 'Please Please Me' (Beatles)

1964

World News

- Plans revealed to build the World Trade Center, New York

- The Beatles arrive in New York: "Beatlemania" has begun
- Cassius Clay beats 'Sonny' Liston
- Richard Burton and Elizabeth Taylor marry for the first time
- Rolling Stones' debut album
- *Mariner 4* lands to take pictures of Mars
- *Goldfinger* premieres in USA
- Sir Winston Churchill dies
- Harold Wilson becomes Prime Minister
- BBC 2 commences broadcasting
- Aberdeen typhoid outbreak – 136 cases are diagnosed
- TV ban on advertising cigarettes
- Forth Road Bridge opens
- Work starts on the Edinburgh/Glasgow M8 motorway
- Radio Caroline begins broadcasting

Dundee News

- Bomb scare in 4,100 seater Green's Playhouse cinema
- Johnny Hudson appears at the Chalet; admission costs 4 shillings
- Jute workers meet in Caird Hall looking for a 40 hour week (it is currently 43 hours)
- Tram procession for employees with 20+ years' service

Films

- *A Hard Day's Night*
- *My Fair Lady*
- *Mary Poppins*

- *The Sound of Music*
- *Goldfinger*

TV
- *The Man From UNCLE*
- *Gideon's Way*
- *Tomorrow's World*

Pop Music
- 'My Boy Lollipop' (Millie)
- 'Anyone Who had a Heart' (Cilla Black)
- 'I Love You Because' (Jim Reeves)
- 'I Won't Forget You' (Jim Reeves)

1965

World News
- Diet Pepsi is introduced
- *My Fair Lady* opens
- Jim Clark, racing driver, wins Indianapolis 500
- Ian Smith announces UDI for Rhodesia
- NHS prescription charges end
- Cassius Clay gives an exhibition bout in Paisley
- BP platform strikes natural gas in the North Sea.
- Death penalty is abolished
- 70mph limit is imposed on UK roads
- Race Relations Act is passed
- Stanley Matthews, aged 50 plus five days, plays his last First Division game

Films
- *Dr Zhivago*
- *The Sound of Music*

TV
- *Morecambe and Wise*
- *Des O'Connor*

Pop Music
- 'I'll Never Find Another You' (The Seekers)
- 'Tears' (Ken Dodd)
- 'Mr Tambourine Man' (The Byrds)

1966

World News
- John Ridgeway and Chay Blyth row the Atlantic
- Chi-Chi, London's giant Panda, goes to Moscow to meet An-An
- US space probe lands on the Moon
- Francis Chichester sets out to sail around the World
- Ground broken on World Trade Center
- *Star Trek* is first broadcast
- The Road Safety Act (Breathalyser) is passed
- *The Frost Report* TV show commences
- Harold Wilson wins General Election
- Government notifies that decimalisation will start in 1971
- Hovercraft Channel service begins
- England win the World Cup, beating West Germany 4-2

- Aberfan mining disaster in South Wales

Dundee News
- Tay Road Bridge opened by the Queen Mother; car tolls are 2/6d (12 ½ p)
- Three Killed in Clepington Road building collapse
- John Cairney appears in stage play *There Was a Man* by Tom Wright

Films
- *A Man for All Seasons*
- *Grand Prix*

TV
- *Till Death Us Do Part*
- *The Adams Family*
- *The Avengers*

Pop Music
- 'Distant Drums' (Jim Reeves)
- 'Strangers in the Night' (Frank Sinatra)
- 'These Boots Were Made for Walkin'' (Nancy Sinatra)
- 'Yellow Submarine' (The Beatles)
- 'You Don't Have to Say You Love Me' (Dusty Springfield)

1967

World News
- Donald Campbell killed on Coniston Water

- Dr James Bedford is cryogenically preserved for future resuscitation
- Elvis and Priscilla Beaulieu marry
- 400 Million watch first satellite broadcast
- The Beatles release 'All You Need is Love'
- *QE2* launched at Clydebank
- Dr Christiaan Barnard performs the world's first heart transplant in Cape Town
- Concorde is unveiled at Toulouse, France
- Torrey Canyon runs aground between Land's End and Scilly Isles
- Scotland defeats England 3-2; this is England's first defeat since their World Cup win
- UK and Ireland apply to join the European Economic Community (EEC)
- First BBC2 colour TV broadcast: Wimbledon Tennis
- Brian Epstein found dead in his home

Dundee News

- Last steam train withdrawn from service in Scottish region
- Caledon Shipyard in merger talks
- Ninewells Hospital construction delay; problems between architect and builder
- Abercraig and Scotscraig ferries sold for £18,000

Films

- *Casino Royale*
- *Bonnie and Clyde*
- *The Graduate*

TV

- *No Hiding Place*
- *The Benny Hill Show*
- *University Challenge*

Pop Music

- 'Release Me' (Engelbert Humperdinck)
- 'There Goes My Everything' (Engelbert Humperdinck)
- 'Puppet on a String' (Sandie Shaw)

1968

World News

- On US TV, white singer Petula Clark affectionately touches black singer Harry Belafonte
- Civil rights activist Dr Martin Luther King is shot dead in Memphis, Tennessee, sparking riots
- Robert Kennedy is shot dead in Los Angeles
- Alec Rose, aged 59, completes solo round the world sail in 354 days
- Ford Escort is introduced
- Abortions are legalised
- Introduction of British Summer Time (BST)
- Enoch Powell delivers his 'Rivers of Blood' speech
- London Bridge is sold to an American entrepreneur
- Manchester United is first English team to win the European Cup
- Last steam train passenger service in UK
- Two-tier postal service introduced
- Russian tanks invade Czechoslovakia

- M1 motorway finally completed
- 5p and 10p coins are introduced, ready for decimalisation in February 1971

Films
- *The Graduate*
- *Oliver*
- *Guess Who's Coming to Dinner*

TV
- *Dad's Army*
- *The Black and White Minstrel Show*
- *Never Mind the Quality*

Pop Music
- 'What a Wonderful World' (Louis Armstrong)
- 'I Pretend' (Des O'Connor)
- 'Delilah' (Tom Jones)

1969

World News
- Boeing 747 'Jumbo Jet' flies for the first time; maiden flight is between Seattle and New York
- Concorde's first Flight
- Apollo 11 puts the first men on the moon: 'The Eagle has Landed'
- First ATM banking machine operates in New York
- Ford Capri is launched
- Lulu marries Maurice Gibb
- First B&Q store is opened in Southampton

- Longhope lifeboat is lost in Pentland firth
- British troops go to assist Royal Ulster Constabulary in Northern Ireland
- *QE2* Makes her maiden voyage from Southampton to New York
- Voting at eighteen years of age is introduced
- Production of half-pennies ceased
- 50p piece introduced
- Colour came to BBC and ITV; Colour TV Licence cost £11

Films
- *The Love Bug*
- *Funny Girl*

TV
- *Please Sir!*
- *The Dustbinmen*
- *The Liverbirds*
- *Monty Python's Flying Circus*

Pop Music
- 'My Way' (Frank Sinatra)
- 'Gentle on My Mind' (Dean Martin)
- 'Nobody's Child' (Karen Young)
- 'I'll Never Fall in Love Again' (Bobby Gentry)

APPENDIX 2
SOME PRICES IN THE 1960s

1960

- Eggs: 2/9d per doz
- Tea: 1/5d per qtr
- Self Raising Flour: 3 lbs 1/10
- Pye TV set, 17inch screen: 62 guineas
- Ever Ready Transistor Radio: 22 Guineas
- Clydesdale KB TV set, 17inch screen: 7/6 weekly
- Hyacinth Bulbs: 10 pennies each
- Daffodills: 4 ½ d each
- Air Fares
  - 17 day Excursions Prestwick to New York £104 ·12/·
  - Prestwick to Montreal £97· 3/· (or by jet £10·15/· extra)
  - Rail Fares
  - Dundee to London Single £8·12/·, Return £17·44/·
  - Dundee to Aberdeen return 12/·
  - Dundee to Glasgow return 24/·
  - Dundee to Edinburgh return 22/·
- Roller Skating
  - Under 15 1/6d per hour, including skate hire
  - Adults 2/6 per hour, including skate hire

1965

- New Zealand Butter: 1/7d per 8 oz
- Danish Butter: 1/10 ½ per 8 oz

- Crosse Blackwell soups: 1/4d down to 1/2d
- Crosse Blackwell Baked Beans: 16oz 1/4d down to 1/1d
- Ribena Blackcurrant Drink: 5/- down to 4/5d
- Chivers Jams: Blackcurrant 1/10d, Raspberry 1/11d
- 6 Penguin Biscuits: 1/6d
- Zip Firelighters: 1/1

1966
- Learn to Drive in a Ford Cortina: 12/6d per 1 hour (£5-10/- for 10 lessons)
- Festive four course dinner and coffee: 19/6d (97.5p)

1967
- Drinks
  - Whisky: 42/11d (save 9/- per bottle)
  - Rum: 45/11d (save 3/- per bottle)
  - McEwans Export and Tennants Lager: 1/11d per can
- Travel
  - Dundee to London (for the England v Scotland football match): Special 2nd Class return fare 112/- (£5.60p)
- Dry Cleaning
  - Miniskirts: 2d per inch

1968
- Ford Escort De Luxe: £635-9s-7d
- Massey's Tea: 1/4d qtr (7p)
- McVities chocolate biscuits: 2/2d (11p)

1969

- Gent's Haircut: 4/6d (22.5p) Boys 3/6 (17.5p)
- Dundee to Arbroath return ticket: 7/- (35p)

APPENDIX 3
PRE-DECIMAL BRITISH CURRENCY

Farthing = 1/4 penny
Halfpenny ('ha'penny') = 1/2 penny
Penny ('copper') = one pence (1d)
Threepence ('thruppenny bit') = 3 pence
Sixpence ('tanner') = 6 pence
Shilling = 12 pence (1s)
Florin = 2 shillings
Half Crown = 2 shillings and 6 pence
Crown = 5 shillings = 1/4 pound
Pound = 20 shillings = 240 pence (£1)
Sovereign = face value of £1 (approx .24 oz. of 22 carat gold).

APPENDIX 4
IMPERIAL TO DECIMAL
CURRENCY CONVERSION TABLE

12 old pennies (d) = 1 shilling (s) = 5 new pence
1 florin = 2 shillings = 10 new pence
1 half crown = 2 shillings and sixpence = 12½ new pence
1 crown = 5 shillings = two half crowns = 25 new pence
1 pound (£) = 20 shillings = 240 old pennies = 100 new pence

ILLUSTRATIONS

A typical late 1960s fascia and interiors from a branch of
Wm. Low & Co. Ltd.

Photographs provided by kind courtesy from the private
photographic collection of Mr John Allardice, with thanks.

Carnoustie branch of Wm Low & Co. Ltd., showing (left to right): Ian Stewart (manager), John Thomson, Alan Longmuir, Margaret Smith, Robert Murray, Isobel Kennedy, Cathy Reid and Kenneth Leiper.

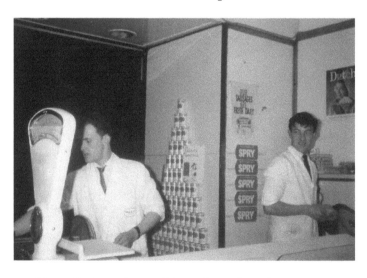

Harry Greig in charge of Logie Street branch provisions department, and apprentice John Allardice.

Staff photo of Dundee Commercial College, Tay Street annexe.
The "S.S. Marie Celeste" sign indicates the centre's nickname.
Photo includes John "Fergie" Ferguson (second from left).

Robbie's teaching registration certificate.

Commercial College walking trip, showing (left to right):
Gordon Laird, John Buchan, George Brown and
Robert Murray.

Expedition to Glen Doll, Angus.

On the walk from Braemar to Aviemore.

A Cairngorms summit!

Robbie, Carys and Gail pictured in 1968.

Robbie with long-time school pal Alan Craigie.

ACKNOWLEDGEMENTS

My brother James (Peem) Murray for his clever sketches.

My colleagues in Tay Writers group for their constant support.

My partner Elaine for her forbearance.

John Allardice and John Thomson, my former Wm. Low colleagues, for photographs.

Gordon Laird, my former college colleague, now 91 years old, for his advice and photos.

Rodger Brunton and Carnoustie's Kinloch Care Centre for their kind use of marketing props.

Tom and Julie of Extremis Publishing Ltd. for expert guidance on all matters.

ABOUT THE AUTHOR

Robert Taylor Murray was born in Barry, near Carnoustie, in 1940. Growing up in Westhaven and later residing in Carnoustie itself, he attended Barry and Carnoustie Schools before becoming an apprentice grocer with William Low & Company Ltd. He qualified as a Member of The Grocers' Institute, and was appointed manager of William Low's Brantwood branch in Dundee, becoming the company's youngest ever manager at the age of 19. He later oversaw the Logie Street branch in Lochee.

Robert went on to manage a larger third branch in Dundee and then, after attending further education management courses, discovered he was sufficiently qualified to successfully apply for a post as a lecturer in distributive trades subjects at Dundee Commercial College – a position he held for five years. Realising how much the retail trade was changing and feeling he was less in touch to reflect the current scene, he applied to join The Grocers' Institute and was appointed Training Development Officer for part of London and east England, where he advised companies and colleges on training in the retail grocery trade.

After two years he returned to the Dundee area when he was appointed Training Officer for Watson & Philip, a national wholesale food distributor. He remained with that company for thirty-three years, during which time he was appointed Personnel Manager and eventually became Group Personnel Manager with responsibility for three thousand employees and, latterly, in the London area.

Robbie's recollections of his early days in the grocery trade, *The Grocer's Boy*, was published by Extremis Publishing in 2018.

Following a company acquisition he became redundant at the age of sixty-two. In retirement he has again been actively involved in amateur theatre. He is a member of Tay Writers – a Dundee based writing group – and Angus Writers' Circle, and writes short stories.

He has written a stage presentation on the life of Robert Burns, *The Spirit of Robbie Burns*, which has been performed several times by amateurs in Tayside. The script was published by Extremis Publishing in 2019.

Robbie has two daughters and four grandchildren. When he is not writing, he enjoys travelling, hillwalking and golfing.

The Grocer's Boy
A Slice of His Life
in 1950s Scotland

By Robert Murray

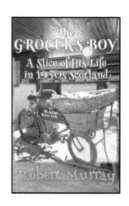

The 1950s in Carnoustie: a beautiful seaside town on the Tayside coast, and a place which was to see rapid social and technological advancement during one of the fastest-moving periods of cultural change in recent British history.

In *The Grocer's Boy*, Robert Murray relates his account of an eventful childhood in post-War Scotland, drawing on fond memories of his loving family, his droll and often mischievous group of friends, and the many inspirational people who influenced him and helped to shape his early life.

Join Robert on his adventures in retail as he advances from his humble beginnings as a delivery boy for the famous William Low grocery firm, all the way to becoming the youngest manager in the company's history at just nineteen years of age. Read tales of his hectic, hard-working time as an apprentice grocer — sometimes humorous, occasionally nerve-wracking, but never less than entertaining.

From Robert's early romances and passion for stage performance to his long-running battle of wits with his temperamental delivery bike, *The Grocer's Boy* is a story of charm and nostalgia; the celebration of a happy youth in a distinctive bygone age.

The Spirit of Robbie Burns

By Robert Murray

The whole world knows the legend that is Scotland's national bard, Robert Burns. But what was the story behind the meteoric success of this literary genius, whose works are still performed and enjoyed to this very day?

Appearing in print for the first time, Robert Murray's acclaimed stage play follows the life of Burns from his formative years in Ayr through to his success and celebrity in Edinburgh and later farming life in Dumfries. You will meet his friends, learn of his inspirations, and discover intimate details of his many romantic encounters.

Related with warm wit and keen insight, *The Spirit of Robbie Burns* delves into the life of one of Scotland's most complex and colourful characters to explore his timeless work and the world he lived in. The text of the play is accompanied by performance notes and detailed appendices, which will make it an essential addition to any good Burns Night celebration.

The Heart 200 Book

A Companion Guide to Scotland's Most Exciting Road Trip

By Thomas A. Christie and Julie Christie

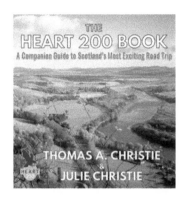

The Heart 200 route is a unique road trip around some of the most beautiful locations in Central Scotland. Two hundred miles running through Stirlingshire and Perthshire, Heart 200 takes its visitors on an epic adventure to suit every taste—whether you are an outdoors enthusiast, an aficionado of history, or simply looking to enjoy yourself in some of the most stunning natural surroundings in the world.

Written with the full approval and co-operation of the Heart 200 team, *The Heart 200 Book* is a guide to the very best that the route has to offer. You will discover the history and culture of this remarkable region, from antiquity to the modern day, with more than a few unexpected insights along the way. Over the millennia, this amazing land has made its mark on world history thanks to famous figures ranging from the ancient Celts and the Roman Empire to King Robert the Bruce and Mary Queen of Scots, by way of Bonnie Prince Charlie, Rob Roy MacGregor, Robert Burns, Sir Walter Scott, Queen Victoria and even The Beatles!

So whether you're travelling by foot, car, motorhome or bike, get ready for a journey like no other as the Heart 200 invites you to encounter standing stones and steamships, castles and chocolatiers, watersports and whisky distilleries... and surprising secrets aplenty! Illustrated with full-colour photography and complete with Internet hyperlinks to accompany the attractions, *The Heart 200 Book* will introduce you to some of the most remarkable places in all of Scotland and encourage you to experience each and every one for yourself. It really will be a tour that you'll never forget.

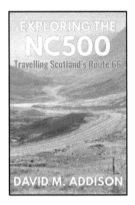

Exploring the NC500

Travelling Scotland's Route 66

By David M. Addison

Travelling anti-clockwise, David M. Addison seeks his kicks on Scotland's equivalent of Route 66. Otherwise known as NC500, the route takes you through five hundred miles of some of Scotland's most spectacular scenery. No wonder it has been voted as one of the world's five most scenic road journeys.

There are many ways of exploring the NC500. You can drive it, cycle it, motorbike it or even walk it, even if you are not one of The Proclaimers! And there are as many activities, places of interest and sights to be seen along the way as there are miles.

This is a personal account of the author's exploration of the NC500 as well as some detours from it, such as to the Black Isle, Strathpeffer and Dingwall. Whatever your reason or reasons for exploring the NC500 may be, you should read this book before you go, or take it with you as a *vade mecum*. It will enhance your appreciation of the NC500 as you learn about the history behind the turbulent past of the many castles; hear folk tales, myths and legends connected with the area; become acquainted with the ancient peoples who once lived in this timeless landscape, and read about the lives of more recent heroes such as the good Hugh Miller who met a tragic end and villains such as the notorious Duke of Sutherland, who died in his bed (and may not be quite as bad as he is painted). There are a good number of other characters too of whom you may have never heard: some colourful, some eccentric, some *very* eccentric.

You may not necessarily wish to follow in the author's footsteps in all that he did, but if you read this book you will certainly see the landscape through more informed eyes as you do whatever you want to do *en route* NC500.

Sit in your car and enjoy the scenery for its own sake (and remember you get a different perspective from a different direction, so you may want to come back and do it again to get an alternative point of view!), or get out and explore it at closer quarters – the choice is yours, but this book will complement your experience, whatever you decide.

Also Available from Extremis Publishing

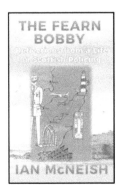

The Fearn Bobby
Reflections from a Life in Scottish Policing

By Ian McNeish

'It's all about the community', the words of Kenneth Ross, Chief Constable of Ross and Sutherland Constabulary, guided Ian McNeish through thirty years of police service. They were true then, back in 1974, and they are true now.

Ian held a police warrant card for three decades, serving communities across Scotland. In that time, his work saw him moving from the northerly constabulary where he policed the rural Hill of Fearn to the social challenges that presented themselves amongst the urban landscape of Central Scotland.

From his formative years in post-War Scotland through to his application to join the police service, Ian has led a rich and varied professional life that ranged from working in iron foundries to building electronic parts for the Kestrel Jump Jet and legendary Concorde aircraft. But once he had joined the police service, he found himself faced with a whole new range of life-changing experiences – some of them surprising, a few even shocking, but all of them memorable.

Leading the reader through his involvement in front line situations, Ian explains the effects of anti-social behaviour and attending criminal court appearances, in addition to dealing with death and the responsibilities of informing those left behind. He considers topics such as ethics, public interest, police and firearms, drug issues, causes of crime, and a lot more besides.

In a career where his duties ranged from policing national strikes to providing comfort and support through personal tragedies, Ian advanced through the ranks and saw first-hand the vital importance of effective management and good teamwork. Whether as the 'Fearn Bobby', policing a remote countryside outpost, as a seconded officer working for the Chief Executive of a Regional Council, or as a Local Unit Commander in Bo'ness, Ian always knew the importance of putting the community first. Comparing today's policing techniques with his own professional experiences and examining both the good times and the harrowing pitfalls of the job, his account of life in the force is heartfelt, entertaining, and always completely honest.

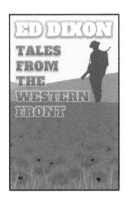

Tales from the Western Front

By Ed Dixon

Tales from the Western Front is a collection of stories about the people and places encountered by the author during more than three decades of visiting the battlefields, graveyards, towns and villages of France and Belgium.

Characters tragic and comic, famous and humble live within these pages, each connected by the common thread of the Great War. Meet Harry Lauder, the great Scottish entertainer and first international superstar; Tommy Armour, golf champion and war hero; "Hoodoo" Kinross, VC, the Pride of Lougheed; the Winslow Boy; Albert Ball, and Jackie the Soldier Baboon among many others.

Each chapter is a story in itself and fully illustrated with photos past and present.

For details of new and forthcoming books
from Extremis Publishing, including our
podcast, please visit our official website:

www.extremispublishing.com

or follow us on social media at:

www.facebook.com/extremispublishing

www.linkedin.com/company/extremis-publishing-ltd-/

Lightning Source UK Ltd.
Milton Keynes UK
UKHW020632161020
371702UK00010B/513